Before Religion

ANCIENT INDIA'S RECONCILING VISION
FOR UNIVERSAL SPIRITUALITY

Nitesh Gor

AVANTI
INSTITUTE

www.niteshgor.com

First published in Great Britain in
2024 by Avanti Institute.

Publisher's note: This edition was sponsored
by the Dharma Endowment Fund.

Every possible effort has been made to ensure
that the information contained in this book is
accurate at the time of going to press, and the
publishers and authors cannot accept responsibility
for any errors or omissions, however caused. No
responsibility for damage occasioned to any person
acting, or refraining from action, as a result of
the material in this publication can be accepted
by the editor, the publisher or the author.

Apart from any fair dealing for the purposes of
research or private study, or criticism or review, as
permitted under the Copyright, Designs and Patents
Act 1988, this publication may only be reproduced,
stored or transmitted, in any form or by any means,
with the prior permission in writing of the author,
or in the case of reprographic reproduction in
accordance with the terms and licenses issued by the
CLA. Enquiries concerning this edition should be
sent to the publishers at the undermentioned address:

Avanti Institute
Wemborough Road
Stanmore, HA7 4NW
Great Britain
www.avanti.org.uk

© Nitesh Gor, 2024
The right of Nitesh Gor to be identified as the author
of this work has been asserted by him in accordance
with the Copyright, Designs and Patents Act 1988.

ISBN: 978-1-7394348-0-9

DEDICATION

To my gurus, Bhakti Charu Swami & Srutidharma Das

You both departed this world within a few months of each other. I miss you every day. I hope this attempt makes you smile...or at least laugh!

mama ratna-vanig-bhavam
ratnany aparicinvatah
hasantu santo jihremi
na sva-svanta-vinoda-krt

'The saints may laugh at me for becoming a jewel merchant, though I know nothing about precious jewels. But I feel no shame, for at least I may entertain them.'
—*Visvanath Chakravarti Thakur*

Contents

Foreword VII
Introduction XI

PART I: PULLING BACK THE CURTAIN
Chapter 1: Spiritual but Not Religious 5
Chapter 2: On Religion 23
Chapter 3: Spiritual Lessons from Everyday Life 37
Chapter 4: Who Am I? 53
Chapter 5: Sources of Knowledge 67
Chapter 6: Cosmic Evolution 79

PART II: SUBSTANCE AND SHADOW
Chapter 7: The Shadow 101
Chapter 8: Karma 115
Chapter 9: Human Behaviour 123
Chapter 10: The Human Condition 137
Chapter 11: Making It Personal 153
Chapter 12: Sins of the Religious 169
Chapter 13: Your Mind and Consciousness 177

PART III: YOUR RELATIONSHIP WITH THE ULTIMATE REALITY

Chapter 14: Radical Personalism 193
Chapter 15: The Power of Three 201
Chapter 16: Reaching for the Spiritual 213
Chapter 17: Universal Love 219

PART IV: SPIRITUAL QUEST

Chapter 18: The Workings of Love 229
Chapter 19: The Object of Love 247
Chapter 20: Living Yoga 263
Chapter 21: Putting It All Together 273
Chapter 22: Help Is at Hand 285

Concluding Words 293
Selected Bibliography 294
Acknowledgements 295
About the Author 296
Other Books by the Author 298

Foreword

Despite the requirements of schools to offer a holistic curriculum, those aspects that are harder to assess, like spiritual insight, have become deprioritised—even in faith schools. And so it is that the founder of Avanti Schools Trust, Nitesh Gor, has written this profoundly important book on universal spirituality. Others will be better placed than me to reflect on the message of the *Bhagavata* and how those reflections can help evolve our view on the role and value of spirituality in all aspects of society, but there is so much here which captures and addresses some of the biggest questions of what it is to be spiritual (and indeed a truly compassionate human) in these challenging times:

> How can we go beyond just respecting and tolerating others to truly accepting them?

> Why, in today's age, is it such a challenge for people of one faith to recognise saintliness within other traditions, while remaining loyal to their own?

> How can we come to accept the truth of each other's experiences and illume each other through dialogue when we might see different aspects of the same reality, speak different

languages, and have different worldviews and cultures? Much is often lost in translation.

How can we learn to ask 'good questions' that prompt contemplation of what we are searching for? How can we be spiritual whilst living out our modern lives? How can we judge whether an experience or encounter 'is as good as I thought it would be', thereby examining the results of materialistic activities and considering whether they deliver on their promise of happiness?

Writing this in August 2024, it is even more evident than ever that there is so much frustration, anger and hurt in this broken society of ours in the United Kingdom today. So much antipathy and antagonism to others, so much resentment that the 'promised land', so often proffered without thought or reflection by politicians, seems beyond reach. But the promised land is not simply reached through affluence, material means, or even academic achievement or reputation. We need more, our children and teachers deserve more; hence, the need for broader educational aims, more focus on well-being, and more contemplation and meditation on the true purpose of education and life. This book poses deep and inspiring questions for us all.

As the author maintains, spirituality is open to all, anyone, anytime, anywhere, and given that those who have typically controlled religious discourse—generally the clergy and aristocracy—no longer have a monopoly on spirituality, it is essential that we all understand what it can offer us, and those in positions of authority and power—in government, in schools, in religions—really open it up to those who follow, to those who teach, to those who learn.

FOREWORD

The *Bhagavata* can help us move beyond sectarian religion and provide a framework for universal spirituality.

In conclusion, I can do no more than echo the author's final thoughts in the closing pages…

> The Bhagavata presents a bold vision of universal spirituality, inspiring spiritual seekers to press forward and deepen their awareness of their essential spiritual identity. This is the most exciting and transformative journey upon which one can embark. Help is at hand, though; we need only take the first step. As Rumi said, 'As you start to walk on the way, the way appears.'

Mike Younger
Cambridge, August 2024

Professor Mike Younger is Chair of the Avanti Schools and was Dean of Education and Head of the University of Cambridge Faculty of Education.

Introduction

Ancient India was the land of spirituality and mysticism. But unlike many later civilisations, Vedic ideas refuse to fit into rigid boxes. Fragments of these ideas spread along global trade routes, but only piecemeal, with neither their philosophical depth nor their breadth intact. As a result, their inclusive and integrative approach remains largely unknown in the West.

This book is offered as a journey through the mysteries of that Vedic civilisation, which once thrived on its sacred texts: texts that avoid extremes and embrace plurality. These hidden treasures offer insight into the human condition, the nature of reality, and a goal that takes its seeker beyond sectarian limitations. Our current problems, with their apparent dichotomies—science versus religion, modernism versus postmodernism, social equality versus individual freedom, sustainability versus development, democracy versus authoritarianism, and so on—are not entirely new. I hope these pages can offer fresh perspectives and powerful insights on how we might respond.

Nowhere are these insights more urgent than the way in which we engage with spirituality and religion. In recent times, religion seems to be jumping from one crisis to the next. With a history of brutal colonisation and plagued by institutionalised hypocrisy, sectarianism, sexual exploitation, racism, and misogyny, religion is viewed by many as intolerably corrupt or, at best, as a naïve and old-fashioned way of living. Scientism is the belief that science is the sole means of determining objective reality, and this has become the new religion of our times. It has supplanted spiritual knowledge as the means to discover deeper truths. But science alone cannot answer all our questions, and nor is it meant to. Bertrand Russell said, 'Almost all the questions of most interest to speculative minds are such as science cannot answer...Science tells us what we can know, but what we can know is little, and if we forget how much we cannot know we become insensitive to many things of great importance.' We yearn for a deeper understanding of human existence:

- Why does anything exist at all?
- Who am I?
- Why is there suffering?
- How can I be happy?

Various spiritual movements have claimed to fill the gap, but without defined principles, solid philosophical underpinnings, and practical solutions to life's real problems, they sound attractive but promise more than they can deliver. In their attempt to 'meet us where we are', they have, ironically, been subsumed into materialism, complete with marketable consumer-friendly products to help us feel good about ourselves. For example, it might result in a message to have faith solely in ourselves, which at first seems appealing but can quickly become overwhelming.

How can a rational person navigate between these seemingly polar opposites to find substance and meaning? Our challenge is to find a *universal* and *philosophical* spirituality that is not limited to any one particular faith tradition but is based on our common spiritual identity—a spiritual philosophy that can be understood

INTRODUCTION

and experienced by everyone everywhere. To transcend nationality, ethnicity, gender, sexual orientation, and, yes, even religion.

The notion of being spiritual but not religious, universal, not sectarian, can be intuitively attractive. But can there also be value in insisting on the specifics of one tradition to the exclusion of others?

We will explore the contribution that ancient India can make to the search for a pluralistic approach to faith and spirituality. Our search takes us to a time before the dawn of the Abrahamic religions and even the ancient Greek philosophers.

Philosophers such as Voltaire and Max Müller have noted ancient India's contributions to world thought, yet in many ways, its Vedic philosophical traditions remain largely undiscovered. Before religion, as we have come to know it, spiritual texts were the very wellspring of philosophy and science. This may sound inconceivable to those who have only experienced religion as standing in contradiction to philosophy and science, or at best, simply borrowing from them to 'fill in the gaps'. In *Before Religion*, we will be looking at some of these ancient Vedic texts, and the *Bhagavata* in particular.

I first came in contact with the *Bhagavata* about 30 years ago; a monk gifted it to me for my 19th birthday. I read the entire 18 volumes quite cynically, looking for logical inconsistencies, irrational dogma, sectarianism, and so on—perhaps a typical young mind. I reasoned that if I could find such instances, I could put the book away. But I couldn't. Instead, I found a text that spoke to me with profound spiritual insight and universality. The words of Ralph Waldo Emerson about the *Bhagavad-gita* came to mind: 'It was the first of books; it was as if an empire spoke to us, nothing small or unworthy, but large, serene, consistent, the voice of an old intelligence which in another age and climate had pondered and thus disposed of the same questions which exercise us.'

There was a time when science was wedded to finding order. That worked well at one level, but as we looked deeper, we found fundamental unpredictability. It needed quantum theory to help us see beyond the constraints of classical physics. Likewise, there was a time when binary approaches to religion and spirituality served a purpose, and as we look deeper, we find the need for universality.

I believe the message of the *Bhagavata* can help evolve our view on the role and value of spirituality in all aspects of society. It addresses some of the biggest challenges of our times: How can we be spiritual but not religious? How can we have an inclusive approach to spirituality without just watering it down to the lowest common denominator? How can we go beyond just respecting and tolerating others to truly accepting them? How can we be deeply inclusive and still loyal to our own traditions? The *Bhagavata* can help us move beyond sectarian religion and provide a framework for universal spirituality.

The Bhagavata
There are three main reasons why the *Bhagavata* is suitable as the central reference text in our search for a universal spirituality:

1) **Intention.** The *Bhagavata* declares right from the start that it will leave aside all materialistic or self-serving forms of religion and practice. It focuses exclusively on essential spiritual truths.

Its framework is grounded in common sense and avoids the dangers of an 'anything goes' pluralism.

2) **Krishna's final message.** The *Bhagavata* includes the *Uddhava-gita*, whose speaker, Krishna, also spoke the famous *Bhagavad-gita*. In the *Uddhava-gita*, Krishna speaks his final and more elaborate teachings. These later teachings bring Krishna's message of universal spirituality to new heights.

3) **A helpful structure.** The *Bhagavata* describes that the first sound in the universe was '*Om*', which is the seed of spiritual awakening planted in the hearts of all living beings. The Vedic texts describe Om as the root and condensed version of all Vedic knowledge. In the *Bhagavata*, Krishna speaks four 'seed' verses, which provide an elucidation of this primordial sound. Krishna's seed verses provide a helpful structure for this book. (A friend reminded me that the scholar and saint, Bhaktivinoda Thakura, used these four seed verses to frame his presentation of the *Bhagavata* in his book *Krishna Samhita*, published in 1880.)

Like any civilisation, ancient India had its own problems. I am not attempting to provide an analysis of its pros and cons, nor an academic treatment of the texts. I am simply trying to convey what I have gained from the *Bhagavata* as a novice practitioner, in the hope that it may help others. Inevitably, my effort will fall short. Therefore, whatever you find helpful in this book is owed to the *Bhagavata*, and whatever you find lacking is owed to my inability.

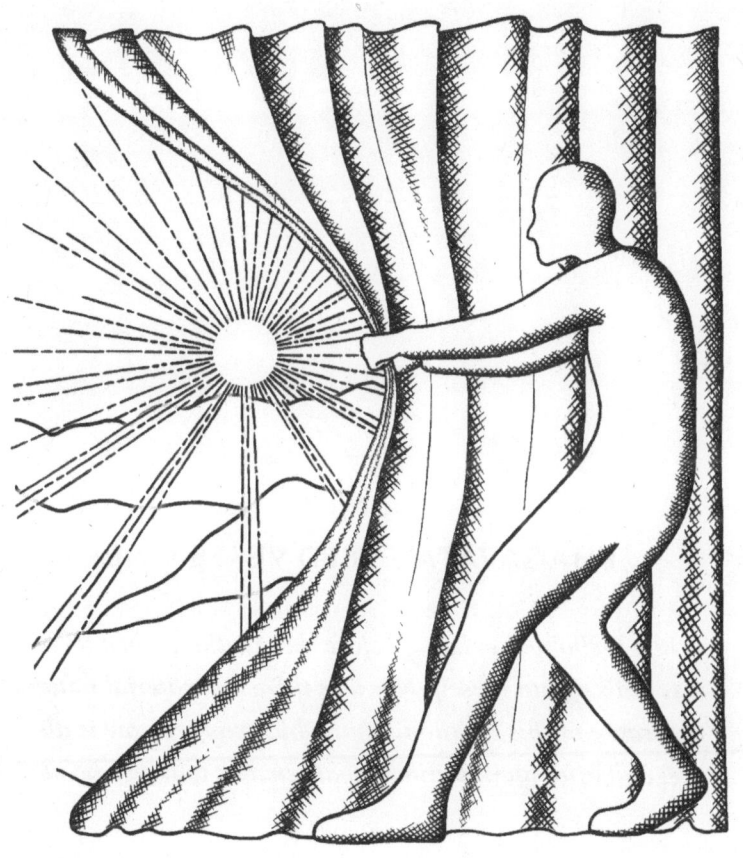

PART I

Pulling Back the Curtain

BHAGAVATA'S SEED VERSE ONE

'It is I who was existing before the creation, when there was nothing but myself. Nor was there the material nature, the cause of this creation. That which you see now is also me, and after annihilation, what remains will also be me.'

SPIRITUALITY FOCUSES ON THE ETERNAL beyond the temporal. Hidden in plain sight exists an unseen and fundamental reality. This first seed verse tells us of an Ultimate Reality that is not tied to any particular sect or creed and that applies to all existence—to the entire cosmos and beyond. Part I looks at what this may mean for us here today.

We start by looking at what we mean by 'spiritual' and how it differs from 'religious'. Next, we cover the role of religion and how we might test it. We move on to how we can draw spiritual lessons from everyday life and then look at the fundamental questions of identity and the nature of the Self. We also explore epistemology, the nature, limitations, and sources of knowledge. And finally, how does this all help to explain the world around us?

CHAPTER 1

Spiritual but Not Religious

*'Hark! O child of immortality,
come to the land of transcendence.'*
—Svetasvatara Upanishad

To be 'spiritual but not religious' is both attractive and convenient. We hear it a lot on social media, in articles, in conversations. There is a clear human desire for spirituality, but left undefined, the notion can be ambiguous and impractical. Getting clear about this will also help us steer clear of distortions pedalled under the guise of spirituality.

How is it possible to define *spiritual* without reference to God? 'Expanding our consciousness', 'understanding ourselves better', 'understanding our relationship with the world', 'self-actualisation', and other phrases have been offered as possible answers. Spirituality is also a process, a quest for a transcendental unity amongst all observable diversities. I find it helpful to explain spirituality using four dimensions:

1) **Finding identity.** We all have different layers of identity: some are contextual (job, family, etc.), some physical (skin colour, ethnicity, etc.), some qualitative ('I am a generous person', etc.). The process of peeling back these layers to get to our most fundamental core—unencumbered consciousness—is essentially a spiritual process. Our spiritual nature is meant to be unbound, hence the urge within all of us that we are meant for more. As we move closer to our core spiritual identity, we naturally develop a profound spiritual connection with all beings and the universe.

2) **Raising consciousness.** We all experience fluctuating levels of consciousness; we have our good days and our bad ones. This second dimension of spirituality is finding those practices that help place us into higher states of consciousness—and keep us there. Meditation is one such practice. By meditation, I mean a state of being, not a technique: it can be an open-eyed, moment-to-moment experience.

3) **Buffering materialism.** By materialism I mean both physicalism (the idea that there is no reality other than inert matter) and hedonism. Spiritual practices buffer us from these limiting mindsets with practices such as stoicism, and techniques such as asking good (deep) questions.

4) **Having purpose.** We feel the need to have purpose beyond ourselves, to contribute. Being part of something greater than just ourselves makes us whole—not in any arrogant or self-serving sense, but in a deeply humble sense: we are a small part of a great reality. Through purposeful contribution, we

find meaning and belonging. As Nietzsche said, 'He who has a why to live can bear almost any how.'

As for its relationship to religion, I like to explain spirituality by saying that religion is a particular practice and belief, whereas spirituality is (hopefully) its essence. As Heraclitus cautioned, 'The oneness of all wisdom may be found, or not, under the name of God.'

Some people consider their spirituality intrinsically tied to their commitment to a particular religion or religious institution. Others may not subscribe to any religion and still consider themselves 'spiritual'. But what more can we say about that term, which science, philosophy, and religion all try to understand in their own way? Spirituality is inextricably linked to consciousness. Usually, science seeks to isolate and measure consciousness, perhaps in areas of study like neuroscience, while philosophy theorises about it, and religion seeks to experience it. The *Bhagavata* combines these approaches; after all, science, philosophy, and religion are all trying to approach truth. The *Bhagavata* does this with various theoretical and practical techniques, including various forms of yoga. When I speak of yoga here, I am referring to practices by which we can connect with spiritual reality, and not simply the colloquial use in terms of bodily exercises and postures (see Chapter 11).

Any group, like a family or a community, is defined by a common denominator. For a family, that's parentage, and for a community, that could be geography or ethnicity. If you think of the broadest grouping, you might get to 'humanity', or even better, 'conscious beings'. Now, the idea of God has the potential to be the 'common denominator' for that all-encompassing group—but the sad reality is that this most encompassing of concepts has instead been used with great effect to divide us into ever-smaller groups.

The *Bhagavata's* means of analysing and experiencing consciousness are accessible to those of any faith or none since they do not demand any particular faith or doctrine. As such, they form the basis of diverse meditation and mindfulness practices. If you have ever done yoga, meditation, or mindfulness, you are, in many ways, following these early teachings of the *Bhagavata*.

The *Bhagavata* centres its approach on the idea that consciousness is central to understanding and developing spirituality. It defines consciousness as underlying all of reality, then explains the stages of consciousness and how to elevate it. Again, none of this requires faith in any particular doctrine. Instead, spirituality is framed as a consciousness-based approach to understanding ourselves and the cosmos, mitigating our suffering, and attaining lasting happiness.

In keeping with this approach, the *Bhagavata* refers to the concept of an Ultimate Reality, where superficially divergent visions of transcendence converge. It reconciles apparent dichotomies, such as impersonal or personal, dual or nondual, transcendent or immanent, and so on. We explore the concept of Ultimate Reality further in this chapter.

THE ELEPHANT IN THE ROOM

The *Bhagavata* explains how spirituality can transcend sectarian religion and how it is, in fact, the essence of religion. Take, for example, the statements of Queen Kunti, who, nearing the end of her life, prayed to be done with everything, including religiosity. This was also expressed by Krishna in the *Bhagavad-gita* when he advised Arjuna to abandon all varieties of religion and simply surrender to him. In these contexts, *religion* refers to the perfunctory aspects of religion—not to its spiritual essence.

This idea of spiritual essence being beyond religion means that no specific religion—or institution—has a monopoly on spirituality. This may seem obvious, but there are many religious groups that claim a monopoly over spirituality. Why in today's age is it such a challenge for people of one faith to recognise saintliness outside of their own tradition?

Religious texts from many traditions acknowledge that there is one divine reality, though called by different names. One 19th-century follower of the *Bhagavata*, Bhaktivinoda Thakura, spoke of how when he visited churches and mosques, he thought, 'Here is my own Lord, being worshipped in a different way.' The *Bhagavata* explains that the names, forms, qualities, and activities of the divine are interpreted differently by different teachers according to their respective scriptures and that divinity accepts the devotion of everyone.

An ancient Indian tale speaks of a group of blind men who came across an elephant. Each man touched a different part of the elephant and came up with their truth of what an elephant was. One felt the trunk and described it as a snake. Another touched the tusk and described it like a spear. Another the leg and thought it was a tree. And so on. We each experience different parts of the same truth. People all over the world experience 'spirituality' but in different ways:

- We see different aspects of the same reality, so we might disagree. One might see a trunk, and another an ear.
- We speak different languages, and have different worldviews and cultures, so, much is often 'lost in translation'.
- We see different aspects of the same reality and, through dialogue, might illuminate each other.

Now, let's take it one step further. What if the blind men are asked to not only understand but also *accept* the truth of each other's experience? This scenario more accurately reflects the true extent of some of our biggest challenges in real life. Is it surprising, then, that universal spirituality is not more common? But if we have information about the concept of an elephant, even if our limited experience doesn't entirely match the whole description, we can at least theoretically comprehend the bigger picture. This will help us make sense of our own experiences and the perspectives of 'differing' others. And through dialogue, and our own evolving spiritual journey, the elephant emerges in all its fullness.

We may spend a great deal of time deciding *which* religion we should follow, sifting through truth claims and asking, 'whom do I worship?' But perhaps a better question is, '*why* do I worship?' This places the onus back on us—we must authenticate our own motivation and purpose on our spiritual path. We will return to this question in Chapter 11 when we discuss *intra*faith.

ULTIMATE REALITY

The *Bhagavata* asserts that a basic premise of spirituality is that underlying all existence is a unity, an Ultimate Reality. In the *Bhagavata*, the term *vastavam vastu* translates as 'the real/factual substance'. This term describes that Ultimate Reality beyond what we perceive with our senses. That is not to say that what we ordinarily perceive is false, but that it is temporary, thus encouraging us to bring into focus that which is eternal—real. As with the example of the blind men and the elephant, reality emerges from the wider relational context.

What is the nature of that 'real/factual substance'? The *Bhaga-*

vata's answer is 'nondual consciousness'. Consciousness refers to our subjective awareness and so is self-evident; it is the only thing we are directly aware of or experience first-hand. We don't require any external validation or experiment to affirm our consciousness; it is a direct and undeniable aspect of our existence. It forms the foundation of our perception and understanding of the world. Matter, the 'known', on the other hand, is a mystery. We do not know its intrinsic nature, only some of its limited properties. Science is clear that the intrinsic nature of the universe remains unknown to us; all that we can say is that it is consciousness.[1] Neither do we have any clue as to how consciousness arises. A materialist might argue that 'Consciousness arises from matter, and we just don't yet know enough to explain how this happens.' The trouble with this argument is that there is absolutely no evidence to support it. That matter arises from consciousness, and not vice-versa, is an important theme for the *Bhagavata*, and we will return to it in later chapters.

Consciousness, the 'real/factual substance', is the *Bhagavata's* focus. This nondual *Ultimate Reality* is the unifying and underlying basis of all existence, including the individual Self and nature. And our encounter with consciousness is what we term 'spiritual'. The reductive approach of physicalism banishes consciousness

---

1) Erwin Schrödinger, from *What Is Life?*: 'Consciousness cannot be accounted for in physical terms. For consciousness is absolutely fundamental. It cannot be accounted for in terms of anything else.' Max Planck (interview): 'I regard consciousness as fundamental. I regard matter as derivative from consciousness. We cannot get behind consciousness. Everything that we talk about, everything that we regard as existing, postulates consciousness.' Werner Heisenberg, from *Physics and Philosophy*: 'The atoms or elementary particles themselves are not real; they form a world of potentialities or possibilities rather than one of things or facts.' Stephen Hawking, from *A Brief History of Time*: 'What is it that breathes fire into the equations and makes a universe for them to describe? The usual approach of science of constructing a mathematical model cannot answer the questions of why there should be a universe for the model to describe. Why does the universe go to all the bother of existing?'

and so is what we term 'material'. This approach to the Ultimate Reality and consciousness enables the *Bhagavata* to apply across traditions, and between science and religion, without getting stuck in biases that so often block the path of non-sectarian spirituality.

> This Ultimate Reality is the ultimate source and cause and transcends designated categories. This allows for a more diverse and inclusive vision of transcendence because it exists beyond sectarian boundaries. The *Upanishads* hint at this approach with abstract references to transcendence, such as: 'Where words cease, and where the mind cannot reach'; 'Outside the scope of religion and irreligion, pious and impious action'; 'What is that thing, knowing which, all other things become known?'

The *Bhagavata* provides helpful insight into the text's philosophical and universal approach with reference to the term Ultimate Reality: 'Learned transcendentalists who know the Ultimate Reality refer to this nondual substance as an impersonal energy, as an indwelling presence within all beings, or as the supreme transcendent person.' One of the key terms of this verse is *tattvam*, 'Ultimate Reality'. The verse relates the word to 'truth' or 'reality' (rather than 'God' or 'nature'). We all—materialists and spiritualists alike—search for the same thing but in different places—and from different starting points. We have our own truths, and real spirituality can provide a vision for their reconciliation.

Spiritual seekers are those aspiring for the Ultimate Reality, even if they don't always know that. They may focus on and perceive Ultimate Reality as an impersonal energy, an indwelling

Superconsciousness, or a transcendent personality. The ability to accommodate various approaches and conceptions of transcendence is a fundamental attribute for spiritual aspirants serious about advancing their journey beyond the beginning stages.

There is, however, a danger that, due to the pursuit of universality, or the attempt to fit the Ultimate Reality into limited parameters like logic, or an inability to conceive of transcendence beyond the impersonal, or for whatever other reason, we will chip away at the attributes of the Ultimate Reality until we eventually reduce it to nothing at all. This is another reason why the systematic approach of the *Bhagavata* explored in this book has such importance for the spiritual seeker.

SEEING BEYOND DIFFERENCE

Bhaktivinoda Thakura continues that we can see one's own object of devotion in the worship of others: 'Since I am committed to my particular practice, I cannot take part in this ritual, but as I watch it, I am developing a greater feeling for my own method of worship. The Supreme Ultimate Reality is one without a second. Therefore, as I offer my obeisances to the form which I see here, I pray to my Lord, from whom this form comes, that this Deity will help me expand my love for him.' We can be inclusive without being unfaithful. It takes maturity in one's spiritual practice to accommodate this approach.

By definition, the Ultimate Reality is one; it is nondual and the original cause. However, we may approach it from various perspectives. Remember the lesson of the blind men and the elephant. It would be foolhardy to insist that truth is attainable only through our own path; there are significant differences even within the same tradition.

A common goal is all that keeps society from splintering and from endless confrontation. This underscores the importance of keeping a universal spiritual reality in clear focus. A.C. Bhaktivedanta Swami said, 'We shall be united on the basis of the prime need of human society, spiritual life.'

In that sense, the *Bhagavata* asserts that it shouldn't matter which specific set of bona fide religious principles one follows, as long as one follows them properly. The *Bhagavata's* message addresses the full spectrum of humanity, to meet each individual 'where they are at'. It can help us all connect with an underlying reality and consciousness in whichever way we can.

Interestingly, this also includes atheists. In the *Bhagavad-gita*, Krishna described the eternal nature of consciousness and then said, 'If, however, you think that consciousness will always be born and dies forever, you still have no reason to lament.' This statement acknowledges that not all people believe in a lasting spiritual Self, which is aligned with a physicalist or atheistic position. Jabali, in the *Ramayana*, argued to Rama that, 'The scriptures have been written by intelligent priests who wished to promote rituals and charity. In this way, they have assured their own livelihood!' He was clearly sceptical of priests, though admittedly not necessarily of God's existence. This is not to say that either Krishna or Rama supported these perspectives, but we can see that both atheism and scepticism were present in the Vedic civilisation. Atheists, for example, were encouraged in their connection with Ultimate Reality through the concepts of time and space (more on that in Chapter 6).

The behaviour and example of saintly people establish the essence of religious principles. And so, the *Bhagavata* extols the virtues of studying the lives of accomplished seekers as a primary means to reconcile contradictions between or within spiritual paths. In the lives of saintly people, we can see their ability to unite people by focusing on spiritual essence. Put another way, you can tell a saintly person by their ability to focus on spiritual essence.

BECOMING INCLUSIVE

The *Bhagavata* places spiritual practitioners into three broad categories: beginners, serious practitioners, and accomplished spiritualists. One characteristic of beginners is their tendency to focus on the *differences* between spiritual paths and develop a sense of exclusiveness. Accomplished spiritualists focus on the essence, and therefore on the *similarities* of different spiritual paths; they detect and perceive divinity everywhere. The group of serious practitioners fills the gap between these two ends of the spectrum as they progress on their spiritual journey.

Seekers of truth, the *Bhagavata* says, disagree only until they acquire a genuine attraction for hearing about and discussing qualities of the divine. The psychology of the initial stage of spiritual development lends itself toward exclusivity, motivated by one having found the 'truth'.

To help us move from the initial to more developed stages, the *Bhagavata* teaches, for example, that since the Ultimate Reality is infinite, so are the names we can use to call upon it. A practitioner achieves their goal most easily by focusing on the name they hold most dear, reflecting both independent choice and the nature of transcendence as attractive to all. The *Bhagavata* approves of various means to approach transcendence. Truth need not be binary—more than one thing can be true, even if it isn't 'your' truth.

As noted above, inclusivity becomes easy when we learn to detect and perceive divinity everywhere, which means all around us and in everyone. Just as some people see everything in relation to making money, the spiritually advanced see everything in relation to divinity. Indeed, this is one hallmark of an advanced spiritual seeker. They seek to please the divine presence in the hearts of all living beings and understand all others to be spiritually equal to themselves. This state of deep empathy is possible for everyone, regardless of occupation, age, gender, religion, or ethnicity. The *Bhagavata* encourages us to practice seeing divinity beyond the coverings and layers of superficial identities. This is the beginning of self-realisation and is characteristic of all spiritual giants.

> ### The Story of King Yadu
> King Yadu met a mendicant (a beggar) and observed that although the mendicant was not engaged in any religious activities or rituals, he had attained an elevated state of spirituality. The mendicant was young, handsome, and eloquent; he had every opportunity to try and enjoy the world. But he was not aspiring or working toward anything mundane. Instead of being 'burned in the forest fire of materialistic life', he was 'like an elephant who has taken shelter from the forest fire by standing in the Ganges River'. He did not even feel the typical human need for companionship. We explore the mendicant's reply in Chapter 3.

This story goes on to explain how our most fundamental need is to offer our love to someone and receive love in return. It concludes that the only way one can be satisfied is to repose that love in transcendence, where it can be perfectly reciprocated. The verse quoted at the start of this chapter speaks to the necessity of universal spirituality. Like the mendicant, we can find this unity when we transcend materialistic and superficial religious practices and focus on the essence of religion.

OPEN TO ALL

Focusing on essence has another important upside: those who have typically controlled religious discourse—generally the clergy and aristocracy—no longer have a monopoly on spirituality. It is open to all—anyone, anytime, anywhere. Some religions claim that this is already the case, but it is found more in theory than in practice, and institutionalised religion has all too often been a means to power instead of to spirituality. We should remember that just as material wealth is not confined to any particular nation, people, or belief system, neither is spiritual wealth.

Celibate monks and renunciates have long held a mystique, in part due to the deep spiritual realisation that strict celibacy requires, and because society values the role of those who have no vested interests or other ethical conflicts.[2] In many cultures, celibates are, therefore, elevated in social status. But Bhaktivinoda Thakura also said that whenever a family glorifies divinity in their home, their activities are immediately transformed into the activities of the spiritual world. Chaitanya Mahaprabhu (1486-1534), a renowned celibate saint in the *Bhagavata* tradition and accepted by followers as an avatar, sought blessings from married people; pure spiritual teachings, he reasoned, were beyond social demarcations. He emphasised that anyone who understood the path of self-realisation could teach others.

The *Bhagavata* advocates spiritual equality for all living beings, including animals and plants. If we ignore a spiritual identity, we cannot have any meaningful sense of equality; based on just the body, no two beings can be equal in any practical sense. Universal spirituality recognises unity in diversity—establishing the underlying spiritual unity while recognising bodily diversity. Many religious groups and institutions have been slow to evolve on gender equality; some have even questioned the spiritual value of women. The personhood of Ultimate Reality is depicted in the

---

2) Celibate renunciates don't have to worry about feeding their families or their next pay cheque.

Bhagavata as having both male and female aspects. There are many examples of women being among the most spiritually advanced sages and saints—Queen Kunti from the *Mahabharata* and the *gopis* of Vraja being two notable examples. The *Bhagavata's* quest to find the most spiritually advanced persons culminates in the *gopis* of Vraja, whose love is so potent that it is described as having 'conquered' even divinity.

Universal spirituality means accepting that every living being possesses spiritual love, and that is a wonderful thing. This love, even when dormant, can be awakened. No other qualification is required.

CHAPTER 2
On Religion

'From the unreal lead me to reality.
From darkness lead me to light.
From death lead me to immortality.'
—Brihadaranyaka Upanishad

In 1965, ruling on the case of the United States v. Seeger, the US Supreme Court paved the way for an expansion of the US government's official definition of *religion*. The Court rejected a distinction between beliefs derived from religious traditions and those derived from purely personal beliefs. It also rejected the notion that belief in a Supreme Being is necessary to be considered religious. The judges cited Paul Tillich, a Christian theologian who claimed in *The Courage to Be* that God cannot be the Supreme Being because that would relativise him to one among many and thus subject him to the structure of the whole. Rather, Tillich claimed, God is being. A past bishop of Woolwich, J.A.T. Robinson, agreed: 'We shall eventually be no more able to convince men of the existence of a God "out there" whom they must call in to order their lives, than persuade them to take seriously the gods of Olympus...to say that "God is personal" is to say that personality is of *ultimate* significance in the constitution of the universe, that in personal relationships we touch the final meaning of existence as nowhere else.' But why must it be one or the other? The elephant story indicates that it need not be a binary choice.

The *Bhagavata's* vision of the Ultimate Reality accommodates and reconciles simultaneously varied approaches to the divine—as the impersonal oneness, the imminent, and the transcendent personal. This is not some naïve shotgun approach, but rather, is characteristic of the comprehensive and systematic descriptions provided in the Vedic tradition. With this approach, the *Bhagavata* acknowledges the wide spectrum of ways in which people throughout time have chosen to engage with the different aspects of the Ultimate Reality:

- **Atheists/agnostics** (those who are convinced that God does not exist or those who are sceptical about the possibility of knowing whether any deity exists). Time and nature are the foci for this group. More on the role of Time in Chapter 6.

- **Pantheists** (those who believe that nature and the cosmos comprise the Ultimate Reality). The Universal Form, a conceptual representation composed of the various elements of the cosmos, is the central focus for this group.

- **Polytheists** (those who believe in many gods). A multitude of deities, each representing various energies or cosmic bodies, is the focus for this group.

- **Impersonalists** (those who wish to finally merge within a Oneness, or who worship imaginary forms of a supreme being). The impersonal, all-pervading, and 'ground of all being' energy, is the focus for this group.

- **Meditators** (those who seek transcendence through mysticism or meditation). The indwelling presence within all beings is the focus for this group.

- **Personalists** (those who cultivate love towards the supreme divine personality). The transcendent personhood is the focus for this group.

As you might now guess from the elephant example, the above need not be framed as mutually exclusive categories: and not or. The *Bhagavata* is structured to accommodate different psychologies and dispositions. The seeker determines which path they most resonate with and dedicate themself to it, appreciating that it won't be the same for everyone. In the pursuit of spiritual realisation, we cannot abdicate our intelligence, or freedom and responsibility of choice. After speaking the entire *Bhagavad-gita*, Krishna tells Arjuna that he must deliberate on what he has heard, and then do what he wishes to do. The focus is on free will and active choice. Krishna is not commanding; he is offering options. It is Arjuna who then must choose.

In making important choices, the *Bhagavata* explains that a sincere seeker should be guided both from without and from within—from the words of scripture or a teacher, and from internal introspection and revelation. This provides a healthy check and balance and, at times, constructive dissonance.

To ensure our choices are true to ourselves, the *Bhagavata* stresses the importance of spirituality being a lived experience and not just theory. Individual experience is key in making informed choices: an important tenet of the *Bhagavata* is that spiritual progress is confirmed by reciprocation with the Ultimate Reality. Without this, our spiritual practice risks being hollow and potentially even harmful, leading to self-delusion and fanaticism. This is a high threshold intended to weed out deception and falsity.

It is said that the Vedas (ritual texts), Puranas (histories), and poetic works instruct, respectively, like a master, a friend, and a lover, and that the *Bhagavata* teaches in all three ways. But even the Vedas, which instruct like a master, always give recommendations, not demands. They are addressed to minds capable of deciding for themselves. The Puranas, like a friend, offer reasonable arguments and encouragement in support of their recommendations. The *Bhagavata* also uses both these methods, and with its exquisite poetic descriptions of the Ultimate Reality, entices us forward on our spiritual journey like a lover.

THE HIGHEST GOOD FOR ALL

The *Bhagavata* comprises a series of questions and answers. It opens with: 'What is the absolute and supreme good for all people?' The *Upanishads* ask a similar question, 'What is that, which having achieved, no other desires remain?'

The *Bhagavata's* question acknowledges that most good carries some tinge of bad, and that good is often relative—one man's food is another man's poison. Thus, it asks for a good that is 'absolute', one that is true for all time, place, and circumstance. It also asks for the 'ultimate' good—not a temporary or trivial good, but something that brings ultimate benefit.

The quest is for the essence of all spiritual teachings, made accessible to all. Conducting such a search without selfish motivation or an egoistic preference for one source of knowledge or truth over another is a challenge. Let's take a closer look at some of the things we can bear in mind when thinking about this challenge. As a start, we will look at three areas: the role of bias, how we might test religion, and the relevance of ethics on the spiritual path.

CULTURAL BIAS

Everyone thinks of others according to their own perspective. It is how we, with our inbuilt biases, see the world—as an extension of our own selves.

While logic and reason help us overcome bias, logic is only as good as the premises on which it is built. For example, the argument that 'if everything must have a creator, who made God?' poses a premise that spiritual nature must have the same requirement of causation as material nature. This ignores the possibility of an entirely different set of parameters. While physical objects must have a cause, spiritual objects do not have the same requirement. We may agree or disagree with the premises—it is a matter of belief—but for something to be considered logical, it must be internally consistent. Something can't be labelled illogical just because the premise doesn't fit with our worldview.

Many scriptural texts have been composed for a particular time, place, and circumstance, sometimes to deliver a message to a specific audience. This may mean certain aspects of the message are being highlighted while other non-essential messages are being set aside. With this understanding, we can see how a seeker from one cultural context may learn a principle, such as compassion, from someone from a different tradition—perhaps even better than they might from their own.

When considering different cultures, we should be wary of assuming superiority simply because we can't identify with them.

Since Western civilisation has roots in ancient Greece and Rome, there is natural acceptance of those philosophies and philosophers. We may struggle with the idea that other world civilisations may have been even more developed or that ancient Western civilisations borrowed much from them. This was exemplified by colonisers for centuries, who viewed cultures they didn't understand with contempt, labelling them primitive. It was then only a short step to justify their exploitation, enslavement, conversion, and even genocide. Not recognising the spirituality and philosophies that characterised many ancient civilisations, they tried to wipe them out or forcefully convert them to their own brand of monotheism, tainting the term 'monotheism' and showing the danger of interpreting cultures and philosophies according to one's own cultural assumptions.

CAVEAT EMPTOR

Alert now to the possibility of bias, let's look at some of the questions we can ask to test any religion. We accept that moisture is all around us in the atmosphere, but if we want a drink, we turn on the tap. Similarly, religion would claim to be the channel (the means) through which spirituality can be more easily accessed: *religion is the means, spirituality its end*. So, how can you tell if that is really where religion is taking you? And if we are to choose which one to practice, how might we evaluate them? Let's explore some of the tests the *Bhagavata* recommends.

Test 1: what does it promote?
- Does the process have a clear goal? What would be the outcome if you were to 'perfect' it? Everlasting life? Liberation? Peace? Pleasure? Is that the goal you want?
- What qualities or character traits does the path promote? Do the teachings encourage virtues to which you aspire, such as charity, compassion, and nonviolence?
- Does it encourage thought and questioning rather than blind following?
- What behaviours do its followers exhibit? Is there systemic harm to others?
- What is its stance toward outsiders? Is it welcoming or condemning?
- How have these teachings been recorded, transmitted, and preserved over time to maintain their integrity?

Test 2: does it provide solutions to the human condition and the world around us?
- Does it address the human condition with penetrating insight?
- Does it provide a framework to help us move beyond materialistic yearnings and negative emotions like envy and fear?
- What, if anything, does it say about some of the key issues facing us today, such as the environment, poverty, mental health, equal rights, and world peace?

Test 3: what kind of civilisation does it inspire?
Over the centuries, spiritual belief systems have contributed to the development of various civilisations.
- Is this a noble, progressive civilisation with a mature worldview?

- Does it promote the advancement of knowledge or seek to hold back enquiry?
- Do its tenets stand up to philosophical scrutiny?
- What is the nature and the depth of the culture it has inspired?
- What types of music, language, and literature have emerged based on it?

Test 4: are followers filled with spiritual love?
This is the gold standard: the path develops genuine spiritual love. The litmus test of a spiritual practice is whether it can transform hearts and minds.
- Can we identify individuals—current or historic—whose example and character inspire us to follow in their footsteps and take their testimony as reliable?
- Are there examples of followers becoming better people—more honest, kind, dedicated to the happiness of others? Are those who are spiritually accomplished on the path able to rise above their lust, anger, and greed?
- How attached are they to things like consumerism, intoxicants, or sex? It is not that these things are inherently bad, but their minimisation indicates that the practitioners have been able to shift the focus of their consciousness from the sensual towards transcendence.

The more elevated a title or position a person takes when teaching others, the more the *Bhagavata* expects of them. So, these criteria will also help us detect whether we, as individuals, are making progress on our chosen path.

ETHICAL SCAFFOLDING

The tests above alluded much to ethics; that's no surprise because many of the destructive things we have seen come from religion are caused by religious people who believe they are 'above' common ethical standards.

Religious rules and rituals are generally alleged to promote purity over impurity and good over evil. Some religious people claim that these rules and rituals are indispensable when dealing with human nature. So, what happens to ethics if we separate spirituality from religion? Can, or should, seekers be concerned with personal virtue while on the search for spiritual essence? The *Bhagavata* states, 'The self-realised are equipoised, equal to all, peaceful, fully engaged in the service of transcendent truth, devoid of anger and working for the benefit of everyone.'

A successful spiritual seeker is expected to exceed the bar of common virtue. The path to spiritual advancement isn't marked by giving up common ethical standards on the basis that they are everyday or mundane. The *Bhagavata* goes a step further to say that the ability to practice self-control is an objective test for spiritual advancement. Rulers and conquerors throughout history were able to control vast empires and yet remained unable to conquer their own animalistic instincts.

The last part of the above quote—'working for the benefit of everyone'—is critical. Great people want to help others. This is one of the most exalted methods of worshipping the divine, who is present in everyone's heart. The first characteristic of a learned person is that they want to serve.

Some might also accept voluntary suffering to help others suffer less. Advanced spiritual seekers may even see suffering as divine mercy. This can, of course, be abused—especially by individuals imposing this view on others—but the fact that a perspective can be abused does not mean that it should be cast out. There is deep power and freedom in understanding that we are not in control of everything that happens to us and that even in the most trying circumstances, we can find hope and spiritual growth.

The *Bhagavata* explains that it is the duty of every living being to perform welfare work for others with their life, wealth, intelligence, and words. It reminds us that trees give fruit, shade, and firewood, and so may be more spiritually elevated than priests who are not dedicated to the welfare of others!

The *Bhagavata* offers universal virtues to which all members of society—regardless of faith, status, or occupation—should aspire. This includes nonviolence, honesty, desire for the happiness of others, and freedom from lust, anger, and greed. In one section, Krishna provides prompts to help us think deeper about the role of virtues and ethics in our spiritual journey. Here are a few of his examples:

- **Tolerance** means to patiently endure distress and happiness.
- **Steadfastness** means to conquer the senses.
- **Charity** means to give up all aggression or animosity toward others.
- **Heroism** means to conquer the desire to enjoy.
- **Truthfulness** means speaking the truth in a compassionate way.
- **Cleanliness** means detaching oneself from sensual pleasure.
- **Education** means learning to distinguish truth from falsity by understanding the nature of consciousness.
- **Modesty** means feeling remorse for one's past improper actions.
- **Beauty** means possessing good qualities.

- **Happiness** means joy beyond temporary pleasures.
- **Wisdom** means becoming free from illusion.
- **Foolishness** means identifying the Self with the body and mind.
- **Poverty** means being unsatisfied with life.
- **Control** means detachment from sensual gratification.
- **Slavery** means attachment to sensual gratification.

At the end of his list, Krishna says, 'Enough, since even seeing the duality of "good" and "bad" can also be a "bad" quality!' Krishna is not promoting an amoral attitude. He is pointing out the risks of becoming stuck or judgmental when there could well be different perspectives on what is 'good' and 'bad'. He is also saying that as we seek transcendence, we need to go further than materialistic conceptions of 'good' and 'bad' because they can simply be relative if not grounded in something deeper.

The *Bhagavata* also offers a warning to seekers who might be tempted to prematurely remove any distinction whatsoever between 'good' and 'bad' or, put another way, 'material' and 'spiritual'. If nothing is 'bad', anything goes. The foremost modern commentator on the *Bhagavata*, A.C. Bhaktivedanta Swami, said, 'In the ultimate issue, there is actually no material world, but when one forgets the service of the Lord and engages himself in the service of his senses, he is said to be living in the material world.'

In other words, there is no sharp divide between material and spiritual, no sharp dualism. At the same time, distinguishing the material from the spiritual is also not misplaced; it is helpful for our practical purposes. For example, knowledge is a coherent continuum, but the practical purpose of education can be helped by categorising it into subjects.

Rules, especially at the beginning, are helpful as guardrails to safeguard our journey. This should be clear for obvious rules like, 'Avoid harming others.' But it is also true for practices of self-discipline, like waking up early, which can help get us into our spiritual stretch zone. It is later, when we have achieved a degree of spiritual maturity and spontaneously live (and think) in ways conducive to raising consciousness, that rules become less important. Rejecting all and any attempts at self-discipline from the outset of our spiritual journey is unnecessarily risky.

THE GOLD STANDARD

We are now ready to consider the *Bhagavata's* perspective on the essence of religion. Its vision for spirituality culminates in a selfless, loving, and reciprocal relationship with the Ultimate Reality. But we can't artificially jump to selflessness—in the early stages of a spiritual journey, a degree of self-interest is healthy as an impetus for spiritual development. The spiritual journey gradually uncovers our transcendent, selfless nature, and now the expression and reciprocation of our love is finally fulfilled: 'As darkness disappears, to that degree knowledge arises, and as knowledge arises, to that degree pains of the heart disappear.'

The Bhagavata View
The *Bhagavata* clearly states its gold standard for religion: that which leads to divine love is religion, and that which does not is irreligion.
  We are reminded that when religions are compared

based on their sub-religious principles[3], there will always be contradictions and disagreements. Whatever the religious tradition, the question is whether it brings us closer to that spiritual love; this is *universal* spirituality.

The *Bhagavata* describes spiritual love as selfless (*ahaituki*: it is not inspired by external motivations) and indomitable (*apratihata*: it cannot be stopped or limited by time, place, or circumstance). The process of developing such love beyond any sub-religious principles is the non-sectarian and universal form of religion we find in the *Bhagavata*. This foundational principle, the *Bhagavata* says, is the only thing that can truly satisfy the Self and is the root of all religion, the essence of all scriptures, and the highest good for all.

This benchmark of selfless and indomitable love as the benchmark for a spiritual path also has practical benefits. For example, it sets a standard that is less vulnerable to abuse than sentiments such as submission. Since love transcends cultural barriers, with no insiders or outsiders, it also keeps biases at bay. And since it is love that ultimately has the power to change character, this benchmark reinforces morality as a natural consequence of spiritual attainment.

---

3) Bhaktivinoda Thakura categorises the differences in sub-religious principles: different teachers or prophets, different mental and emotional attitudes toward worship, different rituals of worship, different types of affection for and activities in relation to the object(s) of worship, and different names and terminologies.

CHAPTER 3
Spiritual Lessons from Everyday Life

'A person adept in perceiving the world around him and in applying logic can achieve real benefit through his own intelligence. Thus, sometimes one acts as one's own teacher.'
—The Bhagavata

Some of us only want to consider a spiritual journey if it doesn't require *a priori* faith. We may first need to appreciate it as a rational thing to do or have some kind of spiritual experience before we take it seriously. For this purpose, the *Bhagavata* offers ways in which we can gather spiritual insight from everyday life based simply on keen observation, reason, and some helpful prompts for reflection. The Vedic texts often start with philosophy first; it is a unique approach that allows them to cross boundaries and appeal to the rational mind.

PHILOSOPHICAL ENQUIRY

First, some background. Yoga and meditation are widespread globally as methods for fitness, flexibility, and relaxation, but their original purpose was to help bring the mind under control and then help link us with the Ultimate Reality. The entire yoga system draws us from matter to consciousness. Yoga systems are best known for their focus on the breath or posture, and we will explore yoga in more detail in Chapter 11. For now, I want to bring the reader's attention to a lesser-known version of yoga (*sankhya-yoga*) that is based on the idea that through careful observation, reason, and contemplation, we can arrive at spiritual conclusions and realisations. The practitioner of *sankhya* comes to two main realisations: a) that the body is dependent upon something other than inert matter, and b) that there exists a conscious observer.

The first realisation, that there is something beyond (and ontologically prior to) matter, is a result of a process deduction. The seeker in *sankhya-yoga* first categorises the material elements as fundamental building blocks of existence. They then realise that having accounted for all the elements and their combinations, they still cannot account for consciousness. They arrive at this conclusion by deduction, or *via negativa*, which in Sanskrit is called *neti-neti*, 'not this, not that'. What was identified through *sankhya* remains the 'hard problem of consciousness' even today: we still don't understand how a physical stimulus in the brain translates into an experience, the precise transition from a living body to a dead one, or the 'birth' of consciousness. The process of *sankhya* concludes that this is because consciousness is primary and matter is epiphenomenal—not the reverse. This last point has been evidenced thoroughly by Iain McGilchrist in his book, *The Matter With Things*.

The second realisation, that there exists an observer, is sometimes dismissed prematurely by meditators who lean toward nihilism. The *Bhagavata* tells us that the presence of the Self can be detected by three states of consciousness: wakefulness, sleep, and deep sleep. In all three states, the spiritual Self is the observer. That there is an observer can also be inferred by the presence of such things as personality and thoughts, just as the presence of air can be understood by the aromas it carries. This observer is currently in something like a dream state, in which one enjoys and suffers falsely, based on a fundamental misidentification with the body as the Self. To bring us to the point of awakening, beginner meditators are often encouraged to reflect on their breath and body, gradually recognising that since they are observing these functions and bodily limbs, they must, in fact, be different from them, separate from the body. As one continues beyond these initial stages of meditation, a natural sense of spiritual oneness arises as our *material* concept of self begins to dissolve. At this early stage, people feel a sense of relief and peace, and sometimes even the loss of individual identity that comes from feeling part of a whole. For those who progress further in yoga meditation, there is then the emerging *positive* concept of the Self in relation to the Ultimate Reality.

Using solely our intelligence and analytical inclinations, *sankhya* brings us to the brink of spiritual awakening, from where we can glimpse an ultimate reality. We now look at some of the ways in which these principles of *sankhya* come to life in the *Bhagavata*.

LEARNING FROM NATURE

Uddhava was Krishna's cousin and most trusted confidant. It was to Uddhava that Krishna spoke his final teachings. This conversation, recorded in the *Bhagavata*, has become known as the *Uddhava-gita*. As part of that conversation, Uddhava asks Krishna for guidance for those on the path of self-realisation. Krishna explains that we can first act as our own teachers by better understanding the nature of this world and our own limitations. This triggers within us a desire to seek further knowledge and insight from others. There is a sense of self-empowerment here in Krishna's words, confirming to Uddhava that we are, at least initially, able to act as our own guides. He asserts that the human form has primacy amongst all living creatures because the Self in this condition is endowed with the intelligence to understand spiritual knowledge and thus search for the Ultimate Reality.

Krishna also says that those who are adept at observation and logic can raise their consciousness by their intelligence. This is not an insignificant point; it means that we can glimpse the eternal even without a prior faith.

One may see a particular spiritual truth exemplified in many different ways, and these examples become further 'teachers'. In this way, the seeker accepts many congruent teachers. Taking help from good and bad examples, the process of observation and application helps to internalise and deepen our realisation of spiritual truths.

Krishna illustrates this approach with the story of King Yadu and the mendicant Dattatreya. The King's attention was caught by Dattatreya, who had a highly elevated spiritual understanding yet did not seem particularly religious. King Yadu asked him how he had developed such deep spiritual insight.

Dattatreya explained that he had taken guidance from many teachers. He applied himself to observation and analysis, extracting whatever he could from each teacher's lessons.

Dattatreya used his mind and intelligence to contemplate the notion that there is an ultimate unifying reality.

As we begin to see things in this way, our urge to objectify and exploit diminishes, and we can observe without the mind and senses being dragged in a multitude of directions. Gradually, Dattatreya saw each of the material elements as unified and their manifestations as his spiritual teachers. He learned so much by studying these new-found teachers; it was a masterclass in mindfulness. We, too, can reflect on our observations of the world around us as stepping stones toward greater spiritual awareness and realisation.

Let's take a look at what Dattatreya learned from some of his twenty-four teachers and what relevance that might hold for us today.

Earth

Dattatreya's first teacher was Earth. From the Earth, he learned tolerance. He learned that even when harassed by others, one should know that they are acting helplessly under their own habits and limitations, and so one should not become distracted from one's own path. And just as a law-abiding citizen doesn't exploit the property of another, we should try not to exploit the natural world.

Mountains and Trees

As part of learning from the earth, Dattatreya accepted mountains and trees as his teachers. Both mountains and trees devote all their efforts—their very existence—to the service of others, and from them, Dattatreya learned to be selfless.

The Wind
From the wind, Dattatreya learned neutrality. He learned that, just as the wind remains aloof from the places through which it passes, he should not become embroiled when coming into intimate contact with material objects or difficult situations.

The Sky
The sky is one step further removed than the wind. From the all-pervading sky, Dattatreya learned about the quality of spirit. It is everywhere within the universe and yet remains aloof: not mixed with anything, not changed by anything, not divisible by anything, and not tainted by anything.

Water
Water is purifying, and Dattatreya learned that he, too, should be a purifying presence for others. Water is also a transparent medium, and a teacher's role is to nurture another's spiritual awakening by transmitting knowledge without getting in its way or obscuring students' realisations with the teacher's own mundane thoughts and desires.

Fire
Dattatreya learned four important lessons from fire. First, fire remains uncontaminated regardless of what it comes in contact with. Dattatreya learned that by practising self-discipline, a spiritual seeker can become immune from worldly distractions. Applied appropriately, self-discipline can help steady the mind and make it less susceptible to fleeting pleasures.

Second, fire manifests itself differently according to the fuel it is burning—sometimes having a different heat, colour, and/or brightness. Similarly, consciousness is present in all types of bodies and manifests accordingly, sometimes less obviously (like in a tree) and sometimes more obviously (like in humans), but we should know it as the same underlying substance.

Third, a fire's flames and sparks display a constancy mixed with transition. Similarly, our bodies are constantly changing as we age, but we perceive the changes only over long periods of time.

Last, fire blazes when properly kindled, and our consciousness blazes with the kindling of spiritual practice.

The Moon

From the moon, Dattatreya learned to not be distracted by superficial changes. The different phases of life and death do not affect our spiritual existence any more than the waxing and waning of the moon change its underlying identity.

The Sun

The sun performs its service to the world by evaporating water from any source and then distributing it without discrimination, attachment, or hoarding. Similarly, one should appropriately accept things that can be used in service of the divine (which includes service of others) without being attached to or hoarding them for oneself. Dattatreya also observed that as the sun's reflections on other objects do not divide it, so too does the underlying spiritual reality remain nondual despite being manifested in different bodies.

Pigeons

Dattatreya once observed a pair of pigeons returning to their nest to see that their babies had been caught in a hunter's net. Blinded by parental affection, the mother pigeon rushed to help but was herself caught in the net. The father cursed his misfortune, and as he lamented, his mind went blank, and he, too, fell into the hunter's net. Dattatreya learned that we need to keep our equilibrium in difficult circumstances if we are to help others.

The Python
The python is satisfied with whatever comes to it by the arrangement of providence. Just as we do not search for distress, and yet it comes, happiness also comes without being sought. Indeed, the more we seek to maximise happiness by material means, the more it is diminished. Dattatreya thus learned from the python not to over-endeavour for temporal happiness or extravagant bodily maintenance.

The Ocean
From the ocean, Dattatreya learned to be externally undisturbed and internally grave and thoughtful. An advanced spiritual seeker is fixed in transcendence and so is deep like the ocean. And just like the ocean, which does not swell or dry up with the changing seasons, he should not revel in times of plenty or lament in poverty.

The Moth
Dattatreya understood that one who fails to control the senses experiences distraction upon seeing something beautiful, like the moth, which, maddened by the sight of fire, rushes blindly into its flames. Other examples he gives are a deer lured by sound, an elephant by touch, a fish by taste (bait), and a bee by fragrance. Unless we are careful, our senses can lure us to distraction and even destruction. As the saying goes, if you're casual, you'll become a casualty.

Honeybees
Honeybees take nectar from different flowers. From them, Dattatreya learned how one should take the essence from all religious scriptures. Honeycombs are stolen from the bees by force, but we should keep what 'honey' we require and voluntarily give the rest to those in greater need.

The Hawk
A young hawk caught a modest prey, only to be attacked by a larger hawk. The young hawk had to give up its meal to escape. Observing this, Dattatreya learned that many of our attachments, which we think are giving us pleasure, are often the causes of our suffering. He learned to give up such attachments to experience greater happiness.

The Spider
As a spider expands thread from its body, plays with it for some time, and eventually swallows it, Dattatreya learned that Ultimate Reality extends the energy of time, produces material nature, and then later withdraws the entire material creation within.

The Wasp
Once, a wasp trapped a small insect. In its intense fear, all that the small insect could think about was the wasp. It watched the wasp's every move as if in deep meditation. Through this continuous and focused concentration, the insect's existence 'merged' with the wasp's. Dattatreya learned that we need to be careful what we spend lots of time thinking about because that's what we imbibe.

The *Bhagavata* contains many other fascinating stories and examples of how observation and analysis, without any prerequisite religious faith, can be used to develop our spiritual awareness. An important feature of *sankhya* is asking good questions, ones which prompt contemplation. Below are some questions we can try asking ourselves—I have also included some preliminary ideas from the *Bhagavata* to help get the 'conversation' going. We will return to these themes in later chapters.

WHAT ARE WE SEARCHING FOR?

We often find ourselves chasing something 'else', and it is exhausting. Self-help gurus talk about tolerating the duality of pleasure and pain, but to step off the hedonic treadmill isn't always so easy. To develop the patience needed to tolerate the demands of our senses, we should start with the basics. Even though experience tells us that pain and misery exist even in the most heavenly circumstances (mosquitos on a pristine beach!) and that they are impossible to avoid (you didn't know about the extortionate tourist tax), most of us live our lives in a vain attempt to avoid even minor fluctuations in our comfort and to maximise even minor pleasures. But this struggle, the constant chase with its diminishing returns, is itself the cause of far greater stress than the 'first-world problems' we are trying to banish.

Of course, what we would really love is to delight in pleasure all we want and be able to tolerate discomfort whenever we need. But our brains just don't work like that; either we choose self-satisfaction, or we don't. And if we do, that also means being tolerant of *pleasure*—a strange concept. Interestingly, the latest neuroscience findings on the dopamine cycle support this claim:

we are happier overall when we learn to tolerate pleasure, not getting carried away by it.

Every action has a consequent reaction, so here is one way we can reflect on the counterintuitive idea of tolerating pleasure: in good times, we are burning up our 'good' reactions, so there is no reason to get too excited, and in bad times, we are burning up our 'bad' reactions, so we can feel some satisfaction in knowing that better times are coming.

In the words of the *Bhagavad-gita*, 'The impermanent appearance of happiness and distress, and their disappearance in due course, are like the appearance and disappearance of winter and summer seasons. They arise from sense perception... and one must learn to tolerate them without being disturbed.' This might seem like a psychological trick, but it works: having a bit of equanimity amongst change gives us balance. Just like a tightrope walker focuses their gaze on a single point and stretches their arms out for balance, a spiritual seeker is focused on a spiritual goal with self-satisfaction for balance.

DOES IT REALLY MATTER?

Another enemy of self-satisfaction is 'keeping up with the Joneses'. This kind of comparison and competition is harmful and does not make us any happier. Yet despite the consequential rise in depression and anxiety, many of us still do it. When we meet a person whom we think has more than us, we can become jealous. When we meet a person whom we think has less than us, we can become critical or arrogant. And when we meet a person whom we think is an equal, we can become proud or competitive.

Feelings like jealousy, arrogance, and pride are causes of distress; we can do without them.

Flipping our attitude can help us overcome angst. The *Bhagavata* advises that when we meet someone who we think has more than us, we should consciously try to be happy for them; and when we meet someone who we think has less than us, we should cultivate compassion; and when we meet someone whom we consider a peer, we should foster friendship. When we notice an opportunity to do this, we can simply pause and take a moment to reflect on how we can adjust our mindset. Trying to do this consciously may feel artificial at first, but with practice, it becomes second nature and increasingly rewarding.

CAN WE BE SPIRITUAL LIVING OUR MODERN LIVES?

Spirituality must not become a path of blind following or abdication of personal responsibility. While simple faith is highly extolled in many traditions, we should safeguard ourselves from blind faith. One way we can do that is to try and understand the reasons behind what we do (or believe).

The *Bhagavata* tells the story of King Priyavrata, who had retired from worldly duties to focus on spiritual enlightenment. He had done this on the advice of his spiritual mentor, Narada, who had instructed him on the benefits of renunciation. The world situation had changed, however; society was in need of a competent monarch, a philosopher king. Considering this, Brahma, Narada's father, appealed to Priyavrata to accept his royal duties once again, contrary to Narada's advice. Both Brahma and Narada were Priyavrata's authorities and so he found himself in a dilemma.

Priyavrata resolved this dilemma through a principle called *yukta-vairagya*, by which one accepts material things but uses them for a spiritual purpose, converting the mundane into the spiritual. This principle empowers a spiritual seeker to function in the material world, avoiding both world-negation and world-absorption. Priyavrata accepted the throne but carried out his role with the mind of one detached from enjoying the fruits of his labour, dedicated instead to a higher purpose.

The idea of *yukta-vairagya* allows us to use the temporary body to attain the eternal. This idea is described as the 'supreme intelligence of the intelligent and the cleverness of the most clever'. Emotions, too, can be used, which could be as simple as expressing our gratitude and dependence on nature before eating.

The principle also helps keep spiritual novices safe in a materially alluring world. Jesus said, 'It is easier for a camel to go through the eye of a needle than for a rich man to enter the kingdom of God.' Wealth can distract one's consciousness. For someone who uses their wealth in serving others and the divine, though, it can be a means to spiritual progress. Bhaktisiddhanta Saraswati (1874-1937), an intellectual giant and devoted scholar of the *Bhagavata* tradition, said, 'If one is so expert that he can engage everything in the service of the Lord, to give up the material world would be a great blunder.'

When properly aligned, activities, emotions, things, wealth, religious duty—everything really—can be used in loving service.

It is incumbent upon the individual to use their intelligence to determine the legitimacy of religious advice and its application to one's life. This theme of making up one's own mind (after due consideration) is repeated throughout the *Bhagavata*. Life and its ever-evolving challenges can't be ignored, neither by religion nor by its followers. That's what it means to be independently thoughtful. Spirituality involves applying our intelligence and accepting responsibility, not giving either up.

IS IT AS GOOD AS I THOUGHT IT WOULD BE?

The *Bhagavata* also suggests that we deeply examine the results of materialistic activities and consider whether they deliver on their promise of happiness. It asserts that we will find that they do not and that, actually, they produce results opposite to what we expect. This message cuts against the very foundation of what we ordinarily believe, and so, such reflection requires honesty. We typically chase short-term pleasures while ignoring longer-term consequences, feelings of regret, and other such negative implications of our actions. The novelty of new purchases, for instance, eventually wears off.

WHO ARE WE REALLY?

The sages Angira and Narada once visited a king called Chitraketu to speak to him about attachment and suffering. These sages categorise suffering as follows: suffering inflicted by other living beings, suffering inflicted by nature and the elements, and suffering inflicted by one's own mind and body.

Angira and Narada explain that it is ultimately through the mind that all these categories of suffering are experienced. As many spiritual traditions claim, control the mind and you control suffering. They then challenge the King to consider his actual identity—is he his body or mind, or is he beyond them? Next, they ask him to consider where he came from, where he is going after death, and why he is suffering. They request him to reflect on these questions and tell him that answering the question of identity ('Who am I?') will bring him peace by transferring his misplaced faith in temporary things to that which is eternal. Through proper deliberation on the temporal nature of the material body, they argue, we can begin to give up our attachment to it.

If we can bring moments of careful observation and contemplation into our everyday lives, the *Bhagavata* promises us that we can glimpse Ultimate Reality and begin to gradually raise ourselves from materialism. We just need to be rational and open-minded in our efforts. We can start by looking more closely at the question: 'Who am I?'

CHAPTER 4

Who Am I?

'Now is the time to enquire about the Truth.'
—*Vedanta Sutra*

The question 'Who am I?' is a good starting point for any spiritual enquiry. Imagine looking at your reflection in an agitated pond of water. You appear to quiver due to the nature of the water. We need to wait till the water is still before we can see ourselves as we truly are. And so it is with the Self—the still, spiritual nature of the Self is at odds with the rippling material nature in which it sees itself. We are duped if we think ourselves like the rippling reflection, just because that's what we first see. We are similarly duped if we mistake our spiritual Self of limitless potential for our material body, with its very limiting constraints. Having attained a human form and the capacity for spiritual enquiry, it behoves us not to waste it but rather search for essential truths: a life less ordinary.

Sanatana Goswami (1488-1558) was the treasurer to the Mughal ruler of Bengal. He was highly educated and very accomplished, so much so that the Mughal ruler once remarked that he depended entirely on Sanatana's advice. But Sanatana's real interest lay elsewhere; he wanted to become a follower of

Chaitanya Mahaprabhu. He was imprisoned for trying to resign from his position but eventually managed to escape. When he met Chaitanya, he expressed that while people considered him a great scholar, he did not even know what was truly beneficial for his own self-interest. He asked, 'Who am I? Why am I suffering? Without knowing the answer to these questions, how can I be benefited?' Such honesty, humility, and sincerity are hallmarks of an ideal spiritual seeker.

YOUR ESSENTIAL NATURE

Every entity has its *dharma*, its essential nature—its qualities and functions. (There are other types of *dharma*—such as contextual, social, moral, and religious—but we will ignore those for now as we focus on our *essential* nature.) Let's use the example of fire; the essential qualities of fire are heat and light. The heat and light of fire remain dormant until there is fuel, something on which fire can act and through which its *dharma* can manifest. The essential functions of fire are to burn and to illuminate. This essential *dharma* is incontrovertible; it cannot be changed. However, improper fuel can appear to temporarily distort it; for example, adding magnesium to a flame turns the flame white. Whatever we focus our consciousness on is the fuel through which our essential nature manifests.

The Vedanta-sutra summarises the essential nature of the spirit as *anandamayo 'bhyasat*, bliss-seeking. It is worth pointing out that using the word 'bliss' to translate '*ananda*' indicates not just pleasure, happiness, or meaning alone, but a combination of all three, resulting in utter fulfilment. Wherever we think there is bliss, be it in money, power, relationships, and so on, there we deposit our faith and work to extract it.

The *Bhagavata* uses the terms *sat*, *chit*, and *ananda* to describe the essential spiritual nature. The Self, being of that same nature, is constitutionally these same three things: eternal and unchanging (*sat*), conscious and the knower (*chit*), and blissful (*ananda*). And this combination of eternity, cognisance, and bliss delineates the full scope of spiritual reality—not eternity alone, not even eternity with knowledge, but eternity, knowledge, and bliss. It is our inherent nature to want to be blissful—we are just looking in all the wrong places.

Our essential spiritual qualities of eternality, cognisance, and bliss relate to our ability to make choices, to understand, and to enjoy. These *qualities and functions* are what distinguishes consciousness from inert matter.[4] This unchanging nature of the Self prompts us to think beyond our usual concepts of self. The Self is not born and does not grow, decline, or die. It is pure perception, an embodiment of pure consciousness, and at the same time possesses the quality of consciousness.

Our nature remains dormant until we choose a 'fuel' on which to focus our consciousness. And as with fire, if we choose unsuitable fuel, by focusing on the temporal, our essential nature—our spiritual qualities and functions—will appear distorted. Only when we choose a suitable fuel do we experience our *dharma*.

---

4) Adapted from Bhaktivinoda Thakura's *Krishna Samhita*, the twelve characteristics of the Self are: *Nitya*—eternal, unlike the subtle or gross bodies it possesses; *Avyaya*—never destroyed when the body is destroyed; *Shuddha*—free from material contamination; *Eka*—devoid of dualities; *Ksetra-jna*—the seer; *Ashraya*—not sheltered by matter; rather, matter is sheltered by it; *Avikriya*—unaffected by any changes in the material body; *Svadrk*—self-perceiving (though not as an objection of material vision); *Hetu*—the root cause of material creation (co-creation due to its desires); *Vyapaka*—not localised to any material place or designation; *Asangi*—though situated in the material realm, unmixed with matter or material qualities; *Anavrta*—not covered by matter.

In other words, a suitable fuel is one that nourishes an entity's inherent *dharma*. Through our own experience, we can see for ourselves what qualifies as suitable fuel towards which to direct our consciousness. Which practices, environments, or people raise my consciousness to experience eternality, cognisance, and bliss? Which help me exercise more free will, understand more fully, and find more lasting joy? Make them your fuel.

Before we go further, it's worth noting the implications of an essential and incontrovertible *dharma* of the Self. They have a significant bearing on the *Bhagavata*'s vision of inclusivity. It means that beyond any 'faith' or 'religion', which clearly can change based on choice, we share a common essential nature that unites us all.

Now, the *Bhagavata* goes one step further by connecting our *dharma* with the Gold Standard of religion we saw in Chapter 1. So, when we ask, 'What is the essential function of the Self?' the *Bhagavata* answers, 'Loving service.' The Self is constantly serving *something* or *someone*. Think about it; isn't it true for us all? It might be serving an organisation, society, family, a pet, or even our own selves—all in a fervent attempt to experience love. But it is only when the Self finally directs this loving service towards its proper fuel, the Ultimate Reality, that its essential function is awakened and its essential nature experienced. It is loving service that requires free will, understanding of the beloved, and results in the experience of ultimate bliss. Loving service constitutes the Self's fullest expression. In Chapter 11, I will discuss the role of loving service as part of the yoga system.

LOVE AND FREE WILL

It is said that the Self is said to possess two attributes: love and the choice to decide where to repose this love—in other words, whether to direct our consciousness toward material illusion (illusion not because it is false, but because it is temporary) or toward spiritual reality. The role of the Self is to choose. In either choice, the Self looks for experiences of lasting bliss and remains dissatisfied until that is found. Whether we seek that eternal bliss in material life or in spiritual life is up to us, but seek we must, for it is our intrinsic nature to do so.

Although we may desire to love many things, we must understand that our current capacity to be practically—and therefore genuinely—loving is not unlimited. Genuine love also necessitates free will; it cannot be forced or legislated. But how do we know our love will be reciprocated if reposed in the Ultimate Reality? Because this is a shared characteristic of the Self and the Ultimate Reality, the part and the whole: both strive toward ever-increasing levels of loving service.

The material realm is a place of exploitation and conflict, where the ruling principle is survival of the fittest. In contrast, the spiritual realm is a place of loving service. The two realms present diametrically opposed approaches to finding happiness and fulfilment. One seeks to selfishly enjoy; the other seeks to selflessly serve.

Endowed with spiritual love, every living being is trying to fulfil the two fundamental needs of the Self: to love and to be loved. In the material world, however, despite our best efforts toward happiness, we make relationships only to become disaffected or, at best, separated at death. We remain (often deep down) unsure whether the same quality of love is returned to us in the way we give it. Spiritual practice is about shifting the focus of our love from the external to the internal. This is an exercise of free will and will be driven by the choices we make and the desires we cultivate. This loving propensity is the Self's original and natural disposition, its inalienable birthright, and it is dormant within each of us, not something to be gained from another source or imposed upon us.

SHINING WITH THE SUN

As we saw in the last chapter, with practised introspection, we can identify ourselves as the constant observer. We can feel ourselves different from this body because the sense of yearning for our natural condition of pure happiness remains somewhere within. We know we are meant for more. These distinguishing characteristics of the Self are usually forgotten in worldly life because we become preoccupied with our senses and fulfilling their urges. However, self-realisation is possible. We gradually perceive ourselves, first in a general, abstract, and possibly impersonal way, then in a more specific, personal way, and intimately related to the Ultimate Reality.

A simple analogy to help us understand our relationship to the Ultimate Reality is sunshine to the sun. We are like individual sunrays, and the Ultimate Reality is like the sun. We are the energetic emanation of the Ultimate Reality. There is no such thing as just *shine* without the *sun*. This is also why the Vedas reference statements such as, 'You, the living being, are the same in substance with that unknown Supreme.' We are, in this very real sense, part and parcel of the Ultimate Reality.

This means that we can extrapolate something of the nature

of the Ultimate Reality by studying our own spiritual nature (eternal, conscious, and desiring to be blissful), like understanding the ocean by studying the composition of a drop of its water.

Having understood the nature of the Self and its relationship with the Ultimate Reality, we can see that we can achieve our true potential once we strip ourselves of our self-imposed limits. As noted by many spiritual traditions, completeness is more about divestiture than acquisition. At a basic level, this involves the divestiture of material desires and, at its most fundamental level, the divestiture of the false ego. By stripping away these extraneous layers, we can arrive at unencumbered consciousness and our true nature.

Throughout our spiritual journey of self-discovery, our individual consciousness becomes increasingly connected with the Superconsciousness of the Ultimate Reality. This Superconsciousness is also described as the indwelling presence of Ultimate Reality within all beings.

This speaks of the two levels of self-realisation: the first is realising our identity as the individual spiritual Self, and the second is reawakening the connection of that Self with the Superconsciousness. We move beyond our limited grasp of reality to the fullness of reality—where spiritual awakening is not only glimpsed but is tangible and lasting.

A BALANCE OF EXTREMES

There are conflicting views about what constitutes the Self—or if the Self even exists. Some of these differences arise when philosophies place extreme emphasis on the Self's distinction from Superconsciousness or, at the other extreme, on its oneness with it.

An absolute difference implies that the Self does not exist as a spiritual reality, characterised by eternality, knowledge, and bliss. Rather, any sense of Self must be found in inert matter. This leads to the loss of any lasting individual identity or existence—spiritual suicide. The *Bhagavata* asserts that consciousness is a product of consciousness, not of the world. Of philosophies that do not recognise the spiritual Self, it states, 'They equate the sky with the clouds, the air with the dust particles floating in it, and think that the sky is cloudy or that the air is dirty.'

Absolute oneness, on the other hand, implies no difference whatsoever between the individual consciousness and the Superconsciousness, between the individual and Ultimate Reality. These philosophies struggle to give a satisfactory account of why we experience awareness limited to ourselves and not all other living beings. They also struggle to explain why we experience a reality that is imposed upon us rather than being controlled by us.

If there is no difference between the individual and the Ultimate Reality, we should possess full unrestricted potency, but this is not our experience. Instead, our free will is restricted, and we are subject to things we do not want. An absolute oneness might also suggest that we, unaided, brought about the entire cosmos, that we are omniscient, omnipotent, and omnipresent. But, as Jiva Goswami says, 'It is unreasonable to propose that the one pure spiritual entity has the power to maintain the external energy and is full of perfect knowledge, and yet, becomes an object of the influence of the external energy and is overcome by ignorance.'

We experience attributes of spiritual reality, but limitedly and not independently. As we saw in Chapter 3, during one's spiritual journey (especially as the false ego thins), one may well experience profound feelings of oneness with the cosmos or other living beings. This is natural; the experience of oneness is part of our spiritual development, but it is not the be-all and end-all.

Some might claim that because the Self is pure consciousness, it cannot possess specific awareness or a sense of personhood. But this contradicts our common experience of how sources of illumination, like the sun, also illuminate themselves as specific objects. The sun helps us see everything and, at the same time, also see the sun itself. Similarly, consciousness reveals itself.

Iain McGilchrist writes, 'Your identity...means that which distinguishes you from others... What makes you the same again and again—from moment to moment—is the very thing that makes you different from others. Internal sameness is a condition of external difference... As we have seen, in some kinds of right hemisphere dysfunction, continuity over time, the glue that holds the forms and patterns of the world together, is lost; thus, your identity is lost. The logical result is that you are no longer unique and that you are at any instant reproducible... Loss of uniqueness is the core deficit in delusional misidentification... We need to see both the unique and the general at once.'

The analogy of the sunray to the sun can now also help us avoid these extremes by the reconciling notion of the Self being, simultaneously, qualitatively the same as, and quantitatively different from, Ultimate Reality.

It might be argued that the Self in deep sleep does not see anything and that this is evidence of the absence of a true Self. However, this is because there is nothing to see, not because there is no one seeing. The senses, mind, and false ego are dormant in deep sleep, and consciousness requires them for perception. With the false ego dormant, the Self falsely takes itself to now be lost. This is like a person who overly identifies with their wealth and then loses it; they feel as though they themselves are lost. If we identify ourselves with inert matter, we will identify with whatever happens to it.

The Self can be indirectly perceived in our experience of sleep. We have noted that during deep sleep our false ego is dormant. Thus, we perceive a mild, temporary version of spiritual pleasure by coming in closer contact with Superconsciousness. Eventually, we must leave this state and awaken because we still have unfulfilled material desires. We are rested and enthused by this daily process. In deep sleep, the Self unconsciously perceives its existence (and indirectly that of the Superconsciousness).[5] This is why, on waking, we remember our own sustained existence through deep sleep yet remain unaware of anything else.

The two extremes of the spectrum—believing ourselves to be absolutely nondifferent from the whole of Ultimate Reality and believing ourselves to be absolutely different, without any real or lasting existence—are actually two sides of the same coin. Both deny the eternal and individual Self. One forces our identity upon the entirety of all existence and so rejects individual existence (and so is called 'impersonalism'), while the other forces it upon the limited material body and so rejects spiritual reality beyond matter (and so is called 'voidism'). The *Bhagavata* says that both are like amputating an infected hand (denying the Self's true existence) instead of removing the infection (material desires) and restoring its proper function (expressing the Self's intrinsic nature)—they are extreme solutions.

For emphasis, the *Bhagavata* uses the word *agrahana* to refer to a failure to grasp or understand our eternal spiritual position.

---

[5] Ayurveda describes how 72,000 subtle *hita* nerves expand from the region of the heart and converge at a juncture with a single nerve, the *puritat*. During deep sleep, the Self becomes detached from the *hita* nerves and enters the *puritat*.

Agrahana also has another meaning: 'killer of the Self'. The word makes the point that these extremes deny a spiritual reality. Apart from the philosophical difficulties, the ethical implications of either extreme are equally disturbing. What happens when we consider that we are absolutely everything? Or that we are absolutely nothing? What actions might be justified? The consequences could be totalitarianism or nihilism.

A LONG-STANDING DEBATE

The theory of absolute oneness was introduced by Shankaracharya (700 AD). His theory, sometimes referred to as Advaitin Vedanta, was an attempt to interpret the Vedic scriptures in a new way, to act as a bridge to Buddhism's notion of the Self's 'absolute difference' that had swept through India: a version of voidism claiming nonexistence of the Self as the inherent nature of reality—i.e. there is no Self. Buddhism's reaction to the prevalent deviations amongst Hindu priests was the rejection of the Vedic scriptures in their entirety—a central theme of which is the Self's relation with Ultimate Reality.

To counter Buddhism, Shankaracharya's reinterpretation of the Vedas took the other extreme by promoting the notion of the Self's 'absolute oneness': a version of impersonalism claiming that any individuality of Self is illusory—i.e. there is only one whole Self. As it turned out, this was an astute argument since the two extreme positions of Shankaracharya and Buddhism, though seeming to be opposites, are, in reality, very similar because they both deny the eternal individuality of the Self. Shankaracharya's contribution thus appealed to Buddhists and simultaneously paved the way for the Vedas to regain prominence in India.

> As a child, Chaitanya and his mother once brought this centuries-long philosophical debate to a practical conclusion. He sat outside his home, eating earth. When his mother reprimanded him, he asked why she was angry since she had always given him earth to eat in the form of food. After all, he argued, playfully imitating Shankaracharya's philosophy, all food was simply earth transformed. His mother retorted that if everything was 'one', without distinction, why did all people not actually eat earth for their meals? And then she answered her own question: because regular food provides nourishment, whereas eating earth leads to disease. There is an underlying oneness, but the difference is also undeniable and important in achieving our desired end. Hence, simultaneous oneness and difference.

A RECONCILING MEDITATION

The *Bhagavata* beckons us: 'What is the value of a prolonged life which is wasted, inexperienced by years in this world? Better a single moment of full consciousness because that gives one a start in searching after their supreme interest... Do the trees not live? Do the bellows of the blacksmith not breathe? All around us, do the beasts not eat and mate?' We are meant to be more.

The *Upanishads* recommend 'meditation on the internal subtle space' to progress toward realisation of the Self and union with the Superconsciousness. Many traditions are familiar with meditation—a universal approach to a universal issue. It typically begins with a turning of awareness from external matter back to the source of consciousness—the Self. As St. Francis of Assisi said, 'What we are looking for is what is looking.'

Ultimately, sustained conviction of the existence of the Self requires personal experience, and with such experience comes freedom from material desire and detachment from the dualities of life. Try this simple test to see how far you are progressing beyond duality: to what degree are you no longer angered when criticised or pleased when praised? As one progresses in self-realisation, the Self observes the perfections of transcendence rising until it reaches union with the Superconsciousness. This union, the *Bhagavata* says, is real oneness: a nonduality in which our existence continues but is *aligned* to Superconsciousness. Situated in its true nature, the Self's inherent spiritual love rushes forth and expresses itself fully. Only once reposed in this love does the Self function naturally and experience unmitigated fulfilment.

CHAPTER 5
Sources of Knowledge

'Dry arguments are inconclusive. Philosophers have to differ. The scriptures are varied. The firm truth of religious principles is hidden in the heart of self-realised persons.'
—Mahabharata

So far, I have focused on themes that might be simply intuited or gleaned through careful contemplation. Before we move on to more knowledge-dependent themes, let's take the opportunity to reflect on the validity of our various sources of knowledge. What are the tools and sources of evidence by which we can verify what we think we know? Epistemology, the study of the nature and grounds of knowledge, can help us distinguish between beliefs that are justified and those that are not. As you might imagine, this has always been a core subject of religion.

In this chapter, we will look at the role of testimony, reason, sense perception, and inner voice, all of which the *Bhagavata* says play important roles as valid sources of knowledge, so long as we understand their respective strengths and limitations. As we will see, the *Bhagavata's* approach is flexible and differentiated according to the seeker and their purpose.

For thousands of years, the West has faithfully stuck to Plato's Justified True Belief as a working definition of knowledge. According to this definition, knowledge means three things: something that I have good reason to believe, it is factually correct, and I genuinely believe it to be true. This was all fine until 1963 when Edmund Gettier upturned our whole perspective on it. One example used to illustrate Gettier's objection is the idea that a broken clock is 'right' twice a day: if a clock is stuck at 1.27pm, and I just happened to look at it at exactly 1.27pm, I would be justified (it's reasonable to assume the clock is telling the right time), it would be true (by chance), and I would believe it (why would I not). But it could hardly be called knowledge since it was just a coincidence. We are left with no clear definition of what we even mean by knowledge.

Now add into the mix the implications of Gödel's theorems, which show that there are inherent limitations in formal systems used for mathematical proofs. This implies that there are *intrinsic* limitations to what we can establish as true. This has implications beyond mathematics, particularly to do with epistemology. It implies that there are always going to be truths that we simply cannot prove within any given set of rules or axioms.

The *Bhagavata's* take on knowledge diverges from the accumulation of information or factual understanding often emphasised in Western epistemology. Rather, knowledge is closely tied to *realising* (experiencing) deeper truths by discernment between the real and the illusory. Let's take a brief look now at the main broad categories of knowledge sources.

TESTIMONY

Testimony is evidence taken from a reliable person, like an expert witness. It obviously relies upon the credibility and knowledge of the person providing the testimony. To some, this kind of 'descending' knowledge, which has been handed down, represents the antithesis of science's 'ascending' approach to knowledge, where we seek to grasp that beyond our current reach. They might argue that while not all of us have seen through an electron microscope, and so we generally accept what we read about atoms in textbooks, all areas of scientific knowledge are still subject to critical inquiry.[6,7] In contrast, the knowledge in most religions' scriptures is never up for debate by the believer. This is a notable objection and why the *Bhagavata* says that testimony can and should be verified by observation, reason, and personal experience.

Most religious systems accept testimony in the form of scripture as authoritative. The *Bhagavata* accepts testimonial evidence as particularly helpful for accessing spiritual knowledge that is beyond the grasp of sensory perception or logic, though it does so with tips for verification to avoid blind following.

---

6) It is worth noting that what is held as axiomatic in one context may not hold in another, or that with the evolution of science what we believe as axiomatic may also evolve, as it did with the development of quantum theory. This seems to contradict the very meaning of axiomatic and forces us to concede the limitations of the term.

7) It should also be noted that the idea of science in the real world being unbiased and repeatable is naïve. Leading scientific publications including Science, Nature, and BMJ, have evidenced this. For example: repeating a psychology experiment drops the significance rate from 97% to 68%; more than 70% of scientists failed to reproduce another scientist's experimental results, and 50% failed to reproduce even their own results; 1 in 7 falsified findings in order to be published in BMJ, 1 in 3 admitted to data mining to get the results they wanted, and 1 in 3 couldn't find the data they used. Peer reviews are also badly flawed, as shown by BMJ who deliberately inserted *major* errors into papers for review: not one reviewer found all the errors, some didn't spot any, and most reviewers only caught a quarter of them.

Doubt is listed in the *Bhagavata* as one of the five aspects of intelligence, but such doubts can be mitigated by reliable information. Doubt, after all, has its limits. Descartes recognised that Aristotle's empiricism was limited because sense perception is limited and fallible. He insisted that the mind must arrive at the fundamental certainties of existence by reference to itself alone, thus arriving at his famous *cogito ergo sum* ('I think, therefore I am'). But, such an approach still doesn't bring us to reliable truth, only to *possible* or limited truth. For example, Descartes, while convinced of his own existence, found himself still able to doubt the existence of others.

The *Bhagavad-gita* advises us to consider things carefully, with intelligence[8], and in the association of a genuine spiritual teacher. When considering testimony, we are advised to also consider and reconcile other sources of evidence, including both sensory and rational. Jiva Goswami, a medieval scholar and saint of the *Bhagavata* tradition, points out potential hazards in excluding other forms of evidence while accepting scriptural truth claims. This is common sense, but it is dangerously ignored by some approaches to reading scripture. Examples of hazards include:

1) Some scriptures contain principles that are subject to time, place, and circumstance.

2) Scriptures may be accepted as having divine origin, but they are conveyed to us through human sages and prophets.

---

8) Kamandaka Muni in his *Kamandakiya Nitisara* lists the aspects of intelligence as: the inclination to hear what others say; actually hearing what others say; the capacity to grasp the meaning of what others say; retentiveness; reasoning in favour of a proposition; reasoning against a proposition; insight into the meaning of what others say; and true wisdom.

3) Scriptures do not negate ordinary sense perception; otherwise, we would not be able to hear or read them.

4) The domain of knowledge for scriptures is largely the transcendent, whereas our experience tells us that the physical world can be reliably known through other means.

5) There may be apparent contradictions between scriptural descriptions and those we perceive in the phenomenal world that require either direct or indirect interpretation.[9] At least in such cases then, our understanding of scripture can be influenced by our perception or reason.

Such exclusions point to an important claim of the *Bhagavata*: the underlying reality of the world can be known by our mind and senses, proportionate to their refinement. As Plotinus said, 'Never did an eye see the Sun unless it had first become sunlike.' Testimony can assist us in that process of refinement. Thus, without needing to reject reason or perception, carefully selected testimony is asserted as a valid means of acquiring knowledge.

CAN WORDS ANSWER?

The *Bhagavata* addresses the following doubt: scriptures, being made up of letters and sounds, are limited to describing the qualities of material nature, but the Ultimate Reality is devoid

---

9) An example from the Vedic tradition is the phrase *gangayam ghosah*. The literal translation would be 'The hamlet on the Ganges.' Our experience and reason tell us that this meaning requires an indirect interpretation in line with the obvious intention of the phrase to mean 'The hamlet is on the bank of the Ganges.'

of material qualities, being transcendental to all material manifestations and their causes. So, how can the scriptures describe the Ultimate Reality, which cannot be described in words? Such doubts have led some traditions to conclude that divinity must be impersonal and beyond any type of description and that any such references must be interpreted as merely symbolic. The *Bhagavata* has a different response: ordinary inert matter also has spiritual potential. Just as we can use our material intelligence and senses to gradually elevate our consciousness, similarly, ordinary paper, ink, and words can also be infused with spiritual potency to make the indescribable at least *somewhat* describable. The Ultimate Reality is, after all, nondual.

Another argument that is sometimes made is that the historical dating of scriptural texts is not important because their significance should be self-evident, not dependent on when they were written. But historical precedence is a sign of both authenticity and validity and thus carries major implications. The test of time is also significant; some might argue that it is the only measure of validity or usefulness.[10] The test of time takes into account the centuries, even millennia, of accumulated intelligence, analysis, and experience. Of course, the downside is that over long periods of time, testimonial truth can become lost or corrupted by human neglect or intervention. This is why our first test of religion in Chapter 2 questions how teachings have been recorded, transmitted, and preserved over time to maintain their integrity.

Different faith traditions claim to hold testimonial truth—though their 'truths' may be different, even contradictory. This raises the question of what makes one testimony more authori-

---

10) See Nassim Taleb's *Skin in the Game*.

tative than another. Here are some guidelines that you may want to consider for evaluation:

A) Do you clearly understand the basic *meaning* of the statements? If not, what is the process for understanding them? (For the *Bhagavata*, there is a word-for-word translation from the original Sanskrit.[11])

B) Do you know how to verify that the statements are *true*? Once you've understood them, how does the tradition say that you can verify for yourself if they are true? (For the *Bhagavata*, this means through your own personal experience as you engage with the process of spirituality.)

C) Do you have good evidence for believing it? The tests of religion in Chapter 2 are a summary of this.

Scriptural testimony, along with the guidance of a genuine spiritual teacher, is a very effective way to start penetrating the secrets of transcendence. The path requires honesty and humility because transcendental subject matter is a living truth, revealed from the heart rather than grasped by the force of intellect. Chapter 3 explored how we can get a glimpse of this reality with our intellect and without any *a priori* faith. The idea is that those glimpses will give us enough confidence to consider scriptural testimony at least worthy of further investigation.

While testimony can further open our eyes to transcendent

---

[11] Published by the Bhaktivedanta Book Trust, the world's largest publisher of India's spiritual classics.

truths, reason and perception retain an important verification role on the spiritual journey.

SENSORY INPUT

Modern science recognises that our observation interferes with our understanding of underlying reality; thus, the ancient notion that, 'We see things as we are.' We also know that our sense perceptions have many frailties; we have no real basis for claiming that what we perceive is the truth, the whole truth, and nothing but the truth. The plethora of optical illusions makes this point obvious. So, if we cannot always be sure of our senses, it should be no surprise that the *Bhagavata* says that it is futile to try and understand transcendence *purely* through them—that is, until they become attuned to perceiving consciousness.

But don't we know that our ordinary sensory information of this world is valid because it corresponds with our experiences? And if our experiences are not valid, we would be in a bind: we would never be sure that the rope is not a snake. The *Bhagavata* accepts this, but it is not the whole story. As long as our senses are driven by 'left brain thinking' and so unattuned to consciousness, their objects will appear like shadows of spiritual reality. A shadow is also real in that it exists and has some properties, but it is not the same as the original object. Similarly, a dream is real in that we experience something while sleeping, but it is not 'reality'. In the rope example, we need to first convince ourselves to relinquish the notion of it being a snake before we can appreciate the real nature of a rope. Unfortunately, our predicament is that we struggle to conceive of both a conditioned and liberated state, much like someone who is dreaming doesn't realise that they are dreaming. As the ancient Chinese text, *Zhuangzi*, states, 'Once upon a time, I dreamt I was a butterfly, fluttering hither and thither, to all intents and purposes a butterfly. I was conscious only of my happiness as a butterfly, unaware that I was myself. Soon I awoke, and there I was, veritably myself again. Now I do not know whether I was then a man dreaming I was a butterfly, or whether I am now a butterfly, dreaming I am a man.'

The idea that there is nothing beyond inert matter is founded upon an inherent illusion. Things are simply not as they appear to be. It is only when we wake that we can realise that we were only dreaming. The process of spirituality is the process of awakening. The material world is real but temporary; we are not all in some completely fictional state of existence, but neither do we perceive the underlying reality.

The *Bhagavata* says, 'Actually, the visible forms of this world are just an imaginary arrangement resorted to by illusioned persons in order to facilitate material affairs'—an accurate statement in terms of the reality of how our consciousness experiences physical matter. Obviously, our senses provide at least some limited scope for reliable evidence when dealing with the simple and tangible: if we want to know the time, we are better off looking at a clock (one that's working, please!) than turning to scripture. However, we should know that our senses (again, in their current unattuned state) essentially provide us with simplistic hacks rather than the underlying reality. A computer's user interface provides a hack so that we can ignore the underlying 'reality' of the code and back-end electronics, but we shouldn't be fooled into thinking that the interface is all there is. We will come back to the workings of our senses in the next chapter.

REASON

Reason and logic are powerful means of convincing our intelligence of what is and is not true, but we cannot afford to ignore their limits. Trying to prove the existence of God using only reason and logic is an example of a debate that has raged for millennia, based mostly on teleological, ontological, cosmological, or moral arguments. But long before Hume, saints of the *Bhagavata* tradition acknowledged the limitations of such arguments. Ramanuja (1017-1137), a foremost philosopher and saint, argued why teleological and cosmological arguments ultimately fail in proving the existence of God. The role of logic, and reason more broadly, is important in helping open our eyes to the possibility and reasonableness of certain truths. They bring us to the threshold, but they cannot get us across. Pascal said, 'The last proceeding of reason is to recognise that there is an infinity of things which are beyond it.'

Logic is born of our mind and intelligence, but as spiritual beings, we demand more. It is only as valid as the axioms on which it is built, and those are vulnerable to incompleteness, bias, and mistake. Many people would consider the laws of logic to be absolute and the most fundamental truths we can know. But even when we consider these laws (e.g., the laws of identity, mutual exclusivity, and collective exhaustivity), we see that they are not absolute; for them to be meaningful in context, they must be caveated. Here is Einstein: 'As far as the propositions of mathematics refer to reality, they are not certain; as far as they are certain, they do not refer to reality.'

Another reason for logical incompleteness is the limited information or perceptibility at our disposal. The *Bhagavata* says that in the spiritual realm, time is absent, and, in its stead, there is a state of the eternal present. A state of 'no time' existence is inconceivable to us, like someone living on a two-dimensional plane trying to comprehend a three-dimensional reality: it can't be done. So, the information at our disposal imposes a cap on our ability to reason; we need new information to make further progress.

INNER VOICE

Beyond the information that comes to us from 'outside' (testimony or our senses) or that which we convince ourselves about (reason), what about when we feel a truth deep down inside ourselves? Like an inner voice or intuition? The *Bhagavata* speaks strongly about the importance of inner voice, stating, 'Of all forms of evidence for establishing the truth, experience from one's own life is the strongest.' It grows with spiritual maturity and reveals from within, emerging from our connection with the Ultimate Reality.

To ensure a grounded approach to listening to our inner voice, we can cross-check it with other forms of evidence. There are spiritual truths that are beyond the grasp of our mind and senses, and though testimony can point us in the right direction, such truths can be perceived and understood only through direct experience (revelation).

The importance of inner voice is as significant in science as it is in spirituality; this should not be surprising at first, since both disciplines seek deeper truths. Einstein said, 'To these elementary [physical] laws there leads no logical path, but only intuition, supported by being sympathetically in touch with experience.'

WHAT IS THE ROLE OF FAITH?

The Sanskrit word for faith, *sraddha*, translates as 'where we place our heart' or 'that which holds our heart'. The concept of faith, then, is intrinsically tied with love. As we saw in Chapter 4, we are bliss-seeking beings. Wherever we think there is pleasure, there we deposit our faith. Typically, that might be money, or power, or relationships, and so forth. In a spiritual context, faith means to be confident that all worthy things are accomplished through spiritual connection and love. Many traditions have beautiful stories about simple, sincere faith being the gateway to spiritual flourishing. Once such faith is established, the *Bhagavata* assures us that spiritual practice quickly bears fruit.

Whereas much discussion about faith in the context of religion involves 'head' arguments based on perception and reason, the Sanskrit word *sraddha* encourages us to be alert to what appeals to the heart—to our feelings and intuition.

An appeal to the heart is, in many ways, a good measure of philosophy. It can take you beyond external considerations such as its country of origin, surrounding culture, or other physical manifestations. The *Bhagavata* emphasises the difference between such externals and underlying spiritual principles. Just as one's eyes see colour and one's ears hear sound, the Self, enabled by faith, can perceive the reality of transcendence. This is, in fact, the core function of faith. Saint Anselm said, 'I believe in order that I might understand.' Our postmodern cultures drive us toward faith in ourselves as isolated individuals; the *Bhagavata* encourages faith in our relationship with the Ultimate Reality.

CHAPTER 6
Cosmic Evolution

'The total material substance is the womb, and in that great Brahman I place the cosmic embryo, making possible the births of all living beings.'
—Bhagavad-gita

In this chapter, we are looking at the nature of the cosmos and our role in manifesting it. We are here because we want to be, and the cosmos is where we get to act out our desires (the good, the bad, and the ugly). The universe then responds to our changing desires, not as a beholden servant but as a neutral broker.

STUFF

There is a subtle reality beyond atoms and subatomic particles—a fact the modern world is only recently coming to appreciate through quantum theory. One of the ways we try to understand the nature of reality in chemistry and physics is to try and understand the fundamental building blocks of matter. But we still don't know what that is: I spent much of my university years in chemistry labs looking through powerful microscopes or at spectrometry outputs, and this became abundantly clear. We have some ideas about the nature of subatomic particles, but we do not know what 'stuff' they are made from. Leading physicists understand that our very approach, and thus the search for 'fundamental particles', is misleading.[12] According to Quantum Field Theory, 'stuff' is basically made up of excitations (quanta) of quantum fields. And what are quantum fields? Abstract mathematical entities that give rise to both matter and energy. They are not located in any one place (they extend across the entire universe), and they do not have mass. Thus, they are not categorised as matter (matter has mass and is spatially present). What arises from these fields can be discrete and can have properties like mass, charge, and spin. And while this all seems pretty far-fetched for those without a PhD in physics, fascinatingly, our descriptions of quantum fields do not contradict the *Bhagavata's* descriptions of the underlying basis of matter. And lest the reader think that we can simply insert quantum fields to update the old reductive approach, here is Niels Bohr: 'There is no quantum world. There is only an abstract quantum physical description.'

Let's take an example: if you want to know what an apple is made of, you can cut it up into increasingly small pieces. If you keep going long enough, you will get to a molecular level. This is

---

12) Mark Bickhard: '...the best contemporary physics demonstrates that there are no particles at all. The fundamental constituents of the world...are dynamic quantum fields in a dynamic space-time...The quantization is reminiscent of particles, but it is in fact a quantization of wave-like processes, not particles. This is akin...to the quantization of the number of wavelengths in a guitar string. But there are no guitar sound particles, and, similarly, there are no physical particles either. And David Tong: 'Physicists routinely teach that the building blocks of nature are discrete particles such as the electron or quark. That is a lie. The building blocks of our theories are not particles but fields: continuous, fluid like objects spread throughout space.' And 'No matter how closely you zoom in, you will not find irreducible building blocks.'

what science is generally good at doing. But somewhere during this process, you will have 'lost' the very essence of what an apple *is*.

A reductive approach can have utility—after all, much of our technological progress has been based on this—but if we want to understand the *nature* of reality, it can also cripple the very goal of scientific enquiry: finding truth (not just utility). As Carl Woese put it, 'Molecular biology could read the notes, but it couldn't hear the music.'

The *Bhagavata* answers the question of the fundamental building blocks by pointing to non-reducible and fundamental qualities—not particles. I recognise that this will be a huge paradigm shift for most readers, but it is not contradictory to science, and it resolves the gaps we find in the reductive approach popular science takes to the nature of physical reality.[13]

MATERIAL AND SPIRITUAL ENERGY

Before we go further, a basic categorisation of the energies within the Ultimate Reality will help us set the stage for this topic:

- Internal energy refers to unencumbered, nondual consciousness. As we saw in Chapter 4, it is characterised by eternality, cognisance, and bliss. It is the basis of the spiritual realm. It is also the basis for the following two energies.

- External energy refers to the transformation of the internal energy, sometimes called the shadow. It *appears* independent of and separate from the internal energy, like ice appears

---

13) See translation and commentary on the *Sankhya Sutra* by Ashish Dalela.

different to water. It is the basis of how we generally experience the cosmos.

- Marginal energy refers to individual units of consciousness as minute extensions of the internal energy. Since these individual units are also consciousness, they share the same characteristics as the internal energy, but to a limited degree. It comprises the spiritual Self of all living beings.

The realm of the internal energy is eternal and infallible—the 'spiritual world'. The realm of the external energy is temporary and fallible—the 'material world'. In the material world, spiritual reality is present and all-pervading but not (generally) perceptible. This is why, as spiritual beings, we find materialism ultimately lacking, which explains our perennial need for spiritual fulfilment. Spirituality, in one sense, is the journey from the material world to the spiritual world.

For the remainder of this chapter, we will focus on the material realm and return to the spiritual realm in later chapters.

IN THE BEGINNING...

With the above (somewhat lengthy—sorry!) introductory remarks, let's get started. The cosmos—including time—comes from the Ultimate Reality and then merges back, just like water comes down from the sky and then, through evaporation, returns. It exists in alternating states, cycling through manifest and unmanifest states, just as the body's senses are always present but not manifest (active) when we're asleep.

For the cosmos to become manifest as we know it, the internal energy takes on certain 'material', or limiting[14] qualities, thus transforming into the external energy. The cosmos can, therefore, be seen as 'spiritual', 'material', or both, depending on your perspective.

The Ultimate Reality is sometimes called *nirguna* or *nirvana*. Both terms denote the absence of temporality or any other qualities of material nature. When the internal energy transforms into the external energy, we get *saguna* (*sa* meaning 'with', and *guna* meaning 'material qualities').[15] 'Qualities' of nature are thus explained as the most fundamental way of understanding and perceiving reality, rather than physical particles.

This transformation of the internal energy into the external energy is the first stage of cosmic creation; its resultant state is a state of potential (*Pradhana*), in which there is no activity, time, manifestation, or even awareness. This state is thus dormant—a vast, *almost* nothingness; 'almost' because it is like a void but is pregnant with potential—like zero is *almost* nothingness with unlimited potential. It has been compared to being in a completely dark room: you can't see anything, including yourself.

It is said that this dormant potential state 'was agitated by the glance of Transcendence'. The *Bhagavata* goes on to explain that this *glance* is composed of the combination of time and the unlimited living beings. Time represents the *will* of Ultimate Reality, and the living beings (the marginal energy) arrive with their respective destiny and desires (carried over from past cycles of similar cosmic development). Observation directs consciousness,

---

14) There is an interesting point here that an omniscient and omnipotent Being could be said to lack something, and that is *limitation*. But that is not so, according to the *Bhagavata*.
15) The words *saguna* and *nirguna* can also be used to different effect: *saguna* can mean with *transcendental* qualities, and thus refer to the transcendent personality of Ultimate Reality, and *nirguna* can be taken to mean without *any* qualities, and thus refer to the impersonal energy of Ultimate Reality.

and this has effects. As one passage describes, 'Exactly as a piece of iron moves under the influence of a magnet, inert matter moves when you glance over the total material energy.' Without this glance, the dormant state would always remain dormant, and we would have no first motion. The infusion of time and the marginal energy allows material nature to move from its dormant state to a primordial state (*Mahat-tattva*) and then on to the activated state (*Prakriti*). You can think of it as 'ready-set-go': the potential state to the primordial state to the activated state.

Once the activated state has begun to 'move', it becomes increasingly attractive. As a result, living beings become progressively absorbed in it, engaging with it to fulfil their pending destinies and desires. At first, it appears that the activated state is dancing to our tune, responding to our desires. However, the dance soon becomes so mesmerising that it is *we* who become enslaved by our absorption.[16]

The *Bhagavata* describes innumerable egg-shaped universes of different sizes, varying from just billions of miles in diameter to far larger, emerging because of the above process. These universe-bubbles are seemingly lifeless for eons. According to the *Bhagavata*, the last time this occurred was trillions of years ago.

In Chapter 4, we discussed how the nature of the Self is pleasure-seeking, and how that original spiritual pleasure is to be found in loving service. But we are also capable of desiring to seek pleasure through exploitation. This entire material creation is a bit like a virtual reality theme park, created to give us an opportunity to play out wayward desires that are incompatible with our original spiritual nature of loving service. In order to facilitate this virtual

---

16) This paragraph is based on part of a Religious Studies A-level lesson by Dr A.D. Srirangapriya Ramanujadasan, delivered at Avanti House Secondary School in London.

reality experience, we need to adopt our new false identity—that we are independent enjoyers. The Sanskrit word for this false identity is *ahankara*, which translates as 'maker of the Self' —we adopt a made-up identity. 'I am an enjoyer', and therefore, 'let me enjoy'. In other words, it is our desire to enjoy independently that generates a false ego, which means misidentification. False ego is the first step, or transformational activity, that takes place in the primordial state.

Now, the false ego can interact with the *gunas* to generate the mind and body, and material elements, that will help the misidentified Self 'enjoy' this world. We start with an abstract concept of false ego and then journey through infinite and specific varieties of false ego by which we hope to experience and enjoy the world as masters.

This account of 'creation' is notably different from the standard scientific or religious *ex nihilo* explanation—where the universe emerges out of nothing—in that the possibility of creation exists in nature itself. This possibility is sometimes manifest and sometimes unmanifest. So, when the universe is destroyed, it hasn't absolutely ceased to exist—it can spring up again and again.

In providing its account of creation, a verse from the *Bhagavata* points out that, 'There is no direct engineering by the Lord for the creation and destruction of the material world. What is described in the Vedas about his direct interference is simply to counteract the idea that material nature is the creator.'[17] The Vedic texts present various ways of understanding the infinite complexity of creation and their sophistication is often missed when the above purpose is not understood. Matter has no initiative of its own. It superficially appears to exhibit initiative, but that's only after it

---

17) I am grateful to my younger son for highlighting the significance of this verse to me.

is set into motion by consciousness. Many of the Vedic creation stories exist to help us avoid the fallacy of attributing initiative to inert matter.

To help conclude this section, we can frame the above in the context of causal categories. The *Bhagavata* uses pottery as an example that overlaps with Aristotle's categories:

1) Material cause = the clay = Potential state

2) Efficient cause = the wheel and the force applied = Time

3) Formal cause = the blueprint = Universal Form
(see Chapter 2, and below)

4) Final cause = storage vessel (the purpose) = Self's desires

COSMIC EVOLUTION

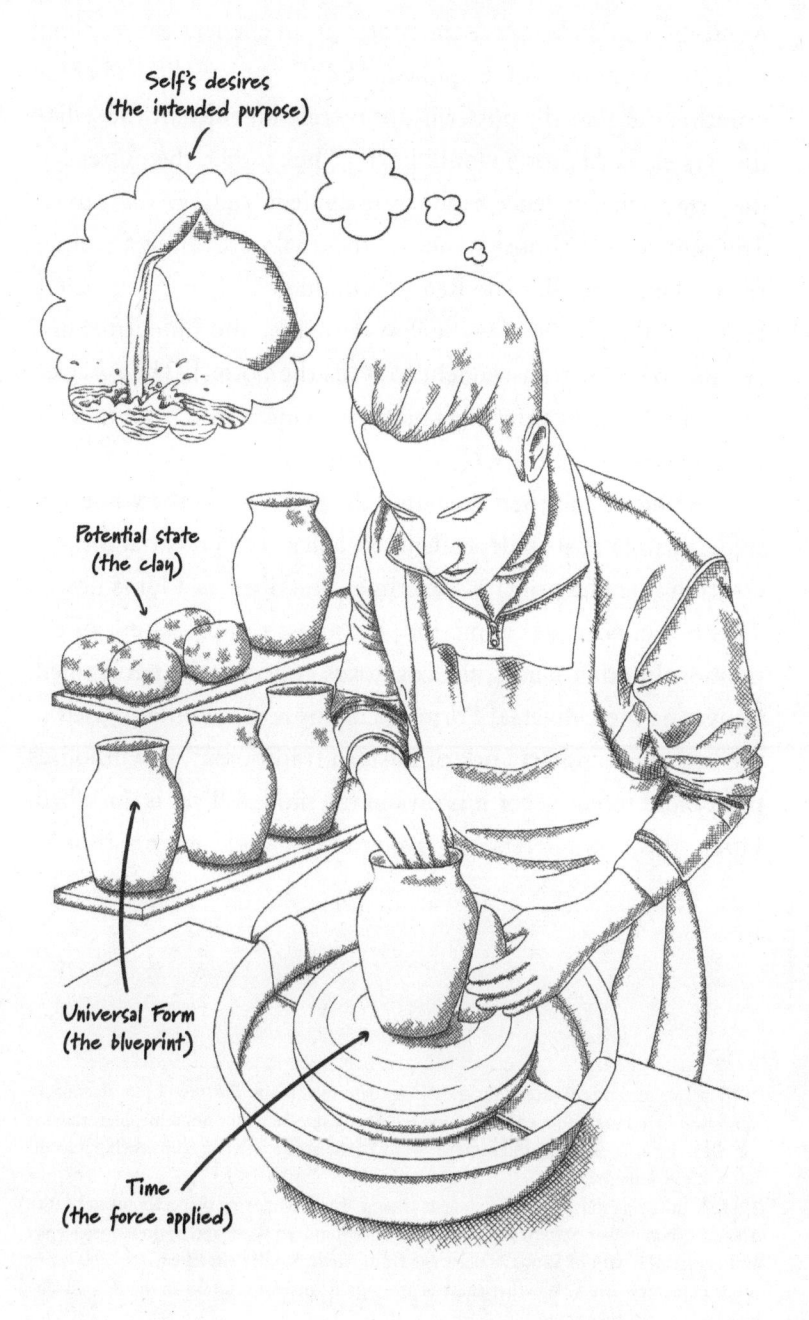

Aristotle would also place the potter as an efficient cause, along with the wheel and force applied. The *Bhagavata* differs here in pointing out that the potter is not merely an efficient cause like the wheel, as Aristotle would have it, but rather, the potter has their own independence as the transcendent 'cause of all causes'. The potter must choose to accept the goal of creating a storage vessel. Thus, the Ultimate Reality simultaneously pervades every aspect of the cosmos (as the clay, process, and blueprint) and yet also remains transcendent to it (as the potter). The *Bhagavata* describes it as akin to a spider weaving a web from its own energy, inhabiting the web it has created, retracting the web by consuming it, and then repeating the process; all the while, the spider maintains its independent existence. The potential form of creation (the blueprint) is sometimes described as a lotus flower. This is a conceptual depiction, or 'artist's impression', of the cosmos. In other places, the cosmos is conceptually personified, known as the Universal Form.[18] The lotus is commonly used in the literature and artwork of Eastern traditions.[19] It symbolises purity and serenity, for it grows in the mud and yet is unsullied. Often, this is in reference to 'Being in the world but not of it.'

---

18) The two methods of ascending knowledge described in the *Taittiriya Upanishad* of the *Yajur Veda* are *vyasti*, to meditate on the self as a fragment of the Supreme, like studying the ocean by a single drop, and *samasti*, study of the entire universe, considering it as the body of the Supreme.

19) It is intriguing that flower-like designs emerge when overlaying planetary orbital paths. The first such flower pattern was illustrated four hundred years ago by Johannes Kepler and depicts the path of Venus as observed from Earth. Similar effects emerge by layering other planetary orbits. Whether there is any significance or relation to the *Bhagavata's* lotus reference is unknown.

COSMIC EVOLUTION

Aspects of Ultimate Reality according to the Bhagavata

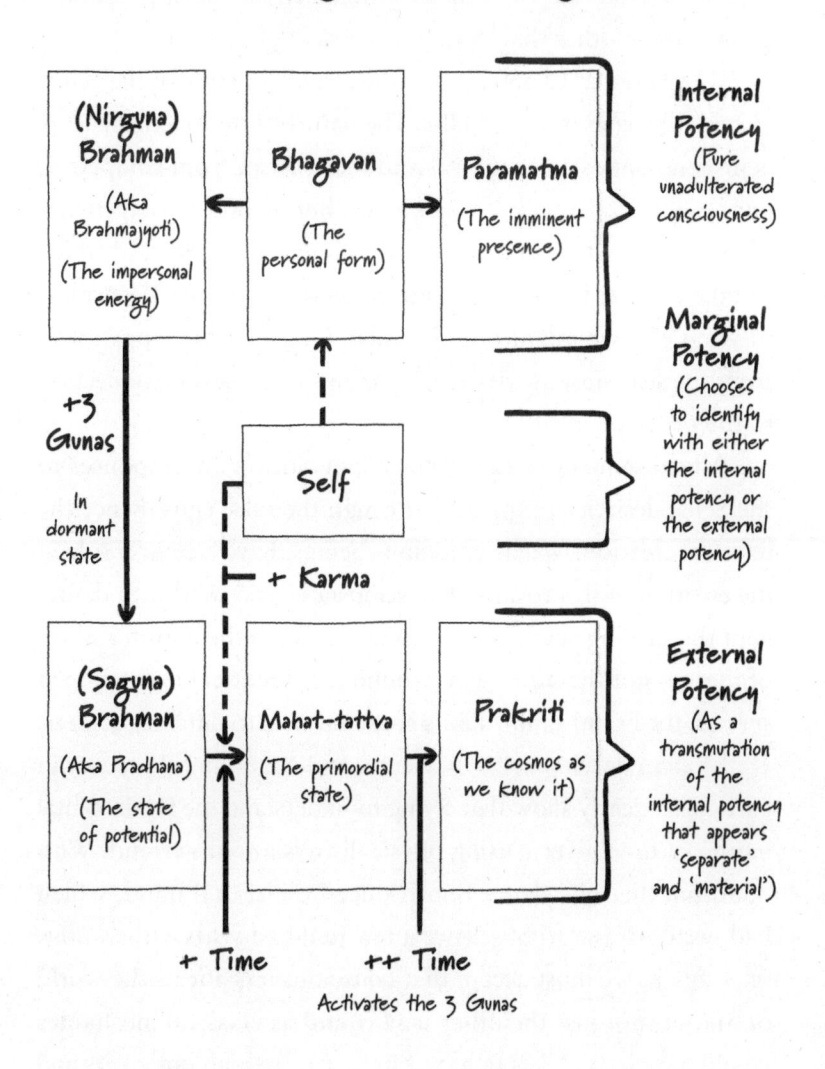

(Nirguna) Brahman (Aka Brahmajyoti) (The impersonal energy)

Bhagavan (The personal form)

Paramatma (The imminent presence)

} **Internal Potency** (Pure unadulterated consciousness)

+3 Gunas — In dormant state

Self

+ Karma

} **Marginal Potency** (Chooses to identify with either the internal potency or the external potency)

(Saguna) Brahman (Aka Pradhana) (The state of potential)

Mahat-tattva (The primordial state)

Prakriti (The cosmos as we know it)

} **External Potency** (As a transmutation of the internal potency that appears 'separate' and 'material')

+ Time   ++ Time

Activates the 3 Gunas

FALSE EGO

As described earlier, the false ego will help it identify with the external energy's foreign environment so that it can 'fit in'. This is the first subtle step in how a spiritual Self mistakenly identifies as something other than consciousness.

We learned in Chapter 4 that the essential nature of the Self is eternality, cognisance, and bliss. The nature of the external energy is just the opposite: temporal and inert. Also, from Chapter 4, our essential function is loving service. But, in order to experience our essential nature in the external energy, we are instead trying to take charge. However, we are a fish out of water. Regardless of what else we might offer it, a fish just can't be happy away from the sea—just as we can't be happy without our connection to the ocean of spirit.

All subsequent stages of cosmic evolution are responses to the Self's desires as expressed through the false ego—hence the term *co*-creation. We, as conscious beings, have a central role in the creation of this cosmos. Consciousness, endowed with desire, is in the driving seat: consciousness leads to the manifestation of matter, not the other way around. And matter (in developed species, the brain) simply limits consciousness to different degrees.

Modern developments in science, and quantum field theory in particular, clearly show that trying to understand the fundamental nature of the universe using physicalism is a fool's errand. With quantum theory, science reintroduced the causal mind, which had been cast out from science a few hundred years earlier: now, once again, we must accept that consciousness affects the world of matter; not just the other way round as classical mechanics would have it. As Niels Bohr put it, '…we are both onlookers and actors in the great drama of existence.' And, of course, well-known phenomena like the placebo effect show this to be true in practice.

THE MATERIAL ELEMENTS

We called the initial dormant potential state the material cause (clay) because it contains all the necessary 'ingredients'. Because material qualities (*gunas*) are still dormant and inactive, this state is, in one sense, the threshold between the spiritual and material. That state of potential hosts the subtle, abstract forms of raw perception: sound, touch, form, taste, and smell. (This is an important part of the puzzle, so please bear with me.) The word subtle indicates potentiality, a state where information exists for future manifestation. Just as a thought or plan to act transforms into tangible form (the act itself), as soon as there is an opportunity, the subtle forms of raw perception develop into their tangible manifestation: the elements. The entire process of cosmic manifestation takes place first on the subtle level, then on the tangible.

Within the now-manifesting universe arise the first signs of the elements—the subtle vibration of sound. It is said that we can perceive this subtle (inaudible) sound vibration when we stop all external hearing.[20] We perceive it from within. It is said that through meditation on this subtle sound, the seed form of all spiritual knowledge, mystic sages advance in spiritual realisation.

From this subtle sound arises the first syllable, Om, composed of three sounds (A, U, M) representing the three aspects of the Ultimate Reality described in Chapter 2: the impersonal energy

---

20) Stopping all external hearing is not as easy as it may sound (no pun intended!). The quietest places in the world are lab rooms that bring the background noise reading down to about -9.4 decibels.

(*Brahman*[21]); the imminent Superconsciousness (*Paramatma*[22]); and the supreme transcendent person (*Bhagavan*). All other sounds are derived from this Om, the 'secret essence and eternal seed', and it exists in the Self of every being. You might be familiar with Om from meditation or yoga classes; this is the meaning and origins of it.

When the desire to hear arises, sound transforms into Akash[23] (ether). Ether—the first 'element'—is the medium for thoughts, concepts, and the subtle levels of sound.[24] Its presence evokes the power of hearing, after which sound moves from subtle to audible. So, ether arises to manifest sound; air arises to manifest touch; fire arises to manifest form; water arises to manifest taste; earth arises to manifest smell. The attributes are cumulative in the above order, so that by the time we get to earth, it contains all of them. For example, the element 'air' is defined as all matter that possesses touch (and sound) but not form, taste, or smell. Therefore, matter that is invisible (e.g., dark matter) is classified as 'air'. Since 'air' contains touch (as well as sound carried over

---

21) The word *Brahman* is used with different effect across the Vedic literature. It is often used to refer to the nondual spiritual reality that is the basis of all existence, including the individual Self and the material nature. It can also refer specifically to the impersonal aspect of the Ultimate Reality, sometimes *Brahmajyoti*, where the suffix *jyoti* indicates effulgence/light.
22) *Param* meaning 'supreme'; *atma* denotes the Self, i.e., Superconsciousness.
23) It is the concept of Akash that Carl Jung referred to in his theory of the 'collective unconscious' in which we access the wisdom and experience of our ancestors, and from which the term Akashic Records arises. Nikola Tesla also seemed to refer to this idea when he said: 'My brain is only a receiver. In the universe there is a core from which we obtain knowledge, strength, inspiration. I have not penetrated into the secrets of this core, but I know that it exists.' Without such an 'element', we remain unable to explain quantum entanglement over space and time.
24) Before we speak, we have the concepts and the specific thoughts of speech. This happens so quickly that we often don't pay it any attention. These are examples of the subtle levels of 'sound' that precede audible sound. The Vedic texts describe a total of four levels of sound, only the last being audible (in common terminology). This also explains why ether is stated as the medium for (subtle) sound, whereas we would normally assume air to be the medium for sound.

from ether), such matter explains sensations of touch, such as 'heaviness'—which is exactly how we know dark matter exists. This is, of course, different from how modern science would define the word 'air'; there is much lost in translation. We can apply the same logic to 'fire', 'water', and 'earth', which possess the cumulatively increasing sensations of form, taste, and smell, respectively. Modern science tells us that light gives rise to mass, which in turn gives rise to form: how is this any different to the *Bhagavata's* version that fire gives rise to form? Since the process is cumulative, it is within earth that the peculiarities of *all* elements exist. The progression can be summarised as follows:

Concept of Sound (desire to hear) → Ether
(medium for transmission, including thoughts) →
Power of Hearing → Sound

Ether + Sound → Concept of Touch (desire to touch) → Air
(medium for sense perception) → Power of Touch → Touch

Air + Touch → Concept of Form (desire to see) → Fire[25]
(medium for distinguishing) → Power of Sight → Form

Fire + Form → Concept of Taste (desire to taste) → Water
(medium for fluidity) → Power of Taste → Taste

Water + Taste → Concept of Odour (desire to smell) → Earth
(medium for solidity) → Power of Smell → Smell

---

25) Depending on context, the principle of fire can also be translated as fire as we usually refer to it, or as electricity, or in the context of the body it refers to acid, enzymes, and bile.

At first glance, these 'elements' may seem simplistic or identical to Naïve Realism, but they are anything but. Remember, these descriptions are based on a radically different perspective—one that is fundamentally qualitative rather than just physical—so we must consider what these elements *represent* in a universal context, in addition to our standard physicalist way of interpreting matter. They are referred to as elemental because, for the reasons outlined at the beginning of this chapter, qualities (and not particles) are elemental. They are the real 'stuff' the cosmos is made from. Science is catching up with this concept: Donald Hoffman writes, 'I am postulating conscious experiences as ontological primitives, the most basic ingredients of the world. I'm claiming that experiences are the real coin of the realm.'

We perceive sense perceptions (the effects), not the underlying objects or functions themselves. For example, we perceive heaviness but not the gravitational field—we simply infer the gravitational field. This is true for all objects and all functions. We perceive the redness, taste the sweetness, and then infer the apple. Therefore, it is the redness and sweetness that are elemental. Through these *qualitative* elements we can arrive at a more comprehensive sense of reality.

Bertrand Russell, in *The Problems of Philosophy*, writes on this problem: '...although the *relations* of physical objects have all sorts of knowable properties, derived from their correspondence with the relations of sense-data, the physical objects themselves remain unknown in their intrinsic nature, so far at least as can be discovered by means of the senses.' We will pick up this point in the next chapter.

A SACRED UNIVERSE

There is one last dimension to this account of the cosmos. Recall the role of the Universal Form, the blueprint and conceptual personification of the cosmos. This concept indicates a nested or fractal structure of the cosmos. What is true at an individual level is reflected in the cosmos, and what is true at a cosmic level is reflected in the individual. Spiritual practices often aim at revealing these connections.

David Bohm writes of how the universe is 'much more reminiscent of how the organs constituting living beings are related, than it is of how parts of a machine interact.' This personification of the cosmos as the Universal Form ties our sense perception with that of all other living beings and the universe itself. Deep contemplation of our own sensations can become a meditation on our connection with the universe and provide spiritual nourishment.

When viewed through the lens of an energetic form of Ultimate Reality, the universe takes on sacred significance. And viewed through the lens of co-creation, the onus is firmly on us to act as custodians. Ecological responsibility is a means to enhance our spiritual life. We are inextricably linked with the creation of the universe at a most subtle and fundamental level. We simply can't be at peace, internally or externally, until there is harmony between humans, animals, nature, and the divine.

PART II

Substance and Shadow

BHAGAVATA'S SEED VERSE TWO

'Whatever appears to be of any value, if it is without relation to me, has no reality. Know it as my illusory energy, that reflection which appears to be in darkness.'

THE MATERIAL REALM IS a reflection of the spiritual realm. As we know, this is where the Self wanders about over lifetimes, seeking pleasure and fulfilment. But when our attempts are without relation to the Ultimate Reality, without consideration of the consciousness underlying everything, they have no lasting effect, no reality. This is the illusion: we have mistaken a reflection for the real thing, and so we hopelessly think it can satisfy us in the same way.

In Part I, we looked at the nature of the universe and an underlying spiritual reality. We also explored the nature of the Self and the role of the Self in co-creation. In Part II, we pick up from this foundation to take a deeper look at the 'reflection in darkness', the shadow. Importantly, we will now learn what the *Bhagavata* has to say about the *rules* of this shadow place and, thus, how to navigate our human experience. Chapter by chapter, we will gradually make our way through the ideas of subtle reality, *karma*, human conditioning, suffering, yoga, and evil, and conclude Part II with an introduction to the relationship between the mind and consciousness.

CHAPTER 7

The Shadow

'Anyone who can bring the mind under control becomes the master of all the senses.'
—Bhagavad-gita

Our lack of grounding in spiritual reality gives rise to an underlying sense of fear, increased by our almost complete (mis) identification with a temporal material body that is destined to 'die'. This fear is part of a wider sense of insecurity—the Self has an eternal nature and yet is repeatedly forced to compromise that in a temporal world. We want permanence because it is our nature, but we can't have it—all things must pass. This world is impermanent, and no matter how hard we try, our attempts for permanence can't succeed. This is about maintaining not just life, but also the status quo, our thoughts and emotions, our expectations—everything on which we have built our false ego. We don't want to be disturbed, yet we are constantly disturbed. Our entire mental construct is trying to avoid pain, and when we see possibilities of pain all around us, we are naturally fearful. This is a universal human state, existing before any religious designation. While religion can offer answers, the solution only comes if we have meaningful experiences of transcendence. If not, religion simply becomes another outlet for transposing our insecurity and fears, such as through imposing our religious views on others or finding comfort in the herd.

The material realm is what we know as our reality, so the *Bhagavata* helps us find our bearings to navigate through it; once we know the goal and rules of the game, we can get better at playing it. Our reality is subtle and complex: so much of it exists within our minds. The *Bhagavata* gives us valuable insights into human psychology and our underlying fears and emotions. This helps us better understand our inner workings and positions us to better manage our lived experience.

We saw in the last chapter how the external energy, the realm of matter, is a transformation of the internal energy of the Ultimate Reality. It is both real and illusory, like a red line caused by whirling a firestick. This shadow realm functions like a cloud: a cloud is created by the sun and yet covers the sun from our observation. The external energy is created by the internal energy, but like the cloud, covers our perception of the underlying spiritual reality. But that spiritual reality, like the sun, remains self-luminous.

Another way we can think about the transformation of the internal energy is in comparison to how we use energy ourselves. Energy in the form of electricity is used, for example, by an air conditioning unit to produce either heat or cold. The original internal energy of the Ultimate Reality can also produce different effects, one of which we call the external energy.

The Self thus finds itself in the external energy, the material universe, *apparently* separated from its connection with spiritual reality. And yet, since any effect still gives at least a glimpse of its original cause, we detect glimpses of the Ultimate Reality even here.

We saw from the last chapter that the Self's journey in the

material universe begins with a false ego, or our misidentification. As we also saw with the process of cosmic evolution, the tangible is derived from the subtle. The subtle false ego similarly develops a material body suited to fulfilling its desires. Now encaged, the Self mistakenly transposes the qualities of spiritual reality—eternality, cognisance, and bliss—onto the material body and the wider material reality. The Self does this because when we see something that we don't immediately recognise or understand, we instinctively revert to what we know and try to transpose our knowledge of that to make sense of the unfamiliar. We thus accept our body and the world as our own. The confused and captivated Self thus chases after eternality, cognisance, and bliss, like one chasing a mirage in the desert. This gives rise to conflicting emotions as we feel both connection and disconnection with this world.

SUBTLE SENSES

For our minds to understand sensory inputs (for sight, that would be colour, size, shape, and so on), we need to already possess these concepts *first*. We don't figure out the concept of colour by analysing different colours; we already know the concept, and only then do we go about identifying and distinguishing specific colours. Similarly, for each sense and their respective universal concepts: for example, sound has pitch and loudness; touch has pressure and temperature; sight has colour and shape; taste has the primary taste categories; and smell has the primary odour categories. This is not to say that we will experience the same object in the same way, since that depends on how our minds are conditioned to combine and interpret these signals, but that we all have universal concepts we already know.

So, before we 'see' anything, we have the faculty of understanding colour, size, shape, etc. This faculty is an extension of the mind, and because it comes prior and deals with *concepts* rather than *things*, is called the 'subtle eye', or, in modern terminology, the 'mind's eye'. It reflects our capacity to 'perceive' without the physical sensory input. This principle applies to all the senses. Our physical sense organs receive inputs, which are then processed by the 'subtle senses' to form something our minds can recognise as a unified object. This means that we are not just receiving information via the physical senses; via the subtle senses and mind, we also *reach out into the world* to create meaning.

Redness, sweetness, and hardness all exist in a particular combination of qualities at a particular time in a particular space, and my mind and senses detect these and combine them into an object that I call an apple. While philosophers and physicists might be used to thinking in this way, most of us are not, and it takes some reflection to appreciate the point. Here is another example that hopefully clarifies the point further: we see an ocean wave and a plastic bottle. We think of one as an object (the bottle) but not the other (we see the wave as a fleeting transformation of the ocean). But both are temporary transformations—one just lasts much longer than the other. The bottle will not remain a bottle forever. In that sense, there are no 'objects', only temporary combinations of qualities. This *reaching out* to create objects out of underlying qualities is us directing our consciousness, creating a connection between the subtle senses and the object.

This is not just idle philosophy; it has profound implications. Ashish Dalela, in his *Material and Spiritual Natures: A Scientific Commentary On Sankhya Sutras*, explains that it is this directing of consciousness by the subtle senses *reaching out* that overcomes the problem of indeterminism in modern science: '...we believe that light enters our eyes, creates an impression in our brain, whereby we see the objects. This is not false. However, what is not recognised is that light is not emitted automatically from a source to a destination...the emission of light is unpredictable—(a) when it is emitted, and (b) to which destination it is emitted. To overcome this problem of light emission, we have to understand that our senses establish contact with the world, and overcome this indeterminism. When our consciousness is directed to a specific thing, then the light from the source is transmitted into our eyes. This process of the senses triggering the emission of light can be called the "collapse" of the quantum wavefunction...The sense movement is under the control of our desires.' This means that where we direct our consciousness matters because our subtle senses become entangled with their objects. Therefore, anyone who can control the subtle senses—a pivotal goal of yoga—can reduce this entanglement and begin to experience greater degrees of free will.

THE SUBTLE BODY

We have learned that material elements are brought about in response to the desires of the Self. Like bubbles form when water meets the air, material bodies form when the Self meets the external energy. Desires rise out of the Self, where they meet the material energy and express themselves through subtle and physical form. We have also learned that the false ego allows us to build a false concept of ourselves, behind which we can hide: an artificial filter applied to pure consciousness.

Krishna explains in the *Bhagavad-gita* that the senses are superior to dull, lifeless matter, that the mind is higher than the senses, that intelligence is still higher than the mind, and that the Self is even higher than intelligence. The false ego leads to the development of both the mind and intelligence, as well as the subtle senses already described above. Together, these constitute what Krishna refers to as the 'subtle body' (also known as the psyche or 'ethereal body').[26] The subtle body mediates the Self's entire experience of physical matter.

The subtle body is one level of abstraction higher than the physical body. I can think about this like the relationship between me and my finger: my finger's existence is dependent on me, but my existence is not dependent on my finger. The higher the level of abstraction, from object to concept, the more essential and encompassing it becomes. So, the physical body is dependent on the subtle body, but the subtle body is not dependent on the physical body.

This subtle body is a superimposition of the Self onto the parameters of matter. Matter forms the boundary conditions, and the Self imposes meaning onto this by misplaced identification. This idea can be contemplated by the Kanizsa Triangle:

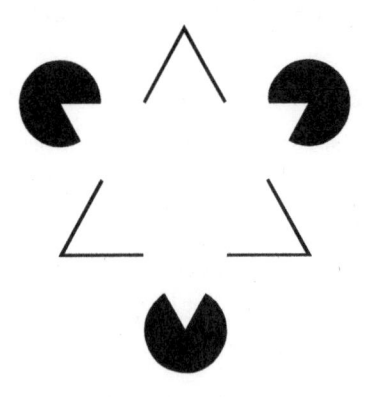

---

26) There are varying and sometimes very technical ways in which the Vedic texts describe the functions and components of the subtle body, but the essence across all texts is the same. For our purposes, we will use the version presented in the *Bhagavad-gita* and *Bhagavata*.

The Self can be likened to the white paper behind, and the subtle body 'emerges' from the apparent limitations placed on the Self. There are no triangles or circles here, and yet we perceive them. We superimpose meaning, i.e., make sense of the image, by completing the incomplete image in our minds and end up perceiving things that are not actually there. We see ample evidence of this in the phantom limb phenomenon, where approximately 80% of amputees experience the sensation of a limb that has been amputated. This is true even for 20% of those born without a limb. We also notice that the white triangle appears with greater luminance; similarly, on superficial inspection, the mind rises to prominence as the apparent Self.

Our function of discernment is labelled 'intelligence'. This includes the ability to see similarities between what appears unrelated. And then there is the 'mind', as a repository of desire, contacting matter through the senses. The mind's function is to simply accept or reject things based on experience, not discernment. Last is the subtle form of the senses, which are always evolving to match the latest state of the mind. The subtle body (comprised of the false ego, intelligence, mind, and subtle senses) causes the Self to transmigrate to fulfil our various desires.

In the *Bhagavad-gita*, Krishna explains some of the basics of transmigration: 'As a person puts on new garments, giving up old ones, the Self similarly accepts new material bodies, giving up the old ones.' And later, 'The Self obtains a particular set of senses for hearing, seeing, touching, tasting, and smelling. These senses are grouped about the mind, and the Self pursues their objects.'

The mind is shaped by our actions, and our actions are guided by our mind: it is a continually iterative process. What the mind considers pleasurable and detestable changes through its experiences of pleasure and pain resulting from our actions and their reactions. Responding to these changes in the mind, the subtle forms of our senses then accommodate the changing mind. If our mind changes to now enjoying violence, for instance, our subtle senses evolve to become attuned to engaging in violence.

The Self follows the subtle body in pursuit of fulfilling its desires, which it can do only through the medium of a gross physical body and a subtle body of accumulated thoughts and actions. We all have experience of our gross and subtle body changing from childhood to adulthood while our identity remains the same. Just look back at photos of when you were a child. Your body was different, as was your psychological state, but you still identify with that person in the photo as 'me'. Krishna explains, 'As the embodied Self continuously passes, in this body, from boyhood to youth to old age, the Self similarly passes onto another body at death. A sober person is not bewildered by such a change.'

This is how our thoughts and actions shape our mind and subsequent actions, thus determining our next destination as naturally as a magnet attracts iron. Our next destination is a reciprocation of our past actions and desires—it *expresses* what we've spent a lifetime focusing on. Just as a dying tree produces the seed of a future tree, the dying body develops in the subtle body the seed of one's next physical body.

The mind is a repository of past thoughts and experiences, and based on those experiences, the mind also stores desires, which are then expressed when opportunities arise. In this sense, since our material bodies are a consequence of our desires, the mind can be considered the cause of different bodies. Just as a caterpillar moves from one leaf to another by part-landing on the next leaf before fully leaving the present one, we 'land' on another body by our subtle body, first developing into a new form before we leave our present physical body. Our subtle body does this based on our thoughts and desires. After death, we go on to inhabit a physical form that matches our new subtle form that has already been created. We know from quantum field theory that nothing takes the form that it does independent of consciousness; our bodies are no exception.

The mind is so wrapped up in the objects of its immediate attention that it knows nothing else. This is why the mind, even though it continues on, seems to 'die a death' when forced away from what it knows at the time of physical death, as the old experiences are forgotten. It quickly becomes absorbed in the objects of its new body, making it feel like a 'new' mind. As birth is identification with a new body, death is forgetfulness of one's previous identity. When a person experiences a dream, they do not recall their previous dreams. Similarly, we also think we have just come into being because we do not recall our past identities. We don't remember all our past, perhaps for the same reason that we don't remember what we were doing this time last week: part of our brain's function is to limit our memory to prioritise short-term/left-hemisphere focus. And because the mind is so identified with the body, considerations such as race, colour, gender, and status appear relevant to the Self. But these have nothing to do with the Self.

When we walk into a well-lit cinema room before the movie has started, we see the 'reality' of everything around us—the screen, other people, the seats, the walls, etc. This is like our original state of consciousness; we see things as they are. Once the lights go down and the movie starts, we become captivated and exclusively focus on what is being projected onto the screen and the accompanying sounds. The screen is like the mind, where the movie is displayed. Everything else 'disappears'. Whatever is happening on the screen is now our adopted reality, and we feel all the emotions associated with it. This carries on until either the movie ends or we choose to step out of the reverie. The Self faces a similar situation, except this 'movie' will keep going until we choose to step out. And when we do, not only do we perceive the reality of the Self, but we can also go on to perceive the 'person sitting next to us', the immanent presence of Superconsciousness.

The outward flow of consciousness via the subtle body and projecting onto the world, leading to our attempts at happiness, can be illustrated as follows:

THE SHADOW

The layers of our subtle body create the lenses through which we see and engage with the world. Our experiences create feedback loops that constantly adjust what we are attracted to and what we are repulsed by.

False Ego	Intelligence	Mind	Senses	Action
Consciousness seeking bliss	Identity	Concepts	Specific idea	

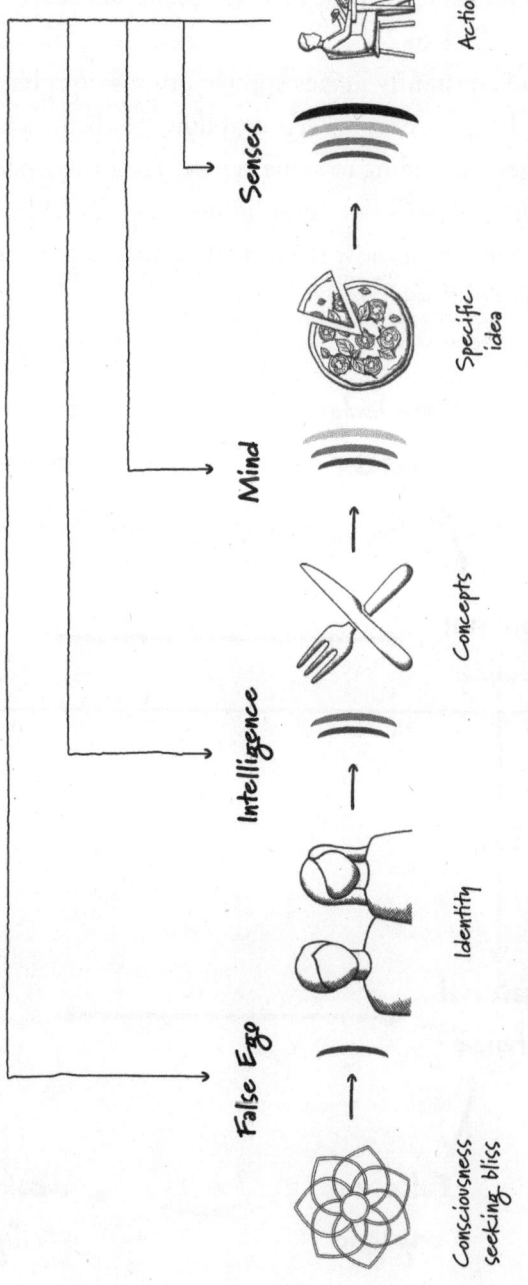

(Adapted from a presentation by Nimai Lila from the Govardhan Ecovillage yoga team.)

In summary, the false ego imposes layers of identity; the intelligence discerns concepts of happiness that match our identity; the mind constantly makes specific propositions based on accumulated experience; the senses follow the dictates of the preceding stages, all leading to some action. The experience of our actions then reinforces our conditioning at every level. In Chapter 11, we will look at how the aspects of yoga can disrupt the different stages of this chain.

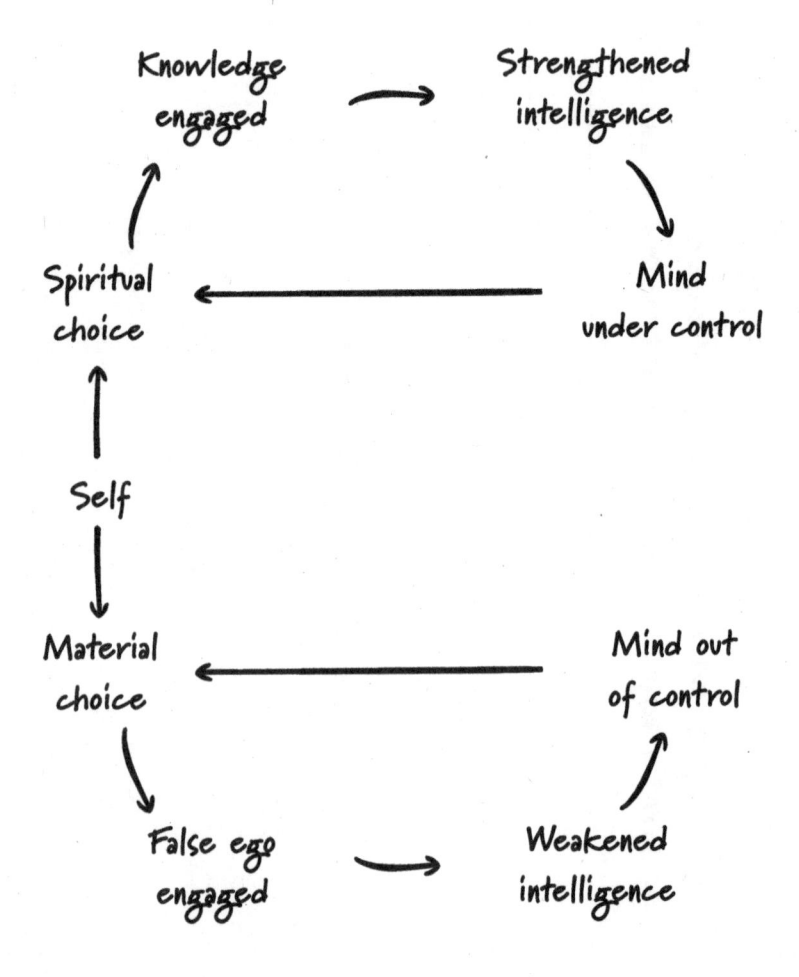

```
        Knowledge  ──→  Strengthened
        engaged         intelligence
            ↑               ↓
    Spiritual  ←─────────  Mind
     choice                under control
        ↑
      Self
        ↓
     Material  ←─────────  Mind out
      choice                of control
            ↓               ↑
        False ego  ──→  Weakened
        engaged         intelligence
```

INTRODUCING OUR FIRST LAW: TIME

We have explored who we are at subtle, physical, and spiritual levels. We will now look at some of the key parameters, or laws, of how the material realm works. We have already come across one of these: time.

Time can be a source of fear, reminding us that we seek eternity where it cannot be found. We are often oblivious to its influence. However, for the spiritually attuned, time can also be a source of inspiration, reminding us of our spiritual quest and destination. Spiritual practice can help us overcome fear and use time as an ally.

For its role in moving the latent potential state into a manifest cosmos, time can be referred to as the material cause of creation. Bhaktivedanta Swami offers an interesting insight here: the cosmos is separated from the Ultimate Reality by means of time, like a tape recording is separated by time from the person's voice. References to time in the *Bhagavata* indicate a nuanced understanding of time as not just a form of measurement (as we commonly understand it) but as flow itself.

Several stories of the *Bhagavata* also tell how our experience of time is relative to our location within the universe.[27] For example, one day on certain planetary systems is equal to six months here

---

27) We know that the speed of light is closely connected to the theory of relativity, specifically to the phenomenon of time dilation. It is relevant then that in reference to a *Rg Veda* verse, early 14th century commentator Sayana (minister in the court of Bukka of Vijayanagar) states, 'It is remembered here that the sun traverses 2,202 *yojanas* in half a *nimesha*.' The *Mahabharata* and the *Bhagavata* define a day as 409,050 *nimeshas*, giving us 0.2112 seconds as a recursive decimal. The equivalent distance of a *yojana*, based on various ancient sources of what constitutes a cubit, is between 8 miles and 9.1 miles. Sayana's quote, therefore, provides us with a speed between 166,802 and 189,736 miles per second. This compares to Olaus Roemer's estimate of the speed of light as 140,000 miles per second in the 17th century, and today's accepted value of 186,282 miles per second.

on Earth, while only one moment on Brahma's planet is equal to one year for us.

In addition to referencing time relativity and spacetime as a unified concept, the *Bhagavata's* smallest unit of time is calculated by the interaction of atoms, which is comparative to modern approaches to calculating atomic time and the foundation of 'modern' timekeeping.

The other two laws, in addition to time, are *karma* and *gunas*. *Karma*, the second law, refers to various types of actions human beings perform—and their corresponding reactions. Recall that the *gunas* (the three fundamental qualities) are present but latent in the potential state of material nature. The infusion of time triggers the interaction of the *gunas*, which, in turn, sparks the process of creation. The *gunas* provide a powerful framework for navigating the human condition. Over Chapters 8 and 9, we will look at these other two laws of nature, *karma* and the *gunas*. This will provide us with a holistic picture of the material nature and our condition within it.

CHAPTER 8
Karma

'The activity of beings that brings about their emerging states of being is the force known as karma.'
—Bhagavad-gita

Karma refers to human beings' actions and their corresponding reactions. *Karma* is a natural law—transactional, not proactive. It is often misunderstood and misrepresented, such as when the coach of the England football team had to resign after he made spurious remarks about *karma* in the Houses of Parliament. He told the Times, 'You and I have been physically given two hands and two legs and half-decent brains. Some people have not been born like that for a reason. The *karma* is working from another lifetime. I have nothing to hide about that. It is not only people with disabilities. What you sow, you have to reap.' Unfortunately, *karma* is often misunderstood and sometimes used malevolently.

People tend to make three errors when trying to understand *karma*: projection, judgmentalism, and over-simplification. The first error is failing to recognise that we cannot say with any certainty or objectivity whether a particular situation is good or bad for another person, or whether a reaction is punishment or reward.[28] Whether something is good or bad is best judged by what effects it has on our consciousness and how we respond to it. Even something like a serious health scare could be a 'good' thing if it leads me to make better life choices. Who knows, it might even extend my life. From this perspective, we really are the architects of our own destinies. Neither power, wealth, status, nor even education is necessarily good or bad; history is littered with stories of how some of the most apparently fortunate people were miserable and how some of the most apparently unfortunate people were the most content. We should be careful of projecting our misconceptions or biases onto others.

The second error is an extension of the first: blaming and judging others externalises an internal issue. *Karma* applies to all of us. We each see the world from our limited perspectives, and we seem to always be looking (and even hoping) to identify people who are worse off than we are. We are not built to be able to see things objectively, as they are—we can only see things from our own individual perspective, as *we* are—and we often find it easier to judge and blame than to withhold judgment or forgive. But *karma* cannot serve as a lens for judgment; it is, rather, a lens for empathy. It can help us understand that we are all equal at a fundamental, spiritual level. Though we might be at different stages of our respective spiritual journeys, we are all vulnerable to the same general errors. We would do well to remember the words of St. Francis of Assisi, 'There but for the grace of God go I.'

The third error is the over-simplification of a situation. When we look at the lives of others, we generally only see a snapshot—we don't see what came before nor what will come after. On that basis, how is it possible to make a judgement about their *karma*?

---

28) See Daniel Gilbert, *Stumbling on Happiness*.

KARMA EXPLORED

Here are a few more important points about *karma* and its implications for our lives:

1) Some people mistakenly conflate *karma* with destiny, under the misconception that it is deterministic ('you can't do anything about it—it's your *karma*'). While it is true that *karma* includes 'automatic' reactions to our actions, the Self does not lose free will in performing those actions or in responding to the reactions. We retain agency, though it is not limitless.

2) It is not constructive to rail against one's circumstances. There are obviously instances when determination is required to fight, but when it is simply for purposes of self-gratification, that fight may lead to negative attitudes, depression, and even destructive behaviour. Our inability to cope with apparent failures and feelings of inadequacy are a significant source of mental and emotional distress. *Karma* helps us understand that we have the ability to choose our response to any situation and take action (which leads to other reactions), but also that there are some things not under our control and that we cannot change.

3) This new mindset can liberate us from trying to always be in control or trying to maximise our gain from every small thing. We can do our best and leave the rest. We can love our fate: *amor fati*, as Nietzsche said.

4) *Karma* supports the long-term view necessary for good character, moral decision-making, and honest labour toward a worthy

goal. When tempted by an easy way out, we may not see the immediate benefit of doing the right thing. *Karma* reminds us of the long view; integrity and kindness eventually pay off.

5) *Karma* encourages us to take responsibility. Nothing comes to us that is not an opportunity for our betterment. This can be a difficult message to accept. Psychologist and Holocaust survivor Viktor Frankl's account of Nazi concentration camps in *Man's Search for Meaning* can help us appreciate that the human spirit can thrive even in the most horrific circumstances. It also introduces the possibility of a therapeutic reason for pain. The *Bhagavad-gita* describes this world as 'a place of miseries', and the first of Buddha's Noble Truths is that suffering is an innate aspect of life. We also know from modern psychiatry that the attempt to avoid suffering can be its very cause; by accepting suffering, we can stop it. Most of us are not even fully aware of our suffering, though we have not experienced life without it; it is the voice of insecurity, anxiety, and fear. But we don't need to hide from pain or suffering. An awareness of *karma* can help bring gratitude to our pain, and gratitude is the condition of the heart that not only facilitates spiritual growth but also heals our pain.

6) Fear is a product of the unknown or apparent randomness. *Karma* helps tame our fears by explaining the longer-term relationship between cause and effect. Now, there is no more that is senseless. Spirituality can then open us up to something beyond *karma*—the possibility of breaking free from a pre-determined future and recourse to strength beyond our capacity. This is also why spirituality goes to the very heart of the existence and expression of free will; spirituality lo-

cates free will in the Self, and *karma* reconciles it with the notion of destiny.

7) Why are different people born into such different situations? And how is this just? The transactional nature of *karma* provides an answer to these questions at both the individual and cosmic levels. Every action has a corresponding reaction, and our accumulated actions lead to a complex web of reactions. *Karma* thus provides for a system of accountability at both the individual and cosmic levels and shows evidence of a universe working on the principles of patience and unconditional love: we get endless opportunities to fail before we finally succeed. If we can understand this, we can see that there is no malice, no damnation, no exclusive privileges for a chosen few, and no action without consequence—only endless opportunities for every living being to realise and fulfil their spiritual potential.

8) As in any system, some will seek to cheat it, to escape punishment they have earned or get a reward they have not. They may even appear to succeed. However, *karma* is not a fallible system, and it is not measurable in the short term. As already discussed, judgments based on snapshots fall short of reality; we find it easy to connect cause and effect when they are close in time and space, but it's far more difficult when they are distanced. Think of how a simple mountain echo so intrigues us—because the effect is distanced in time and space from the cause. In even slightly complex scenarios, we can't see any connection between cause and effect. It helps us sidestep the impossible task of having to find causal chains for everything. And so, we invoke 'chance' (which is simply shorthand for 'I don't know') to help us feel better about not knowing the real

cause, describing the circumstance as causeless, something that cannot be explained, or, worse, something that should not be investigated. Randomness is a theoretical idea that helps us sidestep the impossible task of having to find causal chains for everything, but we should not forget that it has no basis. Our minds like certainty, even if it isn't true!

THE FOUR STAGES OF KARMA

The stages of karma are explained in different ways to help us identify and positively influence the spiral of cause and effect. One way to understand these stages is by comparing them to the life cycle of a plant: our desires are like seeds, our decisions are the budding shoots, our actions are the fruits, and the resulting consequences are like picking and eating the fruit. Other explanations incorporate our conditioning as the stages prior to a recognisable desire being formed:

Stage 1: Impressions. Latent impressions stored in our minds as a result of past actions. At this stage, these impressions are imperceptible.

Stage 2: Inclination. Latent impressions that have developed into perceptible psychological dispositions toward future actions.

Stage 3: Intent. Inclinations that have turned into desires and decisions to perform a particular action.

Stage 4: Implemented. Intent results in action for which we experience a reaction.

This last stage creates further impressions, and thus, the cycle continues.[29]

These stages of karma have also been compared to an arrow. The arrows in the quiver represent our stockpile of impressions and inclinations. When we remove an arrow from the quiver and place it on the bow, ready to fire, this symbolizes our impressions and inclinations coming to the forefront, manifesting as desires and decisions. The arrow released and in flight represents our actions and their unfolding consequences. During Stages 1 to 3, you can still change what you do with the arrow, but once you get to Stage 4, it's too late. If we want to exercise free will, the sooner the better.

We have seen above with the echo example that it's not easy to connect cause and effect. This becomes infinitely more complex when we add other 'actors' into the mix, who have their own impressions, inclinations, intents, and actions. Making sense of the complex web of actions and reactions in a world full of people, each with their own *karma* and free will is beyond any of us. We end up requiring a structure like quantum entanglement just to explain the workings of *karma*. One might even ask: if you accept the reality of quantum entanglement, how can you not accept the reality of *karma*? Now, on to our final law of material nature: the *gunas*.

---

29) Lao Tzu said, 'Watch your thoughts, they become your words; watch your words, they become your actions; watch your actions, they become your habits; watch your habits, they become your character; watch your character, it becomes your destiny.'

CHAPTER 9
Human Behaviour

'Actions are all being carried out by the gunas, the modes of material nature. Bewildered by false ego, the Self thinks, "I am the creator of action."'
—Bhagavad-gita

We are sometimes faced with alluring choices which can prompt us to ask, 'What's the harm in doing that?' The answer is often unclear in the moment and becomes obvious only when it's too late. Most of us have an inherent sense that bad choices result from motivations such as greed and fear and from wilful ignorance, but we don't always consider our motivations as part of our explicit decision-making process. The *gunas* offer a way of looking at every decision from both ends—our underlying motivations and the outcomes.

The *gunas* are the three fundamental attributes of material nature, just as the Self possesses and is characterised by consciousness. They are what define the transformation of the internal energy to the external energy. They are described as states or *modalities* of being. The word 'mode' is thus a more helpful translation of *guna* than just 'quality'. The three modes—Ignorance, Passion, and Goodness—correlate with increasing transparency, and so we move closer to our original nature (pure consciousness) as we move up the modes.

Multiple factors define each mode, but the quality of knowledge and motivation are the most important determinants. The three modes are hierarchical: from apathy and laziness in the mode of Ignorance, we move up to personally motivated activity in the mode of Passion and, from there, strive to achieve the balanced and well-informed choices made primarily in the mode of Goodness.

> *A Story of Three Friends*[30]
> An ancient tale illustrates the three modes of Ignorance, Passion, and Goodness. Once, long ago, there were three friends who lived in a small village. The village land was not fertile, so they decided to go to the city to find work. After walking for some time, they rested under a tree, and feeling hungry, they looked for something to eat.
>
> One of the friends spotted a large tree bearing many mangoes, and the eldest friend went to investigate. He thanked God for showing them such a beautiful and magnificent tree loaded with fruit. As he was about to pick some, he noticed that there were ripened mangoes already lying intact on the ground. To avoid unnecessarily picking more, he picked up a mango from the ground and ate it with gratitude. Then, realising that he had gotten the mango without paying for it, he decided to repay his debt by planting the mango's seed, with a small prayer that it might grow into a tree and benefit other travellers like himself.

---

30) Based on a version told to the author by Sacinandana Swami.

> Hearing of his friend's good fortune, the second friend walked over to the tree. Seeing the large and healthy tree, he realised that he could eat a mango and also take some of the tree's fruit and wood to sell in the city. Since he wouldn't need to pay for either, he looked forward to making a great profit, and after eating as much as he could, he broke off a large branch with many mangoes to carry to the city and, pleased with himself, returned to his friends.
>
> Now, the third friend went. Upon seeing the tree, he recalled with indignation how, in his youth, he had once planted a mango seed and watered it, but to no avail. Out of malice, he resolved to first eat his fill and then destroy the tree. Unable to distinguish between the ripe and unripe mangoes, he picked the mango nearest to him, only to find it sour. He tried another, but it, too, was unripe. He grew angry, thinking that the tree had given sweet mangoes to his friends but only sour ones to him. Thus, he set about to destroy it.

This story illustrates the nature of each mode as if the three were distinct, yet all three modes are simultaneously at work in varying proportions in every person and in every situation. The personality traits are constantly in flux, reflecting tendencies or vulnerabilities that we can either guard against or foster. We each can, however, approximate a combination reflecting our personality. This is not a fixed state, but we will typically default to it when we don't make a conscious effort not to; we can think of it as our 'steady' state. Those with a steady state in a particular combination of modes will be heartened (at least initially) by experiences or things in a similar combination that reflect their likes and dislikes.

The Vedic texts dedicate considerable attention to the modes because their framework can help us navigate our complex world, express our free will, and better predict the long-term consequences of our actions. The three-mode framework stimulates our awareness of the *gunas* and *karma* and helps us see through their seemingly impenetrable level of complexity, as well as supporting our journey toward higher consciousness. I feel they offer a more nuanced and versatile framework to diagnose and predict outcomes than even the highly accurate left and right brain hemisphere framework.

Let's take a look at the three modes and consider how we can better understand them in the context of our daily lives.

Goodness
- The tough, mindful choice—prioritising long-term outcomes over short-term pain.
- Motivated by purpose and knowledge, characterised by equity.
- Thinking and caring about lasting and unseen consequences.
- Results in a lasting sense of fulfilment.

Passion
- The alluring choice—the engine of greed, addiction, and risk, but also of creativity and innovation.
- Motivated by short-term pleasure or gain.
- Intense activity to achieve a goal, marked by extremes, pride, and unpredictability.
- Results in an immediate high, followed by a crash.

Ignorance
- The lazy choice and easy way out—favouring risk aversion and abdicating responsibility; procrastination.
- Valuing security above all else, while less interested in the effects of our actions—on others but also longer-term on ourselves.
- A tendency toward blind following, carelessness, cynicism, and other self-destructive behaviours.
- Results ultimately in dejection and depression.

These may seem simplistic, but as with primary colours, the power of the framework comes in the overlap and struggle between the modes and how this leads to different types of motives, behaviours, and results. Due to the contrary and competing natures of the modes, we always end up feeling like we are missing something. This makes it impossible for us to ever feel completely comfortable as long as we are subject to their influence.

MAKING CHOICES

The *Bhagavata* speaks of our worst instincts as something to be acknowledged and tamed, focusing not on our tendency to *do* bad but on our struggle to *be* good. Socrates said, 'The secret of change is to focus all of your energy not on the fighting the old, but on building the new.' But, of course, there are challenges even in building the new. In the *Bhagavad-gita*, Arjuna asks, 'By what is one impelled to sinful acts, even unwillingly, as if engaged by force?' Added to this internal pressure, is our instinctive need to conform even when it goes against what we know to be right (the Lucifer Effect).[31] We experience these pressures daily and in every aspect of our lives.

The modes can flag our susceptibilities and help us avoid just taking the path of least resistance whenever we are tempted. But it is not simply about repressing 'lower' urges; Krishna warns of the dangers of repression: 'Even a man of knowledge acts according to his own nature, for everyone follows his nature. What can repression accomplish?'

The difference between repression and self-control is that there is no transformation with repression—it is a forced imposition, with desires bubbling away just beneath the surface, waiting for an opportunity to burst forth. We must change our nature (here, I don't mean our essential spiritual nature) gradually through the modes by replacing lower tastes with higher ones. Since our nature in this regard is only conditioning built up over time, it is transitory and can be changed to reveal our underlying and non-transitory spiritual nature. If this were not the case and our characters were not at least somewhat malleable, there would be little meaning to education or training.

NEGATIVE BEHAVIOURS

Ignorance and Passion are the more troublesome modes, but the terms are not meant to suggest value judgments. Nor are they evil forces; they are natural aspects of the human condition, and by

---

31) The infamous 1971 Stanford University prison experiment divided a group of students into prisoners and guards and then confined them to a makeshift prison environment to act out their assigned roles. In just a few days the guards became so sadistic and the prisoners so depressed that the experiment had to be cut short.

monitoring their role in our motivations, we can become more thoughtful and purposeful in our decision-making.

Passion has a place, but in our ever-evolving lexicon, it has been elevated to a desired value. We are encouraged to 'feel passionate' about our work and lives and forget that passion has a dark side: 'a barely controllable emotion'. But boom can turn to bust, winning can lose its thrill, tastes can change, relationships can grow stale, and the satisfaction from status can fade. Passion, it turns out, can be a kind of drug, lifting us up and then letting us down. We crave more. Like an addiction, it requires ever-increasing levels of stimulus to yield feelings of equal excitement. And when we don't get that excitement, we retreat into Ignorance.

Krishna's words in the *Bhagavad-gita*, that 'the person who is not disturbed by happiness and distress and is steady in both is certainly eligible for liberation', can help us get started. 'Not being disturbed' by happiness may seem counterintuitive: why would we be disturbed by happiness? The reader will recall from Chapter 3 that an addiction to dopamine spikes—to material happiness—causes diminishing returns and suffering. We can now also see that dopamine cycle effects correlate exactly with what the modes framework predicts. But we may still ask why we should *start* with tolerating happiness: because happy feelings have a weaker hold on the mind than negative ones. The easiest way to train ourselves is to begin by trying to stop identifying so strongly with the highs. When we get used to tolerating the highs, tolerating the lows becomes easier. The stoicism of Goodness aims at a deep and lasting contentment rather than the addiction to peak moments.

Those immersed in Passion and Ignorance believe gratifying the senses is the prime necessity of human life. They are thus implicated in a network of unlimited desires and resultant anxiety.[32] The ancients understood this concept: the Latin root, *passio*, means suffering or enduring. Christ's Passion is the story of Jesus' persecution, not his miracles. Although the popular interpretation has changed over time, the basic nature of passion has not: it is transitory and unsustainable. The cycle of creation (Passion), preservation (Goodness), and destruction (Ignorance), therefore, is no longer a surprise.

To shift out of Ignorance, through the excitement and activity of Passion, and on to Goodness takes practice and hard work until it becomes second nature. Goodness requires an intentional thought process, and that can start out feeling austere. There are some who might argue that if it's hard work, then it can't be natural, and if it can't be natural, then it can't be spiritual. That is a very weak argument: a young child finds learning to walk hard work; it doesn't mean it's not natural. One challenge of Goodness is to accept that the benefits, especially at first, may be unseen or difficult to identify. They cannot be measured in the same way in which we calculate success or failure.

DOING THE RIGHT THING

A leap is required between knowing the right thing to do and actually doing it. Like any skill, it requires practice and perseverance. You can't intellectualise good behaviour; it must become intuitive. The conventional approach to effecting such change is

---

32) The *Bhagavad-gita* summarises this mentality in Chapter 16, verses 13–15: 'So much wealth do I have today, and I will gain more according to my schemes. So much is mine now, and it will increase in the future, more and more. He is an obstacle and I have, or will, remove him. I am the enjoyer. I am powerful and happy. I am the richest, surrounded by my aristocratic friends and relatives. There is none so powerful and happy as I am. I shall perform rituals, I shall give some charity, and thus I shall rejoice.'

to convince ourselves of a new way of acting. However, changing attitudes and emotions can be harder than changing our actions.

The modes offer an alternative: by focusing on what we can control, by changing our actions, we can change our thoughts, attitudes, and emotions. To do this, we should reflect on a few key questions:

- What was my true (be honest!) motivation?
- What mode was I in?
- Did I consider the wider consequences of my actions?

When we work toward Goodness, we begin to realise a sense of greater purpose, a way to become more aware of the consequences of our actions and link our benefit to the benefit of others. 'Goodness' does not imply a state of grace or exaltation, but someone who acts in Goodness will experience happiness or a sense of accomplishment, along with insight and wisdom. We begin to realise that we are more than our job, gender, ambition, religion, or political affiliation—we have a greater purpose. We also realise that our benefit is in giving and is linked with the benefit of others. And we realise that everything we do has consequences that will manifest in one way or another, seen or unseen. In this way, knowledge of the modes—and Goodness specifically—helps us to raise and expand our consciousness. Engaging in this process of self-assessment, we are more likely to do the right thing with greater consistency; many spiritual practices encourage us to apply such reflection to every aspect of life.

All the choices we make, from the minor to the life-altering, are opportunities to do good. But most of us fritter them away, lurching from situation to situation, grabbing at opportunities, and putting out fires. Thinking about motivations and caring about outcomes are the twin imperatives, the bookends of the process. Like life's traffic signals, the modes help us determine when it's safe to go, warn us when to slow down, and tell us when to stop. The framework keeps us alert, away from mayhem, and true to our higher purpose.

The table provides some examples of how you might experience the modes when going about your daily life.

	Ignorance	**Passion**	**Goodness**
Worldview in the modes	• Uncaring of social issues • Smallest domain of concern • Defeatist	• Drive to conquer, subjugate • Superiority complex • Live for today, enjoy	• Aware of a greater purpose • Mindful of consequences • Creating win-wins
State of mind in the modes	• Lack of interest in personal growth • Bewildered, out of balance • Helpless, jaded, angry	• Motivated by profit, advantage • Intense emotions and desires • Agitated, anxious	• Self-disciplined, calm • No personal agendas • Instinctive moral judgement
Happiness in the modes	• Blind to self-realisation • Based on delusion • Arising from laziness and illusion	• Based on sense objects • At first appears like nectar • In the end is like poison	• Awakens to self-realisation • Starts off like poison • In the end is like nectar

HUMAN BEHAVIOUR

	Ignorance	**Passion**	**Goodness**
Food in the modes	• Involves violence • Unhealthy • Damaging to environment	• Difficult to acquire • Intense flavours • Tantalising, addictive, unhealthy	• Fresh, easy to acquire • Wholesome, nourishing • Non-violent
Work in the modes	• Workers commoditized • Performed mechanically • Working mainly just to avoid pain	• Driven by personal gain • Self-identify as heroic • Money and status over ethics and quality	• Care about lifelong learning • Motivated by improving lives • Care about quality
Charity in the modes	• Given begrudgingly • Not interested in how it will be spent • Not caring about the beneficiary	• Offered with pride • Seeking recognition • Desiring prestige	• Not seeking recognition • Know money will be spent properly • Care about the beneficiary

While we all move up and down through the modes daily, and they sometimes appear and disappear from our awareness, all three modes are always present, ready to manifest, competing for dominance.

The modes provide a lens through which we can see the system in which we find ourselves and a map of how to better navigate it. They provide us with an early diagnosis and prognosis and a prediction of likely outcomes and consequences, thus empowering us to take back control of our lives. To practice, we can start with small lifestyle changes to see how working with the modes can tangibly impact our consciousness and well-being.

FREE WILL

If our thoughts, feelings, and actions are determined by the modes, what about our free will? Do we have a choice? As discussed in the context of *karma* and destiny, the *Bhagavata* does not present a purely deterministic view. In fact, the existence of the Self (an 'actor') implies and requires free will. If there is no Self, there is only matter; if there is only matter, there can be no free will since there is no 'one' to have it; if there is no free will, we cannot reasonably hold someone accountable for their actions; and there would then be no meaning to justice, education, or any other human endeavour. Functional society depends upon the existence of free will, and free will depends upon the existence of the Self beyond matter; chemicals don't have free will. The *Bhagavata* integrates the concept of free will with the role of destiny, reconciling the problem of free will versus determinism.

If subsumed by Ignorance, we are rudderless, our minds merely victims of our habits and sensual urges, with little or no free will. There is greater free will exercised in Passion, but we are still goaded on by desires. An estimated 99% of all our psychological reactions are simply 'automatic'.

Acting under the influence of Passion and Ignorance is somewhat like acting under the influence of an intoxicant: it may feel momentarily liberating, but the mind is still running the show, so our life is not our own to command. This is a reduction of freedom. Only in Goodness is the mind not so influenced: we begin to experience free will and thus can take control of our actions, reactions, and, ultimately, destiny.

In other words, we often make only one choice: which mode we develop. After that, the modes take over. If we can't control our minds and senses, we are forced to act according to the influence of the modes, even against our conscious desires.

There is one way out: when the modes force us in a particular direction, between the stimulus and our response, there is a gap in which we can exercise free will. That moment, the *Bhagavata* says, is where the 'higher' Self must prevail. That is the moment when we can begin to change destiny. As Viktor Frankl said, 'Between stimulus and response, there is a space. In that space is our power to choose our response. In our response lies our growth and our freedom.'

In Goodness, free will flourishes even if, ironically, it can superficially look more restrictive; it is, after all, the 'tough' choice. But we know from experience that rules can enable free will. If there were no road or traffic rules, for instance, our free will would be restricted, not enhanced. The same principle holds for any system of law and order. We need rules and regulations to enable the expression of free will. We talk about human values because we are supposed to be more than animals who rely simply on instinct and exhibit no real free will.

Free will is also relative, and depending on the choices we make, we experience corresponding degrees of freedom. Consider a team of burglars. Before they decide to break into a house, they have a choice—whether to break in or not. Once they choose to break in, their range of choices narrows. They can no longer decide not to break in; now, they can only quit or carry on. If caught, their choices are reduced further to pleading guilty or innocent. And if they are convicted, their choices—their freedom—are limited severely.

To summarise, first, we observe and reflect on how the modes work on us and how they drive our thoughts and decisions. Then, we can begin to think about our conscious desires. Which mode are they in? We can then start to understand ourselves better, beyond all the 'noise', and prompt ourselves upwards toward Goodness. Once our consciousness is freer, we begin to develop an awareness of spiritual reality and the Self.

CHAPTER 10
The Human Condition

'There is no stronger obstruction to one's self-interest than thinking other subject matters to be more pleasing than one's self-realisation.'
—The Bhagavata

Life is challenging, and we might wonder how life's challenges relate to cultivating spirituality.

I read a fascinating article in Reuters in 2018: 'For most people, prison is a place to escape from. For South Koreans in need of a break from the demands of everyday life, a day or two in a faux jail is the escape. "This prison gives me a sense of freedom," said Park Hye-ri, a 28-year-old office worker who paid $90 to spend 24 hours locked up in a mock prison. Since 2013, the "Prison Inside Me" facility in northeast Hongcheon has hosted more than 2,000 inmates, many of them stressed office workers and students seeking relief from South Korea's demanding work and academic culture.'

Paying money to be locked up in prison! These people wanted a break from the challenges of their lives. It may seem unreasonably negative to think of the universe as a prison, but that is one way it is described in the *Bhagavata*. We are all in a 'faux jail', in some ways, able to choose freedom at any moment, to choose real life over a shadow life—if we wish to do so. The laws of this prison—*karma*, the modes, and time—cannot be overcome without spiritual insight. As with a bad dream, we can counteract it by waking up. So, why do we continue to dwell in our condition, choosing prison over freedom? Because we think the alternative is worse? Or because we don't even know the alternative, let alone experience it?

We have far more limited freedoms than we think, we have far less knowledge of the actual state of affairs than we think we do, and we deprive ourselves of deeper experiences more often than we think. Like a prisoner in Plato's Allegory of the Cave, whose only experience has been the shadows on the cave wall, some people may consider spiritual seekers to be dreamers. They may be unable to conceive of, let alone accept, the freed prisoners' description of life outside of the cave.

Despite what anyone might say, nobody has this world figured out. As we have discussed, we don't even know what matter is made of, not to speak of consciousness.

We think we can become free of the laws of material nature if we just try hard enough. This is clear in our attempts to become free from our dependence on the natural world by trying to either insulate ourselves from it or dominate it. We think the purpose of knowledge is to figure out how to control matter, whereas the *Bhagavata* is telling us that its purpose is to free us from the control of matter. The purpose of a prison is not just imprisonment but also reformation.

THE QUESTION OF SUFFERING

When people question the idea of religion, often their objection is, 'If there is a God, why do we suffer?' Suffering pervades our existence: suffering inflicted by our own mind and body, suffering inflicted by the natural world, and suffering inflicted by other living beings.

When Uddhava asked Krishna, 'To whom does the experience of material existence pertain?' Krishna replied that the Self ignores the spiritual reality and is essentially 'sleeping', absorbed instead in the dream-like identity of the false ego. All these material experiences, therefore, are actually those of the false ego, not of the Self. Remember, the false ego has no factual basis but is our misidentification of the mind and body as the Self. Material miseries are without factual existence in that they are transitory. Yet, as long as we see the body and its senses as meant for our enjoyment, we are captured and imprisoned by the illusion and cannot extract ourselves.

Uddhava learns that this illusion is underpinned by the mode of Ignorance, for nothing can be separate from the Ultimate Reality, even if we may perceive it to be so.[33] When we are ignorant of reality, we imagine many things, and whether they are all true or not, we take pleasure in such distractions. These pleasures and displeasures are as real as dreams—that is to say, they are not false, but they are meaningless: temporary and illusory.

So, the Self, the physical world, and the Ultimate Reality beyond are all real, but that does not make the Self's *relationship*

---

33) There are five broad types of ignorance: 1) accepting the body to be the Self, 2) making sense gratification our standard of enjoyment, 3) anxiety that arises due to our bodily identification, 4) lamentation from the same, and 5) thinking that there is anything beyond the Ultimate Reality.

with the world real; it is a transitory arrangement. Their respective roles and relationships are confused, so illusion arises—just as both a rabbit and horns are real, but a rabbit *with* horns is illusory. We've misunderstood our entire existential situation.

TRYING TO AVOID SUFFERING

The first of Buddha's Four Noble Truths is that life is suffering. It is only once we accept this that we can begin the journey to transcend it. And our attempts to avoid suffering can become a cause of mental illness. As Carl Jung said, 'Neurosis is always a substitute for legitimate suffering.' The supposed cure—our attempts to avoid all suffering—can end us up with something worse than the original illness.

The opportunity to enjoy this world is an illusion, a dream never to be fulfilled. And our endless efforts to enjoy it culminate in our human struggle for existence. It has been said that the definition of insanity is doing the same thing repeatedly and expecting different results. The *Bhagavata* defines madness as the refusal, against all evidence, to realise that trying to enjoy our senses is a waste of time. As a five-year-old child in the *Bhagavata* says, 'Because of their uncontrolled senses, persons too addicted to materialistic life repeatedly chew that which has already been chewed.'

If this all sounds a bit pessimistic, know that the *Bhagavata's* candid and sometimes bleak view of the human condition is balanced with both humour and optimism about what opportunities beckon us. The *Bhagavata* prompts us out of materialistic slumber toward a life of newfound freedom, which can only be born of spiritual awakening.

SEXUAL ATTRACTION

According to the *Bhagavata*, sexual attraction is a basic principle of material existence. This is why the *Bhagavata* encourages celibacy for at least certain portions of our life. Sexual energy is powerful, and sex has the potential to be a spiritual act; in the *Bhagavad-gita*, Krishna endorses sex that is *dharmic*, for bringing children into the world, for spiritual purpose, and which is not exploitative or selfish.

Sexual energy that is selfish reinforces our misidentification with our body and thus maintains our conviction that we are (or should be) the centre of the universe, with everything else meant for our enjoyment. This means, for example, that desires for fame and adoration are subtle extensions of selfish sexual desire.

While this might seem a little harsh, as a result of our fundamental misalignment with the universe, we spend most of our time trying to avoid suffering and maximise enjoyment, even though we are capable of far more—of elevating our consciousness to focus on spiritual love, with service as its natural expression. Our choice is in *what* we choose to love and, therefore, serve: ourselves and our senses or a greater purpose.

HOW TO BE HAPPY?

Ironically, we can really be happy only once we stop endeavouring so hard for happiness! Like an itch screaming to be scratched, our desires don't usually abate when we try to fulfil them: they worsen. The best way to deal with an itch is to tolerate it. This ability grows with Goodness. Obviously, there are some 'itches', like hunger and thirst, that can and should be satisfied in a balanced way.

There is never a time when we feel we have enough pleasure, enough wealth, enough power; we always want more. As the business magnate John D. Rockefeller replied when asked how much money was enough, 'A little bit more.' So, we might pursue our pleasures to some degree, but in Goodness, we do so knowing that:

A) sometimes, destiny will simply not allow it;
B) what pleasure we do manage to derive will be temporary; and,
C) we won't be fully satisfied by it because our real need is spiritual.

While a person in Goodness will also try to fulfil desires, they do so in moderation, trying not to get sucked into the never-ending cycle of desire, temporary fulfilment, disappointment, and repeat. Desires are more manageable when kept in their place, but when they become the focus of our lives, they are insatiable.

Somehow, even in the most horrid conditions, we can convince ourselves that we are enjoying ourselves. This is not a sage's equanimity and self-satisfaction, born of detachment and knowledge, but the delusion that we are 'having a good time', born of Ignorance. We confuse the alleviation of suffering with happiness. This is like the 'happiness' felt by a person being dunked underwater and allowed to come up briefly for a gasp of air.

The external energy casts two kinds of spells: diversion, which impels us to remain absorbed in sense gratification, and delusion, which makes us think we are enjoying ourselves even when rotting in the most miserable conditions. Put another way, the mistaken idea that there is any real pleasure outside of the Self is our ignorance feeding the diversion, and our acceptance of suffering as pleasure is the delusion.

We can even be deluded about our past experiences. Psychologists have seen that our recollection of experiences focuses on our peak and last emotions during those experiences. We tend to omit the in-between stuff, which constitutes the vast bulk of our actual experiences, and retain a skewed version of the past and how much we loved or hated it.

In each species of life, the Self finds a particular type of enjoyment and is illusioned not to question or be averse to that condition. Thus deluded, the Self feels little inclination to think beyond the material body. Each species of life is endowed with the ability and inclination to tolerate its respective tortures. The *Bhagavata* tells the story of a great denizen of heaven who was cursed to become a hog. When the time came for him to be relieved of this curse and take on a heavenly body, he refused, saying that he was quite content in his new hog life! We may not become hogs, but the same delusion affects even the best of us.

An ancient, somewhat cantankerous ascetic named Daksha argues that one cannot give up material 'enjoyment' unless one personally experiences how much suffering it entails. He recommends, therefore, that we cultivate material enjoyment and knowledge simultaneously. His theory is that simply through our experience and suffering, we will eventually find material enjoyment abhorrent. He reasons that those whose minds are changed by others do not become as detached as those whose minds are changed by personal experience. This has become a common line of reasoning. The *Bhagavata* cautions us against this risky strategy since our desires for material enjoyment are so powerful and unending that we almost never become disgusted *enough* to desist. And although we can indeed learn from our mistakes, we can also learn in other ways, including from good advice and from observing the mistakes of others.

It is said that Earth once laughed at the foolish attempts of kings to conquer her, for they couldn't even control their own senses. Unfortunately, we see this unquenchable desire for evermore in many world leaders today.

The *Bhagavata* lists lineages of great dynasties to remind us of the temporal nature of our lives and activities in this world. We all come and go, inconsequentially staking our claims while we are here and making plans for future generations we will never meet. We perceive a world of duality fuelled by Passion and Ignorance: pleasure/pain, hot/cold, mine/yours, friend/enemy. At a micro level, we struggle to tolerate the slightest provocation, even by loved ones. On a macro level, history shows how even intelligent people can easily be misled by warped ideals rooted in such dualistic thinking.

Material duality follows an either-or logic, where opposites cannot coexist. We call it mutual exclusivity. We experience duality whenever we are forced to make trade-offs: we want to have our cake and eat it, but we can't. This is Passion and Ignorance in competition, and they show up as unavoidable antinomies. For example, we want something nice, but we want it for cheap. This contradictory nature means that we can never be quite satisfied, and so it keeps us constantly adjusting our ideas, values, sensations, objects, and so on, trying to find the perfect solution without any trade-off.

Recall from Chapter 6 that the potential state is almost nothingness, where the modes of nature are dormant. This state—a sort of nihilism—has understandable appeal to those frustrated with the world's unrelenting dualism. But there are other ways beyond duality. As a start, Goodness can reconcile the opposites of Passion and Ignorance, and so we get to experience something beyond our everyday false dichotomies. Truth emerges as the combination of opposites: 'and' not 'or'. We can then gradually move towards our nondual nature.

In the *Bhagavad-gita*, knowledge is said to be made up of the knower, the known, and the process of knowing. When related to material knowledge or experience, all three are separate. We don't identify ourselves with the object we are trying to understand or the process of understanding it. But when related to spirituality, all three are nondifferent—the knower, what is to be known, and the process of knowing are all the Self. We get to know ourselves by experiencing our eternal Self. This is because spiritual reality is nondual.

FUTILE ENDEAVOURS

Why do we not tire of our futile endeavours? When we are absorbed in material pursuits, the opportunity for a full human life is imperceptibly lost. We don't miss what we don't know. We do of course at times become aware of the futility of chasing unlimited desires, but that awareness is often short-lived, and we pick up where we left off, chasing after mirages: 'If I could only...' And at the risk of getting a bit too morbid, think about this: even if we *could* achieve our 'ideal' life, death could come at any moment; it's like a person on death row trying to enjoy a last meal.

The *Bhagavata* advises us to respond with forbearance. Only a person who remains undisturbed by the incessant flow of desires can achieve peace. This is not an extreme or repressive stoicism but a stoicism balanced with life-affirming Goodness, one where we gain more than we give up. The *Bhagavad-gita* explains, 'What is night for all beings is the time for awakening for the self-controlled; and the time of awakening for all living beings is night for the introspective sage.' The materially detached person is unaffected by enjoyment, just as a sleeping person is unaffected by their surroundings. We need not be obsessed with death nor with enjoying life at all costs.

Here are a few reflections that can promote Goodness and help us calm the mind:

1) Consider the fleeting nature of material happiness and distress and how sense pleasures do not deliver on their promise of lasting or meaningful happiness.
If we don't have a strong sense of purpose, we will be drawn into creating artificial necessities to fill that void. Our mind, with its insatiable desires, is called our greatest enemy because those desires obviate knowledge of the Ultimate Reality through distraction and degradation down the modes. The *Bhagavata* compares our holding on to those desires to a child's demand for things that are impossible to obtain, like the moon and stars in the night sky.

A materialist might laugh at the notion of a mendicant experiencing happiness amidst material poverty; asceticism is not for everyone. But a transcendentalist might likewise laugh at the notion of experiencing material happiness, knowing it to be temporary at best. For the transcendentalist, material detachment comes naturally with spiritual maturity; Goodness helps us in that process of maturation.

2) Know that this, too, shall pass.
Abraham Lincoln cited the story of a Persian sultan who asked a sage for a single sentence to be inscribed on his ring, which

would be ever held in view and was applicable for all times and situations. The sage wrote, 'And this, too, shall pass.' Lincoln reflected, 'How much it expresses! How chastening in the hour of pride! How consoling in the depths of affliction!'

As reflected in the *Bhagavata*, 'This material world resembles the waves of a constantly flowing river. Therefore, what is a curse, and what is a favour? What are the heavenly planets, and what are the hellish planets? What is actually happiness, and what is actually distress? Because the waves flow constantly, none of them has an eternal effect.'

3) Consider whether the material pleasures that we work so hard and long to achieve are worth the effort.
The *Bhagavata* advises us to think honestly about how much our desires cost us—not just in monetary terms but also in time and energy. What effects do they have on our happiness and our relationships? Of our average 80 years in this life, we spend 33 sleeping, 13 at work, 11.5 looking at non-work-related screens, and 4.5 eating. Once you've added a few years on for exercise, holidays, socialising, and commuting, little time is left for spiritual growth. We can help ourselves by really valuing our own time.

4) Practice austerity, understanding that we diminish our good reactions by enjoyment and diminish our negative reactions by tolerance and self-discipline.
Like the poor and weak, the rich and powerful are full of anxiety; it's only the source of the anxiety that differs. Self-discipline tames the mind and senses, reducing their anxiety, and making them easier to direct toward more important matters. It also trains us to minimise our harm to other living beings. Most of humanity today inflicts pain and death on other living beings in order to

eat them. Performed with thought and reflection, regular doses of austerity—such as abstaining from food born of violence—engender compassion.

5) *Real self-interest lies beyond the material; allow yourself to experience the happiness you'll find on the path of self-realisation.*

Materialism robs us of good qualities: it makes us anxious, distracted, intolerant of others, and undiscerning. It leads us to adopt a 'survival of the fittest' attitude to life, whereas the *Bhagavata's* laws of nature tell us that harming others is also against our own self-interest. But, of course, due to the distance between cause and effect, the materialist can't acknowledge this. Materialism blinds us to the consequences of our actions; the *Bhagavata* urges us to open our eyes. One definition of intelligence in Sanskrit is 'One who has eyes to see the future.'

6) *Cultivate gratitude toward nature and plan reciprocal acts to display it.*

By cultivating gratitude, living in harmony, and reciprocating with nature, we can act for an ever-widening scope of concern. We move beyond just our immediate family to our neighbourhood and community, then wider, to others with whom we may not have an apparent relationship, to those in other parts of the world, and then to all living beings. We must learn to live in happy and natural reciprocation with Earth and its resources; if we plan economic development without maintaining the planet, without gratitude and reciprocation, we are thieves.

*7) **Curb activities in the mode of Ignorance and be wary of those in Passion.***
To prevent society from degrading into an animalistic life focused exclusively on protecting oneself and finding food, sex, and shelter, religion has played an important historical role by laying a foundation of rules and limits—secondary religious principles. This is important, but the *Bhagavata* reminds us that it is secondary to religion's primary purpose: the progressive spiritual advancement of the individual and society.

Though the above are listed as reflections, there are plenty of ways in which we can take practical steps to bring these to life. For example, journaling has become increasingly popular and is a powerful way to recognise and cultivate concepts like gratitude. Another way is to create a shortlist of 'go to' activities, such as nature walks or volunteering, that support our movement to Goodness. And if you're not sure, maybe experiment with a few things and be open to where your inner voice guides you.

The Banyan Tree
In the *Bhagavad-gita*, Krishna's famous analogy of an inverted banyan tree illustrates some of these themes. We experience an upside-down tree when we see its reflection in water. This world is the reflection of spiritual reality. If the sun can be compared to spiritual reality, its reflection is the external energy. A reflection possesses some properties of the real thing, such as heat and light, but not all properties and not to the same extent. This metaphorical tree rests upon the desires of living beings: co-creation, as

discussed in Chapter 6. As a real banyan tree has many shoots and branches, so too does the inverted tree of our activities, linked indiscernibly through a series of actions and reactions, *karma*. The Self, situated within the complexities of this tree, impelled by the modes and enamoured by its fruits, forgets the real existence.

The tree description also points to the fundamental structure of reality. The tree structure represents concepts at the highest levels of abstraction, developing into details through furcation. This movement along each stage of the tree, from concepts to objects and then the specificity of objects, is triggered by choice. As discussed in Chapter 6, the potential of the whole tree is ever-existing; things simply become manifest and unmanifest over time. This metaphor also explains the *Bhagavata's* insight into the evolution of species, which corresponds to the concept of a taxonomic hierarchy.

The branches of the banyan tree are all the species of life through which the Self transitions; the twigs are the objects of their respective senses. The roots are the desires that cause the tree's development. Its real form cannot be perceived, and hence, philosophers speculate about whether it is real, false, eternal, and so on. The tree is aptly called *asvattha*, 'that which will not exist tomorrow'. It is impermanent both for the spiritual seeker, who progresses to transcendence, and for the materialist, who will soon see everything they are attached to destroyed. The *Bhagavata* instructs us to cut down this inverted banyan tree with the sword of knowledge sharpened by spiritual practice.

PREDICTIONS OF A DARK AGE

The *Bhagavata* predicts what the human condition in the future (our present age) will look like if we are not careful. And as you read this list, I am sure many of them will unfortunately ring true today:

- Religiosity, truthfulness, cleanliness, tolerance, and mercy will diminish.
- Wealth alone will be a sign of respectability.
- Law and justice will be applied on the sole basis of one's power.
- Success in business will depend upon deceit.
- Womanliness and manliness will be judged only according to sexual prowess, and couples will form based only on sexual attraction.
- One will be known as a priest only by the external symbols they wear.
- One will be judged unholy if one lacks wealth.
- One will be considered a scholar if one is an expert at word jugglery.
- Hypocrisy will be accepted as a virtue, and appearing saintly will be more important than being saintly.
- Eating will become the goal of life.
- One who is audacious will be considered truthful.
- Principles of religion will be observed only for the sake of reputation.
- The strongest will gain power, and the powerful will be no better than ordinary thieves.
- The meaning of family will not extend beyond marriage.
- Monasteries and hermitages will be like ordinary homes (true renunciation will be scarce).

- People's minds will constantly be agitated.
- People will be emaciated by either famine or taxation.
- People will not properly protect their elderly parents or other family members.
- And on a lighter note, beauty will be based on hairstyle.

Sound depressing? Fortunately, there is hope—let's look at this in the next chapter.

CHAPTER 11
Making It Personal

'An intelligent person, whether full of material desire, without any material desire, or desiring spiritual liberation, must by all means worship the Supreme.'
—The Bhagavata

Rather than comparing ourselves to people of other traditions, we are better off comparing ourselves to our past selves—this focuses us on how much progress we have made on our own spiritual journey. We could similarly look inward to *intra*faith differences rather than focusing on *inter*faith distinctions. This approach helps keep the *Bhagavata's* message non-sectarian. On a sectarian path, the deeper you go, the more sectarian it becomes, ending in extremism. On the *Bhagavata's* path, the deeper you go, the more universal it becomes, ending in universal love.

The Vedic scriptures make recommendations based on an individual's stage and state of consciousness.[34] This leads to varying religious practices to cater for the various motivations and aspirations we might have related to: duty and piety, opulence

---

34) Psychologists have also attempted to categorise stages and states of consciousness, such as the Wilbur-Coombe lattice.

(including fame, wealth, knowledge, strength, and beauty), sensual enjoyment, and finally, liberation.

These four categories of aspiration are generic—they cut across religious and cultural boundaries—and they reflect the varying types of consciousness of spiritual practitioners. The *Bhagavata* explains that the different aspects of the Ultimate Reality appeal to different practitioners depending on their consciousness. We know that, depending on their consciousness, two people can have the same thing happen to them and yet experience it very differently. This applies on a surface level, such as to our tastes in food, but it also goes deeper to motive; we can get different results from the same action depending on which mode our motive is in. The mode of any spiritual practice can be analysed by the nature of its rituals, sacrifices, recommended rules, food, and so forth.

Applying what we know of the modes, and the four categories above, we can analyse our sincerity and motives in practising spiritual life. For example: Are we seeking power or service? Do we desire heavenly pleasures or transcendence? Are we drawn to wealth and power over duty? Such questions are far more important than whether we address the object of our worship in Sanskrit or Arabic, or whether we fast on Friday or Sunday. By focusing on individual motivations and aspirations, we move beyond sectarianism.

MAKING IT PERSONAL

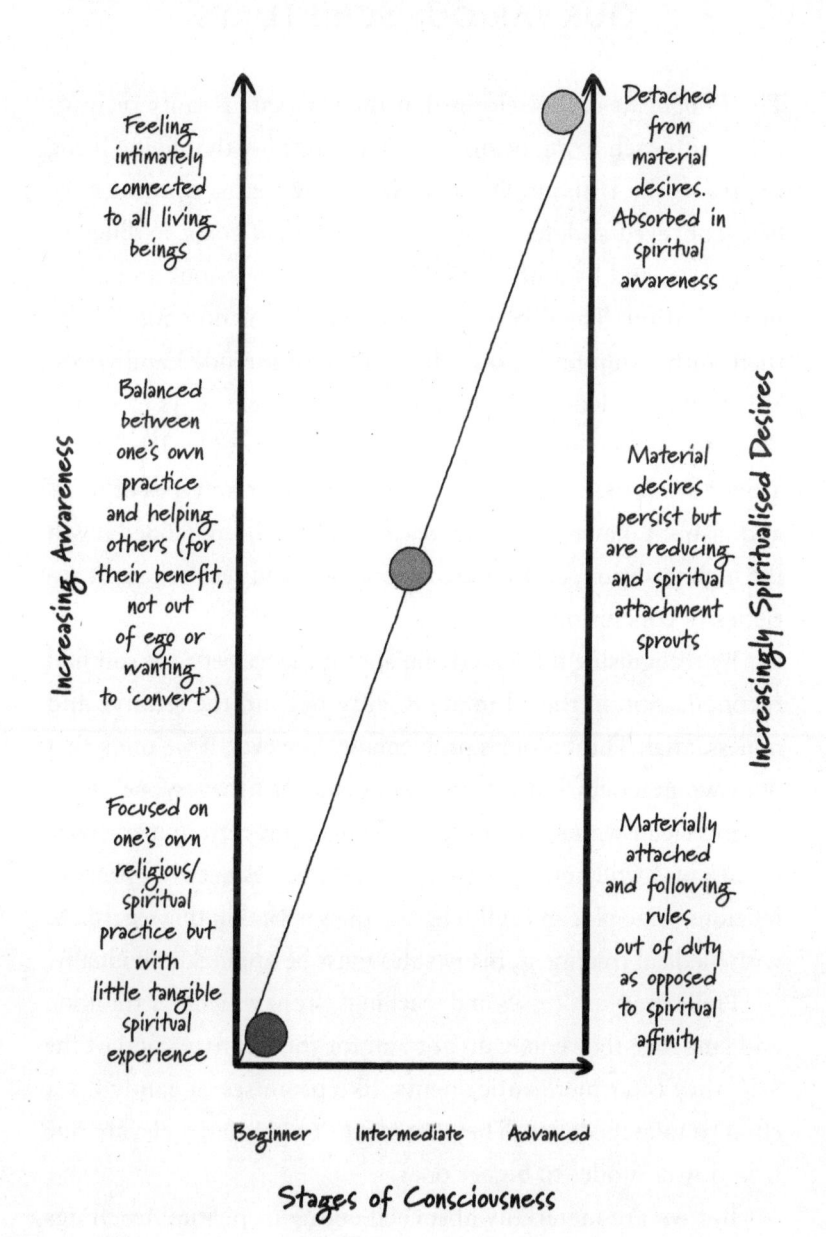

Y-axis (left): Increasing Awareness
- Feeling intimately connected to all living beings
- Balanced between one's own practice and helping others (for their benefit, not out of ego or wanting to 'convert')
- Focused on one's own religious/spiritual practice but with little tangible spiritual experience

Y-axis (right): Increasingly Spiritualised Desires
- Detached from material desires. Absorbed in spiritual awareness
- Material desires persist but are reducing and spiritual attachment sprouts
- Materially attached and following rules out of duty as opposed to spiritual affinity

X-axis: Stages of Consciousness
Beginner — Intermediate — Advanced

OUR VARIOUS SCRIPTURES

The *Bhagavad-gita* discloses that the Ultimate Reality reciprocates with each living being in response to how that living being relates to the Ultimate Reality. We know that scriptures have been conveyed at different times, with different goals, in different languages, and by authors with different convictions and levels of realisation. The diversity of presentation is due not only to their authorship but also to their different intended audiences. Spiritual knowledge is disseminated in different ways to match the different mentalities and desires of various people. Trees along a river drink the same water yet produce different types of fruits and tastes. Likewise, spiritual teachings have been handed down through tradition, custom, and succession and resulted in all varieties of conclusions.

By recognising the underlying aim of this variety, we can find reconciliation in the Ultimate Reality beyond the relative and nonessential. This becomes problematic, however, if we think that our own practices and preferences are meant for everyone. Fresh air and clean water can benefit everyone, but certain medicines, for instance, will not. The distinction between essential or primary religious principles and sub-religious ones is vital in this regard. As with medical treatment, many rules must be applied individually.

Preliminary processes and teachings, from whichever tradition and language they come, do not aim for the ultimate good of the Self; they offer mere enticements, like promises of candy for a child to take medicine. They are meant to gradually elevate one from lower modes to higher ones.

But we are materially absorbed enough; spiritual teachings would not encourage us further in materialism, even if it is of a pious form, without some deeper purpose. The *Bhagavata*, therefore, alerts serious spiritual seekers not to be unnecessarily distracted by flowery words of scripture that promise material rewards. Spiritual love is the only goal worthy of aspiration—a universally applicable rule: the gold standard.

THE LURE OF MATERIAL BENEFITS

Most of us, of course, are still motivated by material benefits. For some, it might be the lure of heavenly pleasures in the afterlife; for others, the cure for a disease in this one. For many, it will simply be a happy, secure, and healthy life for their families.

In all cases, however, the act of seeking a spiritual connection begins a spiritual process. In this sense, there is merit in seeking even material benefits from a spiritual source, via sub-religious practices, rather than through material means that do not acknowledge any spiritual reality. The *Bhagavata* puts it like this: 'For someone who, *for whatever reason*, approaches the Transcendence but in due course of time falls away, there is no loss. But for one who does not approach the Transcendence yet performs his material duties expertly, there is no gain.' However, we must also remember that any material benefit, even if gained by sub-religious practices, still has material strings attached.

STEPPING STONES TO LOVE

Scriptures sometimes recommend stepping stones, stages towards an ultimate goal, which may be discarded on the way. These stepping stones are intended to get people started and moving along the spiritual path. All that is required for a seeker to progress towards their destination is sincerity in their search.

The offer of material benefits and sub-religious practices are an example of such a stepping stone. They bring some regulation and some acknowledgement of a spiritual reality.

The promise of freedom from suffering is another stepping stone. This inspires a serious commitment to spiritual practice, resulting over time in self-realisation. Self-realisation is possible when we begin to abandon the false ego; this is the first major step in spiritual awakening, and it does not yet require love or devotion. With the concept of a false identity removed, the Self first appears to lose all identity and activity. This is *nirvana*, a neutral, impersonal stage that many meditation practices refer to as their goal.

At this stage, we have given up the negative false ego but have not yet replaced it with our positive, *real* ego. Self-realisation brings a sense of freedom and connection to the Ultimate Reality, a deep sense of oneness. Yet the yoga masters, including Krishna and others such as Narada Muni, urge us to continue on the path toward our ultimate goal: spiritual love.

When we love, we yearn to give ourselves wholly for the object of our affection. We see this in different types of love—familial, romantic, patriotic—even when that complete giving of the Self might mean death. But, we do not sacrifice our individuality; rather, we gradually and permanently extend our boundary of concern. Such love brings us into full alignment with the beloved, desiring to serve them. This is the simultaneous loss of self in the egoistic sense *and* flourishing of Self in the spiritual sense.

Scott Peck provides a helpful insight: 'Falling in love is not an extension of one's limits or boundaries; it is a partial and temporary collapse of them. The extension of one's limits requires effort; falling in love is effortless. When limits are extended or stretched, however, they tend to stay stretched. Real love is a permanently self-enlarging experience. Falling in love is not...The temporary release from ego boundaries associated with falling in love, sexual intercourse, or the use of certain psychoactive drugs may provide us with a glimpse of nirvana, but not with nirvana itself.' Falling in love provides a rush with this temporary collapse of individuality (think passion), whereas real love requires joyful effort (think goodness) and leads to the Self flourishing.

LOVE ABOVE ALL ELSE

Why is it that love is so exalted above, say, a formless realisation of Ultimate Reality or awe and wonder? The *Bhagavata* tells of how the great emperor Pariksit was once unjustly cursed to die within seven days for a relatively small mistake. He immediately leaves his palace and goes to the bank of the Ganges where he receives spiritual guidance from the saint Sukadeva. When the emperor asks Sukadeva how one can be freed from the cycle of material life, the saint draws out the answer from Pariksit himself. Sukadeva first suggests piety and atonement as the solution. The emperor rejects this, saying that there is no use in atonement because, despite knowledge of the consequences of our actions, we are again forced to act as though against our will, like the bathing of elephants, who, upon completion of their baths, almost immediately roll around in the mud. Pariksit wants a permanent solution.

Sukadeva concurs and explains that acts of atonement are themselves material and thus cannot liberate us from other material acts—they do not change our fundamental desires, so we may appear pious and yet still be prone to impiety. He next recommends cultivating knowledge of the Ultimate Reality. Pariksit agrees that this is better than piety or atonement, but even when we are armed with knowledge, desires can still rise again, like burnt weeds that return because their invisible roots are still intact.

Sukadeva is pleased with his student's response and provides his conclusive solution: only spiritual love can permanently uproot the weeds of material desires and consequent negative action. Philosophy alone cannot curb the demands of the mind—we must experience higher tastes and joys that will naturally replace our lower ones. Desires, after all, are a symptom of life, so we can't sustainably just negate or deny them; we must seek to transform them from negative to positive, from destructive and toxic to constructive and nourishing. And so, the development of spiritual love reigns supreme.

THE YOGA LADDER

All this brings us to the concept of the yoga ladder. The general idea of the yoga ladder is the gradual elevation of consciousness with an optional fast track. Remember, here we are talking about yoga in its original sense, the notion of reconnecting ourselves with Ultimate Reality, and not just in the way the word is used widely today. The yoga ladder includes general stages of spiritual practice designed to appeal to individuals with different personalities and tastes. The idea is that after a bit of honest self-reflection, anyone at any stage can engage with the yoga ladder and decide for themselves how they want to proceed with their spiritual journey. Let's first look at the basic steps of the yoga ladder.

- The path of action, *karma-yoga*, is best suited to those who are attached to and not yet repelled by the world (world-embracing).

- The path of knowledge, *jnana-yoga*, is best suited to those who are repelled by what the material world has to offer (world-renouncing).

- The path of loving devotion, *bhakti-yoga*, is best suited to those who are neither repelled nor attached (world-engaging).

The steps on the ladder are not totally discrete; as Krishna tells us, 'One who applies himself well to one of these paths achieves the results of both.' These steps are *aspects* of the same path with the same goal. For example, *karma-yoga* is not mutually exclusive from *jnana-yoga*. *Jnana-yoga* involves dropping material desires first and allowing oneself to realise the Self and the Ultimate Reality, whereas *karma-yoga* involves attaching oneself to work for a higher purpose and, therefore, automatically dropping material desires in the process. For most people, one is easier than the other, and we are invited to choose for ourselves.

SUBSTANCE AND SHADOW

Increasing levels of selflessness and love. Aspects of yoga are cumulative as one moves up the ladder →

Practices		Result
Developing spiritual love without selfish motive	← **Unalloyed Bhakti-yoga** → + unmotivated and pure spiritual love; the below aspects are no longer required	Complete realisation of all three aspects
Advanced meditation with full absorption and knowledge	← **Dhyana-yoga** → + control over mind and senses through ashtanga-yoga + advanced meditation on the Superconsciousness	Perception of the formless and the all-pervading aspects
Cultivating transcendental knowledge and rejecting materialism	← **Jnana-yoga** → + cultivation of spiritual knowledge + increasing self-discipline	Realisation of the spiritual Self and the initial awareness of the formless aspect of the Ultimate Reality
Acting to fulfil desires but dedicating actions for a higher purpose	← **Karma-yoga** → + mixed spiritual love + dedicating activities for a higher purpose	Increasingly higher levels of material enjoyment with an appreciation for spiritual aspirations
Acting to fulfil desires in a pious and regulated way	← **Karma** → + sub-religious principles	The moderated pursuit of material happiness but without spiritual awareness
Acting to fulfil desires without care for regulation or restraint	← **Hedonistic Life** →	A reactive life with little to no free will being expressed

MOVING BEYOND BASIC INSTINCTS

The first step of the yoga ladder elevates us from animalistic or hedonistic life to some notion of civility. This allows us to live as productive members of society and cultivate preliminary spiritual knowledge while pursuing our desire to enjoy the material world. We are all compelled to action, and purposeful action in the knowledge of spiritual reality elevates us. Even at the early stages of spiritual practice, we can avoid the frustrations of the deficiencies and suffering that taint every material situation. But if we dedicate the results of our actions to a higher spiritual purpose, we can loosen our entanglement in the four stages of *karmic* reactions (subtle desires, physical acts, acts reinforcing our old desires, and the seeds of new desires).

As spiritual knowledge deepens, we realise that there is no end to our material desires and that their fulfilment is too troublesome. This realisation leads us to a sincere detachment born of rising Goodness, not an artificial, temporary rejection of our duty and engagement with the material world born of Ignorance.[35] Krishna explains, 'One who sees inaction in action, and action in inaction, is intelligent and is in the transcendental position, although engaged in all sorts of activities.' For example, standing by and doing nothing in the presence of crime is an act of omission—it

---

35) Krishna explains in the *Bhagavad-gita*: 'Not by merely abstaining from work can one achieve freedom from reaction, nor by renunciation alone can one attain perfection. Everyone is forced to act helplessly according to the qualities he has acquired from the modes of material nature; therefore no one can refrain from doing something, not even for a moment. One who restrains the senses of action but whose mind dwells on sense objects certainly deludes himself and is called a pretender. On the other hand, if a sincere person tries to control the active senses by the mind and begins *karma-yoga* without attachment, he is by far superior.'

carries *karmic* implications. Whereas a soldier acting to protect others does not carry the same *karmic* reaction as a murderer.

With growing detachment comes the opportunity to meditate upon spiritual reality without the constant distraction of the mind's desires. This is the neutral stage of *nirvana*, the cessation of materialistic life and removal of false ego. And as we contemplate spiritual reality, the early stages of spiritual love awaken. This is not a strict sequence—at any stage, if one is simply genuinely willing, one can fast-track their progress through detachment born of spiritual knowledge and progress to spiritual love.

Our diagram from Chapter 7 can now include the intervention points of the different aspects of yoga. *Karma-yoga* acts to regulate our senses and physical activities. *Dhyana-yoga* acts to regulate the mind, and so changes what the mind thinks is pleasant or unpleasant. *Jnana-yoga* acts to strengthen the intelligence, increasing our ability to understand spiritual knowledge and concepts. And finally, *Bhakti-yoga* acts to chip away at the false ego so that our spiritual ego can shine through.

MAKING IT PERSONAL

The different stages of the Yoga Ladder intervene at different layers of subtlety

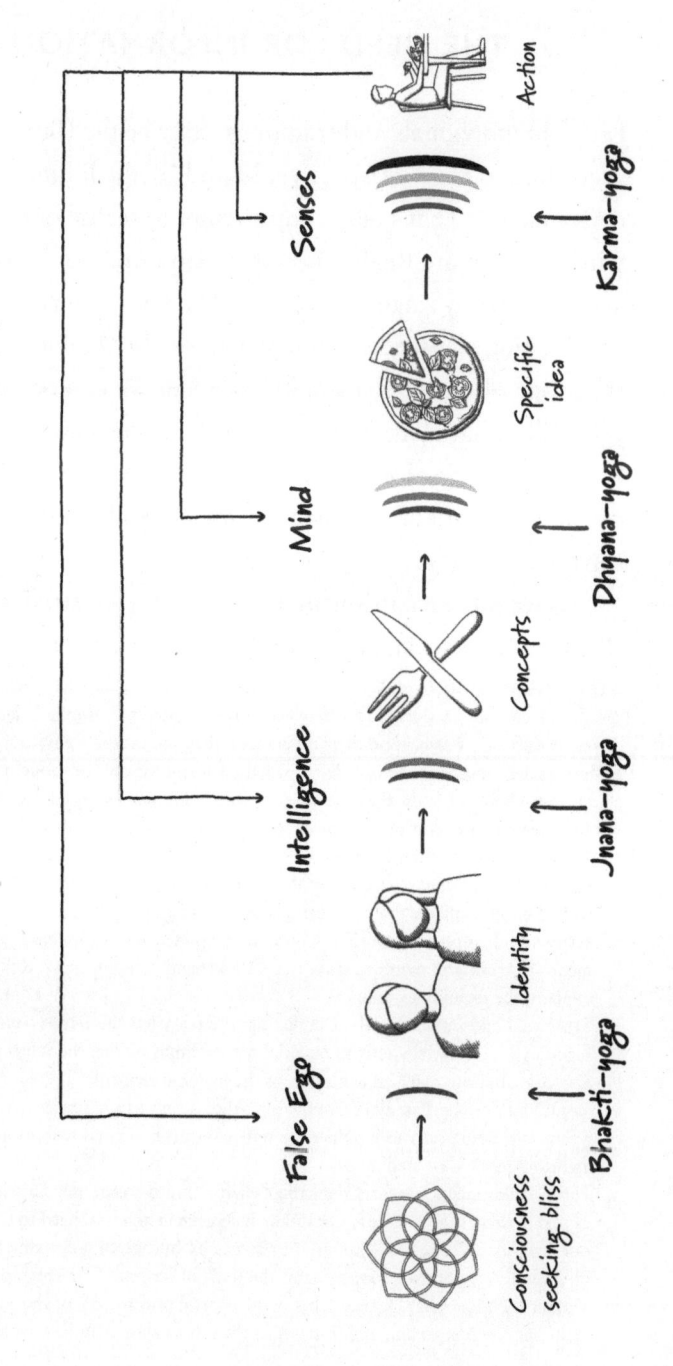

| Consciousness seeking bliss | False Ego | Identity | Intelligence | Concepts | Mind | Specific idea | Senses | Action |

Bhakti-yoga — Jnana-yoga — Dhyana-yoga — Karma-yoga

THE NEED FOR INFORMATION

Different individuals and traditions describe the Ultimate Reality according to their perspective, bound by the limits of their understanding.[36] That's okay; any attempt to realise our connection with the Ultimate Reality is better than none. And more subtly, appreciating any single aspect of the Ultimate Reality is, in a sense, appreciating *all* aspects. But equally, we also do not need to limit the scope of our sources of knowledge. We can be open to the possibility that traditions other than our own contain spiritual knowledge and information about the Ultimate Reality, which can supplement and enhance our understanding and further our spiritual progress.

As we advance in spiritual realisation, we strive to develop the depth and specificity of our knowledge. We desire to move

---

36) As we saw earlier, the modes affect even sophisticated philosophers, leading to many divergent theories. But beyond their differences, they each make significant contributions to developing aspects of philosophy across the various schools of thought. As far as the prominent schools of Vedic thought are concerned, they can appear divergent at one level but display profound convergence at another. These classical schools are:

i. Vaisesika. Philosopher: Kanada. Conflicting belief: seems to accept physicalism and the idea that atomic particles are the ultimate cause and origin of the cosmos. Key contribution: explains the basic categories of reality.

ii. Nyaya. Philosopher: Gautama. Conflicting belief: seems to accept logic as the only means to truth and seems to deny the Self's eternal consciousness. Key contribution: explains the techniques of logic.

iii. Sankhya. Philosopher: Kapila. Conflicting belief: accepts the Self as consciousness, but seems to ascribe activity only to material nature, implying that the Self is purely passive. Key contribution: explains evolution of the material elements.

iv. Yoga. Philosopher: Patanjali. Conflicting belief: seems to acknowledge the existence of a Supreme Being only as a helper for self-realisation. Key contribution: explains the eightfold method of meditation.

v. Purva. Philosopher: Jaimini. Conflicting belief: seems to accept only *karma* and its results as real (if there is a God, he is not totally independent and is obliged to reciprocate with our *karma*), and therefore material existence as eternal, thus denying the concept of liberation. Key contribution: explains the tools of scriptural interpretation.

vi. Vedanta. Philosopher: Vyasa. This is the central philosophy of the Vedic tradition, including the *Bhagavata*, and into which the others above can be seen to converge.

beyond an isolated or abstract concept or sentiment to something more integral, precise, and descriptive. After all, we can't truly love a concept (humanity)—we can only love instantiations of the concept (my neighbour). We also want to know and experience spiritual reality more tangibly. Otherwise, our initial faith may stagnate or wane. As Bhaktivedanta Swami put it, 'Everyone knows he has a father, but that is not sufficient. One must know who my father is.'

With different information coming from different traditions, the *Bhagavata* tells us that we should judge the differences using our intelligence. We should also be able to reconcile apparent contradictions based on the understanding that there are ascending levels of knowledge that are often best understood sequentially. Preliminary instructions might include versions of 'this is the only path; all others are false', which can inspire faith in the weak-minded. Likewise, some teachings instil fear of materialistic life as a means to curb hedonism or prompt spiritual enquiry. Statements like 'God has no name' and 'God has no form' might be divisive from a superficial perspective, but we can reconcile them by understanding the phrases to mean that Ultimate Reality has no *material* name and no *material* form, and to discourage manufactured gods.

When we look beyond the superficial and focus on what will help us in our spiritual journey, we can engage with increasingly integral, precise, and descriptive information about the Ultimate Reality.

CHAPTER 12
Sins of the Religious

> *'A sober person who can tolerate the urge to speak, the mind's demands, actions of anger, and urges of the tongue, belly, and genitals is qualified to make disciples all over the world.'*
> —Upadeshamrita

One ancient atheistic thinker, Charvaka, said that life's sole purpose was to enjoy oneself by any means at one's disposal. He criticised duty and piety as useless in preventing death and spiritual practice as useless in preventing poverty. Of course, we might not agree, but at least this is logically consistent: if you don't believe in a spiritual reality, where is the basis for free will? And if you don't believe in free will, where is the basis for morality? If we, along with our emotions and actions, are merely the result of chemical reactions, neurons firing in the brain, then this implies that there is no free will: chemicals don't have free will. This contradiction is lost on those who accept nothing but physical laws and yet speak on morality. How can we *choose* anything if we are subject entirely to physical determinism? And if we can't choose, then how can we talk about personal or social morality? In fact, there would be no meaning to anything at all.

While we may not like the sound of Charvaka's strand of atheism, we can at least understand the logic of why it justifies hedonism. But those who believe in a spiritual Self that possesses free will and the capacity to love don't have the same excuse.

Bhaktisiddhanta Saraswati described the world as a place of the 'cheaters and the cheated'. Scams and cons abound, and spiritual circles are not exempt from deceit and false promises. Recent research even confirms that mindfulness and meditation can lead to narcissism and a sense of spiritual superiority—the very opposite of what we might expect.[37]

We already know that there are all levels of spiritual practitioner and that many struggle with their practices. But weakness is one thing, cheating another. The *Bhagavata* has some harsh words for such deliberate hypocrisy: 'Distorted interpretations will contaminate the scriptures. Political leaders will consume the citizens. Priests and intellectuals will be devotees of their bellies and genitals. Monks will fail in vows and be unclean. Householders will become beggars (instead of contributing to society). The renunciates will become greedy for wealth. Businessmen will engage in petty commerce and earn money by cheating. Followers will abandon a leader who has lost his wealth, even if he is of saintly character...And those who know nothing will mount a high seat and speak on religion.'

---

37) Study by Roos Vonk, Professor of Social Psychology, Radboud University, Netherlands.

SPIRITUAL TEACHERS ARE NOT ABOVE THE LAW

Many spiritual teachers are themselves bewildered about the purpose of life, but 'the show must go on'. The *Bhagavata* instructs us not to take the role of a teacher unless we are prepared to work to elevate the consciousness of those we guide. That's not to say that we must be perfect before we can teach. The material world is, after all, a complicated place. Krishna says in the *Bhagavad-gita*, 'Every endeavour is covered by some sort of fault, just as fire is covered by smoke.' But while we needn't be perfect in order to teach others, we must at least be sincere. Clearly, this is also easier said than done, for it requires integrity and humility to be sincere.

To drive the point home, the *Bhagavata* tells us of highly exalted priests who acted like fiends and of those who superficially appeared to be fiends but behaved like saints. It also contains examples of persons who rejected their priests if found lacking in sincerity.

THE NEED FOR SCRUTINY

A religion can start with sincerity and truth but, over time, become corrupted. Followers may not be able to distinguish between the original and later messages; increasingly distorted forms of the original teachings arise. Even the best of us can be wrong and make mistakes; this is inevitable over time. And, as the old saying goes, just one drop of poison can contaminate an entire pot of milk. Structures and cultures where a human being can do no wrong are recipes for trouble, even if they involve good people doing 'God's work'.

People can end up promoting strange and sometimes dangerous ideologies. This is sometimes deliberately with bad intent, but sometimes it is innocently with good intent. The latter is often hard to combat because the intent is good, and the outcome may not be obviously bad. Benign though it may seem, we should be aware that even someone with good intentions, if misinformed and holding a gun, can be dangerous. One giveaway of misinformation is that no verification process is offered. Without some degree of verification, we are in the world of magicians, sleight of hand, charisma, and blind faith.

WHERE DO WE TEND TO GO WRONG?

Let's look at four common pitfalls that can cause havoc in our personal lives and social dynamics, particularly in a spiritual society where one might have their guard down.

1) Envy
Once, a poor man was granted one wish. There was only one condition: whatever he asked for, his neighbour would get double. One by one, he asked for all the things he ever wanted. But instead of being able to enjoy what he received, all he could think of was his neighbour having more. No amount of gain could make up for the pain he felt in still having less than his neighbour. Eventually, he asked to be blinded in one eye so that his neighbour would be blinded in both! Academic studies bear out the notion that we would prefer to get £100 and our neighbour £50 rather than get £150 ourselves if that means our neighbour gets £300.

Envy is harbouring ill feelings toward others. Yet, ironically, it is we who suffer as a result, for envy stifles our inner peace and happiness. It is characteristic of the material realm.

We see envy between family members and communities in our daily lives, and between nations and religious groups. Religious leaders who have fallen victim to envy themselves foster it amongst their followers through intolerance. The *Bhagavata* says, 'After worshipping divinity, if one gives trouble to other living beings, his worship becomes fruitless.'

2) Pride

Like ego, there is a dark side to pride when it's all about 'me'. There is a fakeness that we can detect if we look carefully. In a religious setting, it is toxic if it manifests as institutional hierarchy. There may be a practical need for hierarchy, but when it is used to indicate individual worth, there is a problem. A hierarchy within religions based on birth is equally damaging, running contrary to spiritual principles.

The desire for distinction is a stubborn thing; humans like to think we are special in some way. This can be seen in exclusivist forms of faith and religion. Ignoring the possibility that various paths are suited to different people, the proud cling to the notion that theirs is the only way. This also exhibits itself as the need to convert others to their way of thought.

The *Bhagavata* warns the spiritual seeker that even one who rejects the idea of transcendence can still achieve liberation, whereas the proud cannot. Bhaktisiddhanta Saraswati said, 'If one rejects or envies the mood of another, then such feelings are actually targeted toward the Supreme Lord...If one tries to uproot and convert the internal mood of another person into that of his own narrow-mindedness, then the result will be not only criticism of another's religion but enviousness of the Supreme Lord, who is the goal of religion.'

3) Falsity

For some religious people, even after years of practice, falsity can arise because they are still confused about the purpose of their life and the means of achieving it. This confusion can manifest in different ways, including reversion to thinly veiled materialism. If focused on the sub-religious, we can become oblivious to the essentials, paving the way for materialism and even fanaticism as we feel the need to compensate for and externalise our shortcomings.

Falsity also arises when a practitioner tries to imitate a high standard of spiritual love without having grasped the basics. It can be like an actor playing a part—they've learned the script(ure) for the role but haven't developed the associated qualities.

Some people struggle with their spiritual practice but continue because it is a means of livelihood. Others, imposters, deliberately use religion in order to justify premeditated crimes. Some even advertise (or encourage their followers to advertise) themselves as 'God on Earth'!

Hypocrisy has plagued religions around the world and has dissuaded many from adopting spiritual practices. The Sanskrit word for a spiritual leader is *acharya*—one who teaches by example and walks their talk, and the *Bhagavata* sets high expectations for such a designation.

4) Complacency

Religious beliefs can lure us into thinking that we are safe from the fate that awaits the nonreligious (or those of other religions). This can lead people to do all sorts of unthinkable things, confident that they will be saved from suffering the consequences—as if God and the universe owe them clemency. All they need is one of the readily available forms of atonement or confession, and then they're back to whatever they were doing.

It's manipulation on both sides: the institution gains the power of absolution, and the individual gets impunity. To receive pardon for wrongdoing and then commit that act again is worse than committing the original act itself, and over time, it breeds complacency.

Complacency also arises when we fail to recognise that while we may have gained admission to a spiritual path, we are on the journey—we have not yet reached our destination.

In Part II so far, we have been looking at the various aspects of the material realm (the mind and subtle body, *karma* and the *gunas*, human suffering, and diversity of spiritual paths). In this chapter we saw that religious contexts are not immune to the influences of the material realm. We now bring together our learning from Part II and look at the relationship between our mind and consciousness.

CHAPTER 13
Your Mind and Consciousness

'Know the Self as the passenger and the body as the chariot.
Know the intellect as the driver and the mind as the reins.
The senses are the horses, and the sense objects are the roads.'
—Katha Upanishad

In this chapter, we will explore the nature of the mind, along with different levels of awareness and consciousness.

Intelligence has been described (see Chapter 7) as the mind's function of discernment. Intelligence helps us to understand the nature of objects and then direct the mind (and thus the senses) based upon informed choices. A strong intelligence allows us to make choices that are not simply instinctive. When intelligence is weak, the process works backwards: the mind dictates terms, and the intelligence becomes subservient to it, justifying its choices instead of directing it. Intelligence is strengthened by knowledge; thus, the *Bhagavata* emphasises developing knowledge as part of a spiritual process.

The features of intelligence, according to the *Bhagavata*, are doubt, misapprehension (realising what's wrong before we know what's right), apprehension (realising the truth that arises), recollection, and healthy sleep (we have discovered that REM sleep is, in fact, indispensable to our ability to solve problems).

THE MIND AND ITS DESIRES

The mind's natural position is in Goodness, so it is never satisfied by being absorbed in waves of Passion and plans for material enjoyment. It craves peace. This can work to our advantage. Anyone who has practised fasting knows how the mind first fights back, but that through regular practice, fasting can be a powerful way to subdue and eventually bring peace to the mind. A peaceful state of mind allows us to focus our consciousness instead of being dragged in different directions by the mind and senses. But the mind must be fixed on the spiritual to be subdued. And it can be fixed on the spiritual once it is convinced (by the intelligence) of a spiritual reality.

THE MIND AND FALSE EGO

Each of our sense organs has its respective objects of perception—the eyes are perfectly formed to perceive, process, and enable our experience of form, the ears to sound, and so on. The mind is the master of all the senses, but what is *its* object of perception? The *Bhagavata* tell us that the mind's object of perception is the false ego, the very first covering of the Self and the (mis)identification of the Self. The false ego leads to the development of the intelligence and mind in order for us to perceive the false ego—just as in Chapter 6, our senses developed to allow our perception of each of the elements. Thus, the mind and false ego reinforce each other to act out the misidentified Self's material desires.

The story of the Avanti Brahmana, who we will learn about further below, indicates that there are three categories of identification by our false ego with things other than our spiritual identity:

1) When we identify our Self with our body/actions ('I am Italian; I am an architect').
2) When we identify our Self with our qualities ('I am kind; I am angry').
3) When we identify our Self with our experiences ('I feel pain; I feel pleasure').

In all three, the Self remains aloof. Because we misidentify ourselves in this way, we keep reaffirming these other, more superficial identities. We interpret reality through the lens of our mind, which then simply reconfirms our preconceived ideas and identities. So, how does this relate to the spiritual mind?

We can break free of this misconception by focusing on the factual identity of the Self, dissolving the false ego a little at a time. Happiness and suffering take place only in the mind; our *perception* of a situation determines our happiness or suffering. The problem is that we are attached to our minds, thinking, 'My mind is me.' However, when we tolerate the wanderings of the mind and shift its focus to our spiritual identity, we can distance ourselves from our false ego.

Various techniques can help this process. By taking an observer role, for instance, we can observe our thoughts and emotions without judging or becoming entangled in them.

THE MIND AND CONSCIOUSNESS

We know from previous chapters that the Self perceives via the subtle body. The experience of our consciousness, therefore, is dependent on the mind's perception, which in turn is dependent on the brain's interpretation of sensory input. With our spiritual faculties not yet developed, we perceive only subtle and gross matter and remain oblivious to the spiritual reality all around us. It's just about tuning into a different frequency.

One argument that is sometimes made against the existence of an eternal Self is that transitory sensual experiences also cause changes in our experience of consciousness, which means that the consciousness is changing, which means that it is impermanent, which means that it must be material. The *Bhagavata* points out, however, that though the superficial experience of consciousness might change, consciousness itself does not: 'We should distinguish between that which comes and goes, and the point from which it comes or to which it goes.'

During sleep, we forget the identity of the physical body, and during waking, we forget the identity of the mind and subtle body, but in either state, we typically forget the identity of the spiritual body. But we have practical experience of the unchanging nature of the Self: during deep sleep, the senses, mind, and even false ego are dormant. Yet, upon waking, we remember that 'we' were sleeping. This is because the Self, though constituted of pure awareness, is itself an object of its own awareness.

CONSCIOUSNESS AND LEVELS OF AWARENESS

The *Upanishads* and *Bhagavata* describe five *koshas*, or progressive stages of consciousness, each with corresponding levels of awareness of the Ultimate Reality:

1) *Anna-maya*: consciousness is absorbed in a dependence on food and economic development, analysing everything as potential for food or gain, with no awareness of the Self as separate from the body. This is consciousness at the level of the physical world.

2) *Prana-maya*: consciousness is aware of the symptoms of life and is preoccupied with staying alive. This is a more subtle but still physical level of consciousness.

3) *Mano-maya*: consciousness shifts its attention from bodily needs to mental and emotional awareness, absorbed in philosophical thought and focused on thinking, feeling, and willing.

4) *Vijnana-maya*: consciousness distinguishes the body and even the mind from the Self; this is realised knowledge and experience beyond philosophical thought and is the first stage of liberation.

5) *Ananda-maya*: consciousness enters full realisation and absorption in its relationship with Ultimate Reality; the stage of flourishing spiritual life through positive spiritual engagement.

Ananda-maya: Spiritual flourishing

Vijnana-maya: First stage of spiritual focus

Mano-maya: Absorbed in the subtle body

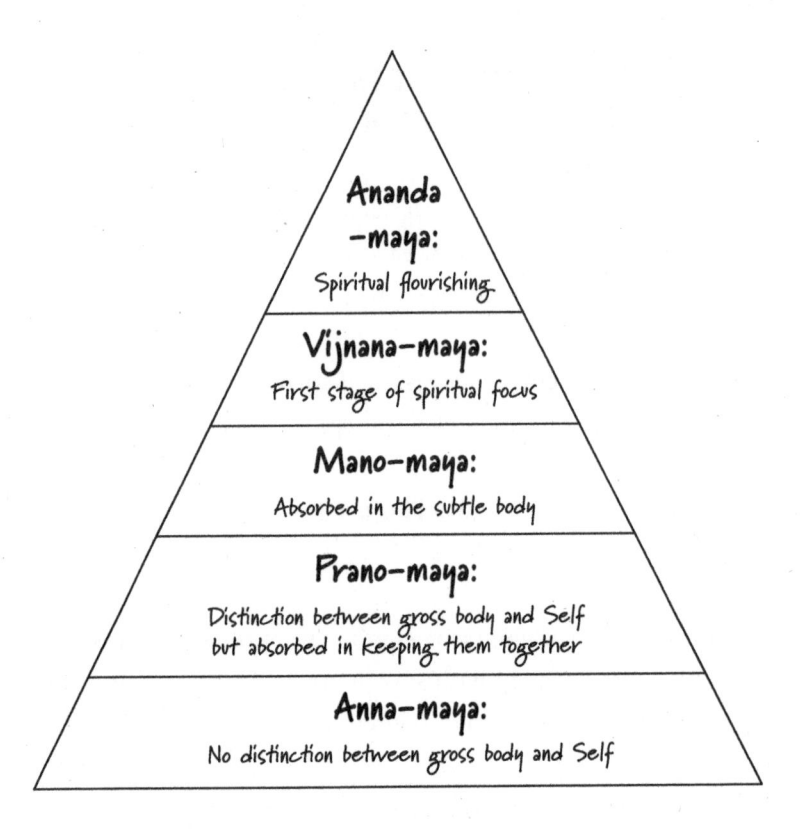

Prano-maya: Distinction between gross body and Self but absorbed in keeping them together

Anna-maya: No distinction between gross body and Self

Effective meditation gradually raises our consciousness through these stages. The common way of categorising states of consciousness is waking, dreaming, and deep sleep. Although dreaming and waking are both experiences of the mind, waking is more important because it is the more persistent and shared reality. Similarly, the *Bhagavata* says activities related to spiritual reality are more important than those related to material reality because they relate to the *truly* persistent and shared reality.

We experience semblances of real things, like shadows, echoes, and mirages, evoking strong emotive responses. Similarly, although our identification with the gross and subtle body is only a semblance of reality, it still generates emotive responses, such as fear, anger, and hope. But for one who has subdued the mind, the universe is seen not as an independent reality but as an extension of and dependent on an underlying spiritual reality. Once we understand the nature of unencumbered consciousness and that we are not currently perceiving the fullness of reality, it's easier for us to develop detachment from our fears and anxieties (which we know are not based on the real picture) and attachment to the true nature of consciousness.

Dealing with the Highs and Lows of Life

The Avanti Brahmana was a teacher from the town of Avanti, one of ancient India's centres of learning, who, after experiencing misfortune, was ignored by friends and family and cut off from society. As the Avanti Brahmana contemplated his misfortune, he experienced a feeling of detachment, resolving to spend the remainder of his life in pursuit of spiritual realisation, beginning with reflections on the mind and suffering: 'These people are not the cause of my happiness and distress. Neither are the celestials, my own body, destiny, my past work, or time. Rather, it is the mind alone that causes happiness and distress.'

He goes on to conclude: 'The mind is stronger than the strongest, and his godlike power is fearsome. Therefore, anyone who can bring the mind under control becomes the master of all the senses. Failing to conquer this irrepressible enemy, the mind, whose urges are intolerable and who torments the heart, many people are completely bewildered and create useless quarrels with others. Thus, they conclude that other people are either their friends, their enemies, or parties indifferent to them. Persons who identify with this body are blinded in their intelligence, thinking in terms of "I" and "mine" and so wander in endless darkness.'

The Avanti Brahmana then contemplates how the Self, which is transcendental to the gross and subtle body and so can never actually be affected by material happiness and distress under any circumstance or by the agency of any person, seems to feel pleasure and pain. What could be causing this experience?

After considering the various possibilities, he concludes that it is, in fact, the false ego that gives shape to material existence and thus experiences material happiness and distress. As long as we are absorbed in the false ego, we accept these experiences as our own. A person who understands this conquers fear.

MOVING BEYOND RELIGION

Note how the impact on the Self—seemingly experiencing material happiness and suffering—is dependent on the Self's misidentification with the mind and body. Without this misidentification, there is a reduction in material happiness *and* material suffering. Instead, material emotions are gradually replaced with spiritual ones, which arise from the conscious Self rather than the false ego.

The message of the Avanti Brahmana helps us understand the layers of our being and the workings of the subtle mind. This can help us understand where neuroscience ends: 'Scientists try to measure thought and feelings through the brain's electrical output, but these brain waves are no more useful for understanding the psyche than the letters of a book written in a forgotten language are for knowing the intended meanings of its ancient author.'[38]

The Vedic texts say that the truth about a person's mind can be known by how they act. And by their mental state, we can understand their past and their future (as guided by *karma* and the modes) unless they seek to break free of this predeterminism. This is why breaking free from the mind is so intricately linked with breaking free of the cycle of *samsara*—it is, by definition, a spiritual path. This is a rational approach that can be accessed by anyone from any background. We all share a basic human makeup, and a better understanding of our makeup with these insights can help any of us.

The mind is the seat for thinking, feeling, and willing: 'The mind's thinking (gathering data through nerves to the brain and then retaining it), feeling (combining and separating the data produces impressions, and then classifies the impressions and so reduces their complexity; then isolates particular items to increase the number again by further analysis) and willing (reasoning by deriving meaning from the impressions) are fuelled by sensory input, but the mind remains unaware of the significance of its contents other than to experience them as desirable or undesirable.'[39]

When our consciousness is influenced by the modes, our subtle body (including the mind) takes form. The mind, in that sense, is a product of the modes, the resultant influence of the modes on pure consciousness. Thus, we have different 'states of mind'. So, when the mind wanders between what it deems desirable and undesirable, based upon impressions of past sensory experiences,

---

38) *Tattva Sandharba* by Jiva Goswami, translated by Gopiparanadhana Das.
39) *Sankalpa Kaumudi* by Sivarama Swami.

it must be carefully brought back by 'intelligence strengthened by Goodness', like an expert rider who sometimes lets their horse have its way and sometimes guides it back on track. Similarly, we are advised to observe the movements and desires of the mind and gradually bring them under control. As the mind is tamed with spiritual practice, the modes gradually desist, and one moves toward transcendence.

Krishna says in the *Bhagavad-gita*, 'For he who has tamed the mind, the mind is the best of friends; but for one who has failed to do so, his mind will remain the greatest enemy. For one who has conquered the mind, the indwelling Superconsciousness is already reached, for he has attained tranquillity. To such a person, happiness and distress, heat and cold, honour and dishonour are all the same.' And we are warned, 'Just as a hunter, after capturing wild animals, does not put faith in them, even advanced souls should not put faith in the mind, which is restless and can cheat us at any moment.' So, the mind can be helpful if tamed, but even then, we should not fully trust it or give it free rein. This is why the spiritual path is not simply an outright rejection of all rules or all religions but rather a gradual flourishing of the Self that, in the early stages, is supported by structure until it is ready to blossom with spontaneity.

As we try to tame them, the insecure mind and false ego fight back to protect their false sense of intimacy with this world, just as the mind wanders when we are trying to focus. The Avanti Brahmana warns us of the hazards generated by the mind and false ego as we try to release the Self from the psyche. One hazard is what he found himself doing—looking for someone to blame when things go wrong. But he learned that since distress occurs in our minds, there is no one to blame. By ruminating on whom to blame, we fall victim to a trick of the false ego—putting ourselves back in the centre of our self-centred universe. By doing so, we inflict greater suffering on ourselves, spiralling down the modes, losing track of our spiritual identity, and realigning with the old mind and false ego.

If we tolerate the mind, the veil of the false ego will gradually thin, allowing our real identity to shine through and enabling our spiritual nature and free will. And once we slacken the mind and false ego's grip on us, we can more easily engage in spiritual practice. As stated in the opening of Patanjali's famous *Yoga sutra*, 'Yoga is the restriction of the movements of the mind. When this is achieved, the witness comes to exist in terms of its true identity. Otherwise, the witness assumes the identity dictated by the movement of the mind.'

Over the past few chapters, we have explored the concept of the Self as pure consciousness and an object of its own awareness. We know that the Self's consciousness is channelled through and directed toward the mind and body, while the Self also remains distinct, like a witness to the three states of material consciousness (waking, sleeping, and deep sleep). We also know that the Self is only the 'doer' in the sense that it desires, followed by attempts to fulfil these desires. But we should not be fooled into imagining ourselves as totally independent actors: from the point of our desires, the rest is also a function of time, *karma*, and the *gunas* acting on us. Having understood the shadow (external energy) and our situation within it, we are now ready for Part III, where we explore in more detail the relationship of the Self with the Ultimate Reality.

PART III

Your Relationship With the Ultimate Reality

BHAGAVATA'S SEED VERSE THREE

'Know that the universal elements enter into the cosmos and at the same time do not enter into the cosmos; similarly, I also exist within everything created, and at the same time, I am outside of everything.'

THIS MAY WELL BE one of the most profound philosophical insights ever. Tragically, its explanatory power and its implications have largely been overlooked. In addition to explaining the spiritual reality, this text also refers to the material elements. In doing so, it challenges everything from Aristotelian logic to a reductive understanding of reality.

Over Part I and II, we looked at the idea of a universal spirituality, had an overview of the subtle and physical aspects of reality, and a perspective on the human condition. In Part III, we are going to look at our relationship with the Ultimate Reality. This relationship is best explained as a simultaneous oneness and difference. Just like a piece of cloth, these threads are simultaneously both a part of and independent of the cloth. We explore this idea of simultaneous oneness and difference from various perspectives, including radical personalism, the integrative nature of the Ultimate Reality, the mind as an ally, and the inevitable conclusion of oneness and difference: universal love.

CHAPTER 14
Radical Personalism

'Anyone who can bring the mind under control becomes the master of all the senses.'
—Bhagavad-gita

Absorbed as we are in materialism, we may not recognise the spiritual reality that resides in every object, every atom. The *Bhagavata* encourages our introspection and answers the perennial question, 'How can I see God?' If a person who has never encountered a car engine hears the sound of one, they won't understand what it is. Similarly, we struggle to understand or even recognise the divinity or spiritual reality surrounding us because we have been so long out of touch.

One way to tune back in, practised in different parts of the world and in various guises, is radical personalism. This is when we conceive of the personhood of Ultimate Reality exhibited in the forms of nature. Building such practical connections can be a powerful spiritual (and ethical) practice. One imagines the rivers as God's veins, the mountains as God's bones, and so on. This is similar in some ways to a naïve pantheism (the universe *is* God), and in more ways to a sophisticated panentheism (God pervades the universe *and* is more than the universe), since it recognises that this is an imaginary construct and that there is also a dimension of transcendence beyond nature. The *Bhagavata's* sophistication is in delineating precisely how this oneness and difference can exist—the energy and the energetic.

FINDING GRATITUDE

One way to spark recognition—and subsequent connection—is by stimulating our awe and wonder of the natural world. Gratitude is a gateway to spiritual awakening, and if we recognise our dependence upon and indebtedness to nature, that will help us in our progress. Different cultures have interpreted this principle in a different way. For some, the sun is worshippable; it enlivens us with heat and light and reminds us of the movement of time. Cooperation between humans, nature, and the divine, can begin with awe, wonder, and appreciation. Bhaktivedanta Swami said that what artists call beautiful nature is but the Lord's smile, and the sweet songs of birds but specimens of his whispering voice.

Expressing the concept of radical personalism, Alexander Pope wrote, 'All are but parts of one stupendous whole, whose body Nature is and God the soul.' The *Bhagavata* draws a similar parallel between our bodies and the cosmos as the body of the Supreme Self.

In the *Bhagavad-gita*, Krishna says, 'This entire cosmos is pervaded by me in my unmanifested (impersonal, energetic) form. All beings rest on me, though I do not rest on them…And yet everything that is created does not rest on me. Behold my mystic opulence!' He goes on to explain that all beings rest on him in the same way that the wind rests on space. His energetic form is all-pervading, while his transcendent form remains aloof. This is how he can exist within everything and, at the same time, be outside of everything. Even without deep spiritual knowledge, just the thought of such inconceivable potency stimulates awe and wonder.

Seeing material nature as connected to and part of the Ultimate Reality transforms ordinary perception into spiritual understanding. As butter can be manifested from milk by churning, or fire from wood by kindling, the presence of the Ultimate Reality can be 'extracted' as we become increasingly sensitive to the spiritual reality all around us.

Cultural prejudices can cause us to dismiss beliefs and practices different from our own as primitive, naïve, or lesser in some way. The *Bhagavata* tells us that different people will connect with the Ultimate Reality in different ways. Belief systems that help one see the imminent divine animating the world as we animate our bodies may or may not present the complete truth, but they can be stepping stones, aiding us on our journey.

WORSHIPPING IDOLS

Radical personalism can also be directed to a deity or divine image. But what is the difference between the worship of such an image and idolatry? One difference is that an idolater does not comprehend the relationship between the idol and divinity; their attention does not stretch beyond the physical. Whereas the other focuses their attention on the Ultimate Reality present within everything made accessible by the image or deity, like windows to the spiritual realm.

Spiritual reality always exists everywhere, all around us; we need only to know how to 'extract' it. The *Bhagavata* does not suggest an 'anything goes' philosophy; it urges us to test any claim by its results and then to accept with humility that others, particularly individuals and cultures with long histories of spiritual development, hold truths from which we may yet benefit.

UNIVERSAL FORM

In the *Bhagavad-gita*, Arjuna asks Krishna to see his unlimited form, the Universal Form: 'I wish to see how you have entered into this cosmic manifestation. I want to see that form of yours.' Krishna agrees, and in the cosmic, awe-inspiring vision he is granted, Arjuna sees the past, present, and future all collapsed into one. He describes this form as immeasurable, the entire creation and its causal elements all in one and speaks of an effulgence more glaring than the sun. Arjuna's mood changes from wonder to fear as he sees the impending death of the soldiers gathered on the battlefield. He prays fervently, and the Universal Form replies with words quoted later by J. Robert Oppenheimer upon witnessing the first nuclear explosion: 'Now I become Death, the destroyer of worlds.'[40]

The Universal Form is described as 'a godless display of opulence', as 'an imaginary form', and as 'materially conceived'. These descriptions may seem odd in reference to the divine if one is not familiar with the role of radical personalism as a stepping stone.

The *Bhagavata* advises people who are too materially attached to focus their minds first on the Universal Form. They can allow themselves to be awed by this 'greatness' and thus develop respect and appreciation for the potency of the Ultimate Reality and the 'body' of the divine. In this way, the sceptic can also 'see' Ulti-

---

[40] A more literal translation of the original Sanskrit would be: 'Time I am, acting to destroy the worlds.'

mate Reality. The Universal Form can, therefore, give physicalists a concept of the Ultimate Reality with which they can identify and thus encourage their cooperation with and respect for the natural world.

The *Bhagavata* correlates the development of the Universal Form to the specific stages of embryonic development. It also correlates it to the composition of a human body: just as individual human bodies are composed of countless cells and microbes, the Universal Form contains all the individual bodies of living beings.

Radical personalism is a way in which many traditions around the world build everyday connections to the Ultimate Reality. It may appear naïve at first, but look deeper, and you will often find a profound and practical spiritual process—one that ties our lives and well-being with that of the natural world and one that today's world could benefit from.

A MIND-BLOWING REVELATION

Learning about the features of the Ultimate Reality, such as the Universal Form, can be stimulating for some and puzzling for others. If we value elevating our consciousness, it is sometimes necessary for us to be provoked from slumber; the *Bhagavata* says that one's consciousness is thus 'agitated and elevated'. Ideas that provoke awe and wonder, or inspire curiosity and surprise, can be helpful in jolting us out of the ordinary, thereby opening us to higher truths.

'Everything rests upon me, as pearls are strung on a thread,' Krishna tells Arjuna to help him perceive the Ultimate Reality in all things. The thread upholds and maintains the necklace, but it goes unnoticed. 'I am the taste in water, the radiance of the sun and the moon, the syllable Om in the Vedic mantras; I am the sound in space and the prowess in men. I am the original fragrance of the earth, and I am the heat in fire.' Later, Arjuna asks to hear more of the ways in which the Ultimate Reality can be seen to pervade the world by physical representations. Krishna obliges: 'I am all-devouring death, and I am the generating principle of all that is yet to be. Among women I am fame, fortune, fine speech, memory, intelligence, steadfastness, and patience. Among all means of suppressing lawlessness, I am punishment, and of those who seek victory, I am morality. Of secret things, I am silence, and of the wise, I am the wisdom. Know that all opulent, beautiful, and glorious creations spring from but a spark of my splendour.'[41]

Seeing extraordinary manifestations of potency, we can be provoked into spiritual contemplation. Even Krishna's mention of 'all-devouring death' is in this vein since contemplation of impending death can be a powerful spiritual practice.

As we become accustomed to thinking in these ways, we can then also detect spiritual connections in even the simplest things, like the taste of water and the light of the sun. Bhaktivedanta Swami once said that even a drunkard fond of wine could meditate upon its taste as the taste of Ultimate Reality and thus become a yogi!

---

41) The *Bhagavata* also includes similar references: 'He is the ultimate goal of those seeking progress, and he is time for those who exert control. He is the equilibrium of the *gunas*, virtue among pious, of subtleties the soul, of difficult things the mind...He is the basis of the *atma*, the *gunas*, and the *Mahat-tattva*; he is everything and nothing can exist without him.'

SEEING THE BIG PICTURE

Our ordinary perception is limited by time, space, and thought. The *Bhagavata* pre-empts the following question: how is it then that we can hope to perceive the transcendent and limitless in this way?

Firstly, because the spiritual process raises us above the 'cloud' of the modes that block the 'sun' of the Ultimate Reality from our vision—this occurs when we recognise our identity as pure consciousness.

And secondly, the Ultimate Reality is self-revealing in reciprocation when the Self seeks connection with it. This occurs when we act based on our newly discovered spiritual identity—such actions are the expression of spiritual love. So, we can begin to perceive spiritual reality not simply by our own limited faculties but facilitated by the self-revealing nature of the internal energy. We have only to want it.

The nature of the Ultimate Reality cannot be fully understood by our own efforts alone. The *Bhagavata* offers us the example of a well-disguised actor whose identity is not evident to the audience. The actor needs to want to reveal themselves, and in the case of Ultimate Reality, this is stimulated by our budding love.

The seed of spiritual love, the essence of bliss, is inherent to every living being. This love attracts the all-attractive and induces the Ultimate Reality to reveal itself in increasing fullness. When this original spiritual loving propensity is directed toward material nature, it becomes adulterated and thus draws the Self toward the world of matter. The path of spiritual love, therefore, is the perfect antidote to our material condition—it reverses the very cause of our situation: misdirected love. So, in this most effective yoga system, having withdrawn the mind from other objects, like a tortoise withdraws its limbs, one absorbs it first in the Self, then in the Superconsciousness, and finally in the transcendent object of love. That may sound simple, but anyone who has tried silencing the mind knows that this is not an easy task, especially with an unruly mind not accustomed to listening.

WHAT LIES BEYOND ILLUSION

According to the Vedic texts, we can be said to be in illusion whenever we consider anything as separate from the Ultimate Reality. It follows then that the Ultimate Reality can reveal itself everywhere and anywhere, in any form and to anyone. There cannot, therefore, be a privileged few. And given the connection of everything to the Ultimate Reality, *things* cannot be considered inherently good or bad. Their purpose is most important, and, therefore, a spiritually informed use of material objects in and of itself can be a spiritual practice. This is the same principle of *yukta-vairagya* from Chapter 3. As we have seen before, this principle is a powerful means by which we can stay in the world but not be of it.

For a beginner, seeing beyond the illusion of separateness from Ultimate Reality is a practical, fast-track approach to starting a spiritual journey without religious trappings. For the advanced, it is the viewpoint of the lover—so captivated are they that wherever they look, they remember and see only their beloved.

CHAPTER 15
The Power of Three

'The Ultimate Reality is perfect and complete, and because it is completely perfect, all emanations, such as this phenomenal world, are perfectly complete wholes. Even though so many complete units emanate from it, it remains the complete balance.'
—Isopanishad

Let's recap and consolidate what we've understood about the nature of Ultimate Reality. We know that it has three features and three energies. Recall the three features are:

1) The impersonal (possessing eternality).
2) The imminent (possessing eternality and cognisance).
3) The personal (possessing eternality, cognisance, and bliss).

The three energies are:

1) Internal (the spiritual reality and basis for the other two energies).
2) External (the material reality).
3) Marginal (the individual Self).

The *Bhagavata* says that the world's diverse spiritual practices engage with this framework in their own ways, terminologies, and categories.

The idea of a Universal Form—not listed above because, remember, it is an imaginary conception—is easily appreciated by materialists, mainly because it is based on matter and doesn't necessarily need someone to believe in transcendent spiritual reality. The impersonal is easily appreciated by philosophers and seekers who are inspired by speculation or a thirst for philosophical knowledge. The imminent is easily appreciated by yogis and meditators, inspired by a desire for mystical connection. The personal is easily appreciated by devotees, who are inspired by a desire for reciprocal spiritual love. These are not mutually exclusive categories, but they can indicate a tendency toward different spiritual goals. They are also cumulative in terms of realisation: someone who more fully comprehends the Ultimate Reality understands all these different aspects.

Since we each see reality from our own limited perspective, we naturally tend to emphasise one thing over another, depending on our preferences. Unable to accommodate the inconceivable, people may sometimes prefer to imagine a void or something impersonal as a spiritual goal. But we need to be careful not to revert to a veiled form of materialism; it's all too easy to use the nebulous as an excuse because it's easy, requires less thought, and challenges us less. If it does become veiled materialism, by definition, we will be dealing only with material things.

The possibility of a transcendent form is a sticking point for many people. Some fear downgrading the divine to the mundane; some insist that any form is limiting; and some claim the absolute inconceivability of the spiritual. According to the *Bhagavata*, acceptance of a purely spiritual transcendent form of the Ultimate

Reality does not compromise inconceivability, limit the Ultimate Reality, or downgrade the transcendent to the mundane.

As fire has form, but its energies of light and heat do not, *Bhagavan* is described in the *Bhagavata* as the source of energy having transcendental form, though its energy does not. In many traditions, the concept of a God with form has shifted over the centuries. Some mainstream religions today started off with a transcendent personal concept of God that shifted over time toward an impersonal one. Many scriptures refer to the hand, face, or back of God, but traditions have often rejected the literal meaning and assumed an impersonal interpretation, blurring the lines between the divine having no material form and having no material *or* spiritual form. This slippery slope can lead first to monism, then to voidism, and eventually to materialism.

Let's now look at what more the *Bhagavata* tells us about the three features of Ultimate Reality.

STAGE 1: THE IMPERSONAL

In the *Bhagavad-gita*, Krishna says, '*Brahman*, the spirit, beginningless and subordinate to me, lies beyond the cause and effect of this material world.' *Brahman* is the end of all energy, the very substrate of all existence, including matter. This impersonal aspect of the Ultimate Reality can be realised simply by applying one's mind to spiritual reflection. However, only things that have form can be objects of the mind's direct sense perception. Thus, to enable its perception by contrast with the *untruth* of matter, the mind perceives *Brahman* as formless concepts like Truth, Beauty, or Virtuousness.

The *Brahman* state of first spiritual contact is a transitional position between the material and spiritual. It is formless, sometimes experienced as void, and without designation—like deep sleep. It is transitional because the fullness of spiritual love and variety is not yet manifest, but at the same time, the *gunas* are dormant, so it is not material either. The happiness of such a state is defined by the absence of suffering.

Liberation is when one awakens from the mistaken thinking that the Self is completely independent and/or that there is no Ultimate Reality. The *Bhagavata* explains that wherever the scriptures provide an impersonal description of the Ultimate Reality, they are establishing that everything in relation to the Ultimate Reality is free of mundane duality and characteristics. Those focusing on the impersonal *Brahman* often like to deliberate on affirmations such as 'That you are' (*tat tvam asi*)[42] and 'I am that *Brahman*' (*aham brahmasmi*). Such aphorisms are warnings that we are not matter. They are preliminary spiritual instructions, leading us to stop illusory activities and thus offer relief from suffering. They also lead one to abandon false identities and mitigate the concomitant suffering due to false identification.

The Self's merging with *Brahman* is also often interpreted as nonexistence—by merging with *Brahman*, the Self loses its own individual identity and existence. It has also been noted that if

---

42) This aphorism is often used to support the claim that the Self is absolutely the same as the Supreme Self. I am grateful to my elder son for the following explanation: '*Tat*' is a neuter term. The person being addressed (Svetaketu) is the son of the speaker. In the line immediately prior, the father uses '*Sa*', a masculine term, to denote a direct relationship between the son and the atma, or individual spiritual Self. Therefore, the use of '*Tat*' over '*Sa*' in relating Svetaketu to '*animan*' (universal subtleness—a synonym for *Brahman*) denotes an indirect relationship rather than a direct one. In Sanskrit, the gender relationship between words is crucial in distinguishing relationships and meanings, and therefore, it seems most likely that this is a precisely curated statement, framed within intentional uses of grammar to express precise theological teachings: you are *like* that, in essence—just as a drop of ocean water is *like* the ocean.

such liberation did mean complete and absolute oneness, it could not contain any sense of happiness because one would not have the faculties of individual consciousness with which to experience happiness. This extreme version of nondifference thus disallows the Ultimate Reality from being a spiritual entity with any qualities or from being a knower or actor. It also leaves open questions of how our illusioned state came about and how it is being sustained.

In summary, there are broadly two categories of those who aspire for the impersonal *Brahman*. The first—less extreme—understands the principle of oneness and difference, the eternal integrity of the Self, and the multiple phases of Ultimate Reality, but still leans toward oneness and the impersonal. The more extreme rejects any sense of eternal individuality, accepting only an absolute nondifference; its concept of liberation is for one to merge into that impersonal state by relinquishing one's individual identity (obviating the principle of individual love).

STAGE 2: THE IMMINENT

Krishna describes the Superconsciousness feature of the Ultimate Reality: 'The Supreme Truth exists outside and inside of all living beings, the moving and the non-moving. Because he is subtle, he is beyond the power of the material senses to see or to know. Although far, far away, he is also near to all. Although Superconsciousness appears to be divided among all beings, he is never divided. He is situated as one...he is knowledge, he is the object of knowledge, and he is the goal of knowledge. He is situated in everyone's heart.'

As the individual Self's consciousness pervades the body, Superconsciousness pervades the universal body, everywhere and without limit, and so is referred to as the Superconsciousness. Because Superconsciousness is all-pervading, it also introduces the possibility of more than one individual unit of consciousness (a living being) connecting with another, with Superconsciousness as the medium. We don't see properly in the dark, but by the light of the sun, we can see everything, including ourselves. Similarly, we can perceive reality more accurately in the all-pervading light of Superconsciousness.

Superconsciousness has three important functions: as witness to the Self's actions in the external energy, as the one who sanctions these actions, and as the provider of sustenance to the Self. It guides the subtle body by providing remembrance, knowledge, and forgetfulness. Such sanctions are transactional, based upon *karma* and the Self's desires. This allows the subtle body to 'know' how to act according to the reactions of past *karma* and desires. In keeping with free will, to those who do not wish spiritual awakening, Superconsciousness remains in the background, invisible and inaudible, but all the while providing opportunity: the Self chooses, Superconsciousness sanctions, and the *gunas* carry out.

Since the beginning of the Self's sojourn in the material realm, Superconsciousness has been present, placing the seed of spiritual awakening in the heart of every living being, waiting patiently for the Self to recognise and act upon it. Superconsciousness is always anxious about suffering humanity, even if they are not awake to this concern. And for those seeking spiritual nourishment, Superconsciousness reveals spiritual insight in proportion to their awakening. At less mature stages of spiritual life, we must be careful because the mind's dictation can be confused with the voice of Superconsciousness, but at advanced stages, the Self experiences a clear direction. Superconsciousness thus manifests to the individual Self according to their spiritual development.

Superconsciousness offers a more complete experience of Ultimate Reality than the impersonal *Brahman* since, in addition to eternity and the alleviation of suffering, it also offers far greater cognisance. But it does not yet manifest the full bliss of spiritual reality.

STAGE 3: THE PERSONAL

In the *Bhagavad-gita*, Krishna says, 'I am the basis of the impersonal *Brahman*, which is immortal, imperishable and eternal and is the constitutional position of happiness.' Just as it is easier to look at the sun's rays than to stare at the glaring sun directly, it can be easier to appreciate the Ultimate Reality as changeless, formless, pure consciousness than as a supreme person with transcendental qualities. The notion that Ultimate Reality is without qualities or that all names and forms are unreal has been prevalent in religions throughout history. Krishna addresses this point directly: 'Those who do not know me well think that I was impersonal before and have now assumed a personality. Due to their limited knowledge, they do not know my higher nature, which is imperishable and supreme.' The notion that any personal form of the divine must be imaginary, born of anthropomorphic origins, is also not new. But the *Bhagavata* makes clear distinctions between that which is imaginary and conceptual, like the Universal Form, and that which is eternal and transcendent.

BEYOND LIMITS

As we saw in the last chapter, religions have debated whether or not the divine has form. The mere fact that such a fundamental principle is a subject for debate indicates that the matter may not be binary. The personal form is described as 'the soul of all qualities' because it 'gives them life' by manifesting their prototypes. This is because without the original prototype, qualities would remain abstract, without exemplification, and thus lifeless; qualities come to life only when a being exhibits them. This transcendent personal feature is called *Bhagavan*. Even more incredible, *Bhagavan* manifests a specific spiritual quality for each living being so that we can appreciate and connect with the Ultimate Reality in our own particular ways. Therefore, a primary name for *Bhagavan* is Krishna, the 'all attractive'. We will come back to this meaning of Krishna in Chapter 18.

It is contradictory to try and limit transcendence from the possibility of having form because form is limiting. Either transcendence is limited, or it is unlimited, and if it is unlimited, then it must be able to possess form. The argument also assumes that any form of transcendence must be limited in the same ways that mundane forms are limited, but that argument is problematic since we would also need to say that transcendence would have to have other attributes of the mundane, including a cause, and thus nullifying the first cause nature assumed of divinity. By definition, that which applies to transcendence need not comply with the same limitations we observe in the mundane—which is as true for form as it is for cause.

Apparent contradictions, such as the Ultimate Reality being both all-pervasive *and* localised or being both neutral *and* partial, have often been misunderstood. The *Isopanisad* says, 'The Supreme walks and does not walk. He is far away, but he is very near as well. He is within everything, and yet he is outside of everything.' These are not contradictions but inconceivable features, and as such, they represent attractive attributes—not faults—of the divine.

In the *Bhagavata*, Kapila says, 'A single object is appreciated differently by different senses due to it having different qualities. Similarly, the Ultimate Reality is one, but according to different scriptural perceptions and explanations, it appears to be different.'

Such contradictions appear irreconcilable until we stop imposing material limitations on the nonmaterial. The *Bhagavata* tells the story of an incredibly powerful and capable tyrant to illustrate the inevitable outcome of falling victim to such mistaken thinking. This tyrant once sought to usurp the universal order and declare war on God. But he mistakenly thought transcendence must also be bound by material laws and limits. He angrily searched the entire universe. Unable to find God, he concluded, 'God is dead.' Our tyrant then assumed that with the old God 'dead', he himself must now have become God. All this time, God had playfully hidden himself in the tyrant's heart, where he never thought to look. These events took place aeons ago, but the faulty conclusion still persists—humans try to play God all the time. We can't even easily conceive of how an entire tree can be contained within a seed, so it's no surprise that the spiritual nature is also not easy to conceive. We cannot expect that just because material laws are the only laws we know, that spiritual nature must also be bound by them.

SPIRITUAL LOVE

If some processes reveal specific aspects of the Ultimate Reality, are there any that reveal the fuller picture? The *Bhagavata* points to spiritual love. Evidence for this is found in the lives of the most accomplished yoga masters such as the Kumaras, meditators such as Dhruva, and philosophers such as Sukadeva—all of whom became attracted to loving service as the climax of their spiritual paths. They were already advanced in piety, knowledge, and mysticism, yet they chose to continue progressing up the yoga ladder toward spiritual love.

Spiritual love also allows us to reconcile apparent contradictions and appreciate how the Ultimate Reality manifests in different ways. Some approach the Ultimate Reality as impersonal, some as the indwelling presence of divinity, some with formality and awe in the worship of a supreme transcendental personality, and some with greater levels of loving intimacy. These are not contradictory any more than it is contradictory for us to have different and seemingly conflicting aspects of our personality or the different roles we play at home and at work.

Such love also enables us to see things in perspective. Viewing just a snapshot of a parent disciplining a child may make the parent seem unjust, but understanding the loving reasons for that discipline and its long-term positive effects can put things in proper perspective. The Ultimate Reality is absolute; any genuine contact with it will positively impact our spiritual journey.

The notion of love implies dependence, but for many of us, depending on someone else does not come naturally. But the right kind of dependence can bring relief and peace. We know that the mind and senses, being symptoms of life, can be tamed but not stopped. We also know that they can become detached only by superior engagement. That superior engagement is the process of refocusing our love—from chasing our own enjoyment to expressions of love for our eternal object of love.

OUR COMPLETE NATURE

On this path of spiritual love, we can experience our complete nature. The *Bhagavata* advises that our love finds its perfect repose in *Bhagavan*, the Supreme Person. The arising bliss has no limit, increasing beyond all other states of absorption. The *Bhagavata* also says this loving dependence is reciprocal.

How we wish to engage with the Ultimate Reality is our choice, and this choice may change over time as we progress on our spiritual journey. There is no need or reason to limit our choices—or to rush them; we can just keep an open mind and let our spiritual practice develop.

CHAPTER 16

Reaching for the Spiritual

'What is the value of a prolonged life which is wasted, inexperienced by years in this world? Better a moment of full consciousness, because that gives one a start in searching after their supreme interest.'
—The Bhagavata

Having described the formless, all-pervading, and personal aspects of the Ultimate Reality, we now explore some useful tips for our journey towards them. As we have seen in previous chapters, the *Bhagavata* prompts us to first acknowledge that there is something beyond the veil of matter and then move toward that transcendence. It all begins with a search for that which lies beyond, then a steady commitment to spiritual life, followed by gradual control over the mind and senses, thus enabling potent spiritual practice.

We've discussed yoga as the various paths to transcendence rather than something you do at your local gym. As we saw in the yoga ladder (see Chapter 11), yoga first moves us up the modes to Goodness. But Goodness is like an airport—a helpful place to facilitate travel, but it is pointless if you miss your plane. We must move beyond Goodness to transcendence. Let's start with the restless mind, which we have heard much about in previous chapters.

THE RESTLESS MIND

Whatever spiritual path we take, we must bring the mind under control; if we don't, it will be our enemy instead of our friend, dragging us toward materialism. With the mind at least somewhat under control, our spiritual practices gain focus and efficacy. Krishna advises, 'From wherever the mind wanders due to its flickering and unsteady nature, one must withdraw it and bring it back under the control of the Self.'

But when our lives are so busy, that might sound challenging. And indeed, Arjuna protests, thinking it too difficult a task: 'The mind is restless, turbulent, obstinate and very strong, and to subdue it, I think, is more difficult than controlling the wind.' Krishna agrees that it is difficult but says that it is not impossible: 'It is undoubtedly very difficult to curb the restless mind, but it is possible by suitable practice and by detachment.'

Spiritual practice and self-discipline will gradually bring the mind under control, and once bridled, the mind can help us to our destination.

Our false ego directs our intelligence toward fulfilling our mind's demands instead of directing it with knowledge. In this state, intelligence can be nervous, weak, and vacillating—evidenced by its inability to control the mind. But as we contemplate our spiritual identity or at least theoretically accept spirituality as a goal, our intelligence starts to become spiritualised. This eventually enables us to discriminate between material and spiritual. In this state, intelligence becomes resolute and strong and can control our mind and its desires. We can then focus on and engage in spiritual practice.

BODY FIXATION

As seen in almost every aspect of our lives, we spend much time focused on our bodies. We strive in so many ways and to such great extent to maximise bodily beauty, physical strength, bodily comforts, and bodily image—well beyond healthy attention to comfort, health, or self-esteem. This can result in obsession, which may, ironically, lead to poor mental and physical health and low self-esteem. Body fixation can lead to the opposite of the peace we desire.

The *Bhagavata's* message is that we must be careful of what we choose as our object of focus, for it determines our future. In our obsession with our current body, we also determine our future body.

BEING CONTENT

The detachment that Krishna speaks of as being key to self-discipline comes from the commitment of intelligence to positive acts. This commits us to act for the benefit of other living beings, which in turn helps free us from negative emotions by replacing them with concern for others, and so brings us peace. Everything in the universe is insufficient to satisfy one whose senses are uncontrolled. And without spiritual realisation, whose ambitions have ever been fully satisfied?

The way of happiness, then, is to be content with that which is necessary. As Gandhi said, 'The world has enough for everyone's needs but not everyone's greed.'

This notion of being content might feel unrealistic because our minds are always demanding 'more'. And that is Arjuna's question: how can we control the mind? How can we make it peaceful and content?

THIS NEEDS FIXED DETERMINATION

Practice and detachment require effort, and there will no doubt be disturbances along our spiritual path. Progress will likely be incremental, but practice leads to success. Yoga typically includes meditation, postures, and breath work, which can help—but in all cases, we need the resolute determination of our intelligence. Without practice and detachment, we may think we're making progress when we aren't—like someone dreaming that they are awake, only to experience a rude awakening.

The *Bhagavata* assures us we can conquer harmful desires by making determined plans. This means we should carefully and in detail consider how we will respond to specific scenarios when unwanted desires surface or negative emotions are triggered.

FINDING KINSHIP

Friendship with like-minded people along this spiritual journey is also important. When we struggle and need honest feedback, the association of trustworthy people who are interested only in our welfare—and ideally are also proficient in spiritual practice—is invaluable. Such relationships also help channel our natural propensity to offer and receive love, making us less likely to direct our loving propensity toward material things or uncaring relationships.

Finding such kindred spirits is not always easy, but they are around. People used to go to places of worship to find them previously. Now, depending on your circumstance, they may be easier to locate online, through podcasts, for example, or in-person, through spiritual workshops and retreats.

KEEPING IT REAL

Since we cannot hope to separate the mind entirely from its objects, it makes no sense to try and artificially reject the material world. Rather, we can use our intelligence to positively engage with the world so that we can progress on our spiritual path with realism and integrity, even as we remain aware of the world's illusory and temporal nature.

One can spend years dabbling in various processes but committed to none. In the name of inclusivity, we may be misled into an uncertain approach to spirituality. We should choose our path carefully (see the tests in Chapter 2) and give it a good attempt.

Loving devotion, direct experience of transcendence, and detachment from other things occur simultaneously for one who has taken the shelter of the divine. I like the analogy the *Bhagavata* provides: pleasure, nourishment, and relief from hunger come simultaneously and increasingly with each bite for a person engaged in eating. When we eat, we get some pleasure, we are nourished, and our hunger dissipates; we have no need for further convincing. If we do not feel any of these three things, we might question whether we are indeed eating. When we progress on a genuine spiritual path, we will likewise experience these three things:

spiritual love arising, increasing direct experiences of spiritual reality, and decreasing material attachments. If these three are not occurring, we should re-examine our practice.

We need to have reasonable expectations proportionate to the time and effort we invest, but we need not abandon the expectation of results that convince us that we are indeed 'eating'.

DECIDING TO ACT

As we progress on our spiritual path, we will likely feel the urge to engage in spiritual activity. This is natural, for the Self's inherent nature is to love and be loved. Some practices stress the importance of mental absorption or remembrance, while others stress action. The *Bhagavata* clarifies that the two are not different. Mental absorption is the offering of the mind, the monarch of the body and senses. The mind's full concentration can properly engage the body and senses in active, loving service without disturbance. Before we achieve that stage of total concentration, our mind is subject to distraction, so the engagement of our body and senses through acts of loving service helps keep us focused. Mental absorption and action can thus act in tandem.

Rantideva was a king who attained the spiritual stage of being able to see with equal vision: he perceived the presence of the Ultimate Reality everywhere and within every being. The *Bhagavata* tells us of Rantideva's great charity and self-sacrifice. During a famine and at risk of starvation, he repeatedly offered his quota of food to others, even a dog. When we are situated on the platform of spiritual realisation, there is an imperative to act for the benefit of others; it is no longer just a theoretical concept.

CHAPTER 17

Universal Love

'May everyone be blessed; may everyone be healthy.
May everyone see goodness, may no one suffer.'
—Garuda Purana

Enlightened by the knowledge of simultaneous oneness and difference, we begin to see the spiritual equality of all living beings. This brings us to the inevitable conclusion of universal love. In this chapter, we look at the idea of universal love, what it is, and how we can move towards this in our lives. Charles Darwin, whose theory of evolution perhaps ran contrary to the idea of universal love, caught a hint of this:

> 'Experience unfortunately shows us how long it is before we look at [men of all nations and races] as our fellow creatures. Sympathy beyond the confines of man, that is humanity to the lower animals, seems to be one of the latest moral acquisitions... This virtue, one of the noblest with which man is endowed, seems to arise incidentally from our sympathies becoming more tender and more widely diffused, until they extend to all sentient beings.'

We recognise our children as our own, of course, and we identify with them. But we also understand that we are *different* from them. Extending that understanding to all living beings forms the basis for universal love.

With this understanding of oneness, we can understand that our ultimate goal and interest, as well as that of our family and all other living beings, is the same. Unlike the man who wanted to be blinded in one eye out of envy for his neighbour, we should instead be happy in the success of others. When we live in this reality, all our thoughts, words, and actions align with the Ultimate Reality.

TO THE BENEFIT OF ALL

In the long-term view of Goodness, the happiness of others also signals our own happiness. One who sees the world in this way naturally becomes dear to everyone, and everyone is dear to them. To rise to such a state, we are advised to start by offering respect and care to all living beings. Krishna says that he considers this process—using one's mind, words, and body to realise the Ultimate Reality within all beings—to be essential for spiritual realisation. Avoiding harming or exploiting any living being is, therefore, an essential spiritual practice.

NO HARM TO OTHERS

Recognising the spiritual equality of all living beings is not contrary to treating them all differently. How we engage in practical terms with different species is a matter of common sense, but the universal point is that it should be with respect and care and not exploitation. The concept of *ahimsa*, non-harm, is key to the ethics of the *Bhagavata*.

The *Bhagavata* tells us that those who are vulnerable to exploitation deserve our highest priority. Stories of great spiritual teachers like Chaitanya embracing and healing lepers epitomise his compassion for all living beings. Chaitanya once sang and danced in spiritual ecstasy through the forest of Jarikhanda, and animals that were usually hostile found reconciliation in his love. Animals are among the most vulnerable (see also below), and we are implored to care for them as we would our children.

The *Bhagavata* tells how Narada once came across a hunter, Mrigrari, who would wound animals and enjoy watching them die. Narada begged Mrigrari to kill his prey outright to avoid inflicting such unnecessary pain, and as Mrigrari heard from Narada about spiritual principles, he had a change of heart. Sometime later, Narada visited Mrigrari, who was now so transformed that he would carefully avoid stepping on even an ant while walking. Narada commented that Mrigrari's new behaviour was not surprising, for a spiritual person is never inclined to give pain to others.

Meditation on Being Kind to Others

The 17th-century saint Visvanatha Chakravarti offers us the following meditation:

> 'The earth, which is always visible to me, is the expansion of the sacred feet of my Lord, who is always to be meditated upon.[43] All moving

---

43) In Vedic culture, the feet of any superior are the object of shelter.

> and non-moving living beings have taken shelter of the earth and are thus sheltered at the sacred feet of my Lord. For this reason, I should respect every living being and not envy anyone. In fact, all living entities constitute my Lord's *kaustubha* gem.[44] Therefore, I should never envy or deride any living entity.'

The *Bhagavata* instructs us that ritual worship, or external religiosity performed while disregarding the presence of the Ultimate Reality everywhere and within every living being, is 'simply imitation' and is rooted in the mode of Ignorance.

As discussed in Chapter 2, it is the duty of every human being to perform welfare work for other living beings. Even simple trees so ably serve others. Without this equality of vision, there is no universal love. Acts of charity, such as feeding or sheltering people experiencing poverty, are, of course, recommended in many religions as an integral part of their religious life.

There was once a highly advanced soul called Jada Bharata. He wanted only to focus on his spiritual journey and wanted nothing to do with what the material world had to offer. He ostracised himself from society and pretended to be mute. As a result, he was mistreated by a society that thought him uneducated or intellectually stunted simply because he didn't conform to their standards. People abused him even though he was only ever a well-wisher to all living beings. As a society and as individuals, when we ignore the spiritual identity in others and in nature, we

---

44) A reference to a favourite jewel that is worn by Krishna.

objectify and thus dehumanise them. This inevitably degrades us to a materialistic, transactional, and exploitative foundation.

BEING KIND TO ANIMALS

There is a parallel here with so-called intelligent people sending innocent animals to slaughter, ignorant of their spiritual identity. There are concessions within the world's religions, including Hinduism, to eat meat, but there is no excuse for the billions of animals that are mistreated and tortured before being sent to slaughter.[45] We need to recognise the breadth and depth of bias and prejudice that exists even in so-called civilised society.

Seeing the world's suffering, Vasudeva Datta once prayed to take upon himself the suffering of all other living beings so they might be liberated. He wanted to save everyone, regardless of their status, religion, or species. And he wanted them to be permanently liberated, not just temporarily relieved.

Such incredible expressions of compassion are rare, but we can follow their example with simple acts of kindness by extending ourselves to others. This includes practical charity towards humanity with our efforts and money, including making lifestyle choices that cause less harm.

It also includes supporting others in their spiritual quest. Taken egoistically, this means we need to 'convert' others, as ours is the only way to salvation. But taken in the light of this chapter, it means helping each person without the egoistic need for them to become part of 'our group'. Religious charities often do valuable charity work, but all too often, there are strings attached.

---

45) See *Diet of Transcendence* by Steven J. Rosen.

Our last section, Part IV, will now explore the nature of our spiritual quest.

PART IV

Spiritual Quest

BHAGAVATA'S SEED VERSE FOUR

'One who is searching after the Ultimate Reality must certainly search for it up to this, in all circumstances, in all space and time, and both directly and indirectly.'

WE CONDUCT OUR SEARCH directly by searching out spiritual reality but also indirectly by letting go of all that would hold us back. After all, that which we don't say or don't do can have just as significant an impact as that which we do say or do. And while love is already established in the hearts of all—not something to be gained from an external source—how can it manifest?

In this last part of the book, we look at the spiritual quest: the journey towards the full manifestation of love. We are encouraged to engage in this search thoroughly to arrive at the essence of that which is universal and eternal. The *Bhagavata* tells us that every goal has its corresponding method of attainment, so it's helpful to be clear about how any method might get us to where we want to be. Part II showed us that the attainment of our material goals is constrained by material laws; Part IV shows us that spiritual goals are available without such constraints. We start by looking at the workings of love, then the object of love, and then the yoga of love, also known as the living yoga. We introduce a framework to help us think about choosing a type of career or work that helps us be our best and can be dovetailed to support our spiritual journey. We end with some essentials for the journey ahead.

CHAPTER 18
The Workings of Love

'My devotee is always within the core of my heart, and I am always in the heart of my devotee. My devotees do not know anything else but me, and I do not know anyone else but them.'
—The Bhagavata

The *Bhagavata* directs spiritual aspirants to its highest goal: spiritual love. This love is described as the reservoir of all pleasure and is, hence, the highest goal. Through the path of love, the heart is engaged, taking us beyond the fruits of basic meditational exercises that aim to still the mind. Once the heart is engaged, the mind naturally follows, giving us access to a profound moment-to-moment life of meditation.

Progress on the journey to spiritual love is typically gradual, and the *Bhagavata* sets out the distinct stages of its development, each qualifying the seeker to advance to the next. Such a framework helps our self-assessment and also wards off complacency.

In summary, one first becomes interested in the idea of spiritual love, seemingly by accident, as an unintended consequence of a positive spiritual act. Initial interest may be vague and tinged with mixed motives. The seed of faith in spirituality sprouts, and the aspirant begins to consider spiritual reality worthy of focus. The door to transcendence is now open, and with sincerity of purpose, enquiry, and effort, deliberate spiritual life can begin. Even in the earliest stages of spiritual practice, the seeker begins to experience relief from distress and a sense of good fortune. This initial experience fuels their application to the spiritual path. They learn spiritual practices, and through dedicated application, the mind is elevated to Goodness, and unwanted habits, desires, and thoughts begin to fade. Spiritual practice is at first often fickle, and the practitioner fluctuates between moments of elevated consciousness and the mundane. This may be experienced when someone takes up meditation but does not practise every day and thus becomes disillusioned with the lack of results. For a while, they stop meditating, convincing themselves that it does not work. Then, they attend a retreat and rediscover the joy of meditation. But alone back home, they struggle to maintain their practice. Gradually, with determination and the right support, our spiritual practice can become unwavering, and our consciousness firmly established in spiritual life. But until that point, the spiritual journey is often marked by a struggle with flickering faith, unwanted habits and desires, a lack of self-discipline, and enjoyment of the material benefits of spiritual practice, such as the accolade of others. As in any form of education, the technique is only part of the story. Subtler and thus more elusive is the development of intent and emotion. After steadiness is achieved, spiritual life becomes natural and is spurred not by duty or discipline but by attraction. Getting to this point of steadiness may take years, but from there, the seed of spiritual love sprouts quickly and intensifies until the point of union with the object of our love.

My Meditation Path

I began practising meditation more than 30 years ago after I first read the *Bhagavad-gita*. I read about various techniques and philosophies of meditation. I began with sitting in silence and observing my breath. I tried clearing my mind. I tried observing my thoughts. I found all of these helpful, but they weren't enough for me. They helped calm my mind. They took some of the negativity away, but that was the limit. By themselves, they felt like mind games.

For me, meditation took on another dimension when I began mantra meditation. I found that I could use the techniques of calming the mind, breathing, and observing my thoughts to help prepare me for focusing on the mantra. I would take a few minutes to prepare and then meditate for about two hours on the mantra. I also found doing this in the early hours of the morning most conducive.

My early experiences were quite a 'bumpy' experience. I think this was because the process of meditation seems so simple from the outside. I thought I could just follow a few simple steps (sit properly, breathe, focus, clear the mind, chant the mantra), and that would be enough. For anyone who has ever tried to clear the mind—you know how unrealistic that is! However, what I did find was that even through these bumpy times, I felt significant benefits in my life. Even though I didn't have daily 'peak experiences', I did feel a constant level of contentment and a gradual slackening in material desires. These were very precious and real changes.

I persisted. Over the years, I was fortunate to have had

guidance from highly successful meditators. Slowly, the mantra came more alive—certainly not all the time, but with moments of connection that I wish I could sustain. Those experiences have encouraged me to continue.

Some claim that this is comparable to drug-induced experiences. That's obviously a riskier alternative. I was once extremely ill with blood poisoning and was hallucinating, seeing all kinds of strange things while awake. One afternoon, while on the one hand, I felt like I was about to die, I also experienced a completely expanded state of consciousness. I felt intense feelings of spiritual longing. I was actually quite enjoying this new me! But I quickly realised that this was just my body-brain chemistry playing up. So, I can well imagine how drugs could have similar effects. And as I reflected on this, I also realised the crucial distinction. My illness was an abnormal state—like a fleeting drug-induced one. My spiritual practice is to recover my natural state, which requires no artificial stimulant. It has sustained benefits every day of my life; it improves my character and motivations, positively influences my daily actions and contribution to the world, and gradually unveils the spiritual reality. That's all simply not on offer with drugs.

SEEING PROGRESS

Throughout this journey, we can measure our progress by the reduction of material attachments and the increase in our spiritual love. We can observe these in our meditation and behaviour. For example, we might become less interested in the latest gossip or in following the crowd. We should take note, therefore, of whether or not our meditation, which often begins as occasional and distracted, is moving in the right direction: to steady meditation with occasional distraction, then to deep absorption, and finally to inseparable spiritual love.[46]

Like all types of growth, spiritual growth requires the 'death' of those things which hold us back. We each have negative attitudes, habits, situations, and maybe even people in our lives that we can categorise as:

1) Easy to let go of.
2) Requiring real effort to let go of.
3) Impossible to let go of.
4) Not wanting to be let go.

It can be a helpful exercise to make such a list and then ask ourselves, 'Are the contents of the third category actually impossible? Or do they belong elsewhere?'

FACING CHALLENGES

In the West, we are conditioned to be self-reliant. We don't like asking for help; it hurts our ego. For example, the notion of 'taking shelter' in a spiritual context can get our backs up. However, unreasonable individualism can lead to negative, disempowering, and even toxic psychologies. We are dependent in so many ways;

---

46) See *The Nectar of Devotion* by A.C. Bhaktivedanta Swami.

to deny this aspect of ourselves is folly. We may mistakenly think that by seeking help, we are surrendering our independence, but this simply isn't the case.

Ramanuja compares how a monkey and a cat carry their young. With monkeys, the baby must hold on. With cats, the mother holds her kitten in her jaws; all that is required from the kitten is faith. The *Bhagavata* tells us that our determined endeavour, sincerity of purpose, and intense yearning—coupled with an appeal for help—draws intervention from the transcendental plane. This requires effort *and* grace: they go hand-in-hand. Bhaktivedanta Swami once commented that an easy-going life and attainment of perfection in transcendental realisation go ill together.

What confronts the spiritual practitioner striving to rise above their lower-nature influences is the nagging realisation that it is difficult to give up one's conditioned nature simply on one's own. Association with like-minded aspirants and those who are more advanced can be catalytic. So, too, is the in-dwelling of the Ultimate Reality. This munificence is described in different traditions with words such as *mercy* and *grace*. The sincere endeavour of a spiritual aspirant draws out this spiritual 'embrace'.

> Chaitanya once took his followers to clean the Gundicha temple in Orissa in preparation for the arrival of the temple deity.[47] He taught each devotee how to clean. This episode shows how the awakening of spiritual love requires us to clean our own hearts. Sometimes, we don't know how

---

47) The re-enactment of this festival, called Ratha Yatra, is still the largest street procession in the world, attracting up to 3 million people in one day.

dirty a room is until we start cleaning; likewise, we don't always know our own shortcomings until we seriously try to practise spiritual life.

Biographers recorded that 'Chaitanya made [the Gundicha temple] as cool and bright as his own heart, thus making it a fit place for Krishna to sit.' The devotees all cleansed the temple a second time, this time taking the finer dust, straw, and sand—for we need first to remove bad habits, and then the subtle unwanted desires and motives we may not have even noticed. After cleaning the temple twice, they cleaned the external grounds so the dirt would not re-enter.

For practitioners, there is a risk that carelessness might open the door for subtle contaminations (e.g., fault-finding and envy) to re-enter. Chaitanya then mopped and polished the marble with his own shawl, for the path of serious spiritual practise invariably involves some level of personal sacrifice. When the devotees had finished, their minds were as purified and pleasing as the clean temple rooms.

REMAINING MODEST

No form of piety or worship can bring about the same level of purification as when spiritual love manifests within the heart. And yet, the *Bhagavata* warns that when such love does appear, we must try to keep it concealed and not make a public show of it. This is an important test, for the lure of cheap adoration can be compelling. The *Bhagavata* cautions, 'That which is very confidential is successful if kept secret.' The higher echelons of spiritual attainment are matters of the heart best kept to oneself. This connects us to the most essential support of spiritual love: humility. Humility can be cultivated as we practise spiritual life, but in its most natural and exalted state, it is concurrent with the emergence of love, acting both as cause and effect.

ON LOVE

Spiritual love is a 'spontaneous ecstatic urge of the Self to fulfil the desires of the Supreme'. The deepest love, unalloyed love, is without personal consideration and is thus called 'oneness' because it is totally aligned with the beloved's desires. Love is a focus on the pleasure of the beloved. Unalloyed love is the Self's original and natural disposition and is the fullness of the Self's true capacity.

Bhaktivinoda Thakura wrote, 'The essence of the soul is wisdom, and its action is love absolute. The absolute condition of man is his absolute relation to the Deity in pure love. Love alone, then, is the religion of the soul and consequently of the whole man.' The sage Pippalayana says of love, '[T]here is one ultimate goal, one highest attainment...[and] one potent means to bring the Lord under control.' Pippalayana says that such love emerges spontaneously from a dormant state within our hearts with divine grace.

If we are not attracted by loving exchanges in the transcendental realm, this intrinsic desire for loving reciprocation will revert toward the material world, seeking selfish pleasures instead of those of the beloved—a perversion of our original spiritual sentiments. For those who desire to make the transition, the Ultimate Reality eagerly awaits: 'As soon as there is a reciprocal exchange by the Self, at once the great spiritual being attracts the small living being, thus freeing him from all material bondage.'

ALL-ATTRACTIVE

As we saw in Chapter 15, the name Krishna means 'all-attractive'. Bhaktivedanta Swami wrote, 'The word *krs* is the attractive feature of the Lord's existence, and *na* means "spiritual pleasure." When the verb *krs* is added to *na*, it becomes *Krsna*, which indicates the Ultimate Reality.'

The Ultimate Reality, being all-attractive, is deserving and capable of reciprocating our love. Thus, Krishna attracts even those yoga masters who are 'beyond all attraction'. One reason I like this meaning is because it is truly borderless: some people are attracted to names and images that are full of power or majesty, and some to compassion or intimacy; all this and infinitely more is accommodated within the simple reference of 'all-attractive'.

With the name of Krishna defined and established as an inclusive and non-sectarian name of the personality of the Ultimate Reality, we will use this name henceforward as we refer to this specific aspect. If you are culturally unfamiliar with the name, please don't be put off—even the word 'God' has Indic roots, so there's no escaping it!

The *Bhagavata* also describes both male and female aspects of the personality of the Ultimate Reality—Krishna and Radha—where Radha is the inseparable and complete embodiment of Krishna's blissful internal energy.

TRANSCENDING ALL

By better understanding the distinguishing qualities of spiritual love, we can develop an appreciation and affinity for such love. This represents a maturing of spiritual aspirations beyond earlier motives, such as desires for peace, liberation, knowledge, and material improvements. These are no doubt noble aims, but love transcends them because when we love another, we want for them the best possible outcome for the longest possible time. With such love, we want the spiritual world and nothing less. Our aspirations guide our spiritual journey. After all, the *Bhagavata* says love can be described in words only to a very limited extent; it must be experienced to be understood. We first understand it theoretically, typically from spiritual teachings. But it remains aloof. We glimpse it through our spiritual practice. But it is not fully revealed. But the *Bhagavata* shows us that when we fully contact spiritual love, it moves us beyond any attempt to understand it and takes us to a reality of its own—the spiritual reality. It becomes our reality, not an understanding or even a temporary experience.

The *Bhagavata* contains examples of spiritual seekers who have progressed up the stages of yoga from self-realisation to ever-greater depths of love. Krishna says in the *Bhagavad-gita*, 'And of all yogis, the one with great faith who always abides in me, thinks of me within himself and renders transcendental loving service to me—he is the most intimately united with me in yoga and is the highest of all. That is my opinion.'

LOVING SERVICE

The *Bhagavata* uses the Sanskrit word *bhakti* when referring to the means and the goal. The word conveys much more than its typical translations—devotion or worship. More accurately, it conveys the notion of 'loving service'. Neither worship nor service alone will suffice since they can be done out of duty, without love, and service alone may not even be carried out favourably. Love necessitates action. Loving service, *bhakti*, then, is both the process and goal—the activities that cultivate transcendental love and the activities of one who has attained it. One paves the way for the other: the process of *bhakti* cleanses and softens the heart, speeding the dissolution of the false ego and allowing the perfection of *bhakti* to manifest. Unlike other practices, with *bhakti*, the goal itself is the means.

Bhaktivinoda Thakura asserts that we attain perfection corresponding to our meditation and practice. The goal of love requires a practice that is enthused with love, a process that not only withdraws us from the negative but also positively engages our minds and emotions. Stilling the mind withdraws the mind from the negative. That brings us to a neutral state, which we can call 'zero'.

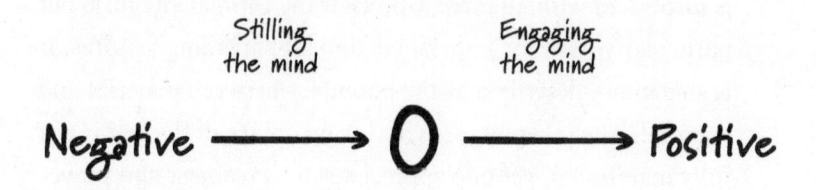

$$\text{Negative} \xrightarrow{\text{Stilling the mind}} 0 \xrightarrow{\text{Engaging the mind}} \text{Positive}$$

This brings great relief. Like all zeros, it seems like a state of nothingness but is pregnant with potential. *Bhakti* is the natural next step, providing positive engagement to take us beyond the stillness of zero. Just as doing no harm is better than inflicting harm but not as complete as actively helping someone, heartfulness goes beyond mindfulness. The anxiety of love is more exalted and relishable than even the peace of self-realisation.

A LOVING RELATIONSHIP

The *Bhagavata* asserts that each living being has an ontological relationship with the Ultimate Reality. Like a sunray to the sun, each living being has a distinctive, reciprocal relationship with the Ultimate Reality. That loving relationship is categorised into five broad categories: appreciation, service, friendship, guardianship, and amorous love. We will look at these five categories, called *rasas*, in turn. The *Taittirya Upanishad* states, 'He himself is *rasa*, the emotional rapture of a particular relationship; one who achieves this *rasa* also becomes filled with bliss.'

As we approach the most advanced stages of spiritual love, our spiritual journey becomes increasingly personal and individual:

- **Appreciation** is a relationship of wonder and observation. It is neutral because it is externally inactive and lacks intimacy. It is associated with all three aspects of the Ultimate Reality, but particularly with the impersonal and all-pervading features. It is sometimes described as the boundary between material and spiritual. The inherent, actively loving nature of the Self is not fully manifested, yet one appreciates the greatness and power of the Ultimate Reality and sees its representation everywhere.

- **Service** describes a relationship in which the majesty of the Ultimate Reality is perceived with awe and reverence.

- **Friendship** can be imbued with the mood of an attendant, and the friend is a well-wisher. Friendship can also be infused with familiarity and camaraderie and manifest as mutual service. Love begins to eclipse the majesty and power of the divine. In this realm, everything becomes subordinate to love—even divinity!

- **Guardianship** manifests for those who desire to engage in a relationship infused with parental love toward the Ultimate Reality. Guardianship exceeds the equality of friendship and is characterised by a protective sentiment.

- Spiritual **amorous love** is hinted at in various spiritual traditions. For many, it is difficult to grasp, and so the *Bhagavata* takes great care in building up to its systematic and full revelation.

These categories help facilitate the different 'flavours', or emotional raptures, of spiritual love. And while each person in that realm enjoys their particular happiness and feels that there could be no greater joy, these categories are equal from an absolute level.

PERFECT RECIPROCATION

Narada says, 'As a jewel appears blue, yellow, or some other colour when viewed from different sides, so the Lord takes on different forms according to how one meditates upon him.' The *Bhagavata* explores the idea of relative perceptions of truth and how reality manifests differently according to the observer. Therefore, transcendental reality is not only about the perception of truth but also how Ultimate Reality manifests in reciprocation to our consciousness. This indicates the responsive nature of Krishna: he manifests a particular quality for each living being: 'He is visible to the devotee according to the devotee's desires', and this all-attractive nature nurtures our unalloyed love.

The way the personal aspect of the Ultimate Reality manifests in reciprocation with the consciousness of the individual can be glimpsed through scenes from the *Bhagavata*, such as the one in which Krishna enters an arena. Various groups of people in the arena regard Krishna in different ways when he enters. The wrestlers, in the mood of fury, see him as a lightning bolt. The cowherd men, in the mood of laughter, see him as their relative. The impious rulers, in the mood of chivalry, see him as a chastiser. His parents, in the mood of compassion, see him as their child. Kamsa, the despotic king, in a mood of terror, sees him as death. The non-intellectuals, in the mood of ghastliness, see him as the Universal Form. The yogis, in the mood of neutrality, see him as the Ultimate Reality. And the Vrishni clan, in the mood of loving devotion, see him as their supreme deity.

AN ALL-INCLUSIVE LOVE

Within this window to the spiritual realm, we see a vision of transcendence that is all-inclusive, reciprocal in nature, and responsive to the unique love of each living being. Even in the spiritual realm, there is an accommodation for variety. We each have our truth, and for any version of universal spirituality to endure, it must respond to that diversity with a compelling vision and secure philosophical basis. There will always be (what seems like) irreconcilable differences, but the philosophical framework gives us the tools to stand above them.

SEEING LOVE EVERYWHERE

When a parent sees the toys or clothes of their child and immediately visualises the child's features and qualities, this is 'seeing through the eyes of love'. One who possesses deep spiritual love perceives their beloved 'face to face' everywhere; it is not an exercise in imagination, artificial meditation, or intellectual manipulation. Such love is the intimate experience of Ultimate Reality when one is conducted 'helplessly' under its control.

Just as a starving person's attention cannot be drawn by anything other than food, one whose heart burns in love cannot be attracted by anything less than their beloved. It has been said that the most extraordinary group of transcendentalists, the young ladies of Krishna's village who embodied the most intense amorous devotional love, brought a standard of unalloyed spiritual love previously unknown to this world. And that just by exhibiting their love, they showed the world great compassion such that we might be inspired by the example and the quality of their love.

THE CROOKED PATH OF LOVE

The *Bhagavata* describes that love—even spiritual love—traverses a crooked path. In pure love, the living being has no desire for personal pleasure; the Self feels unbounded and ever-increasing bliss in the happiness of its beloved. And Krishna experiences the same.

Another aspect of this crooked path is how even calamities

can provide an impetus for bliss. To the uninitiated, the effects of love can seem painful, even devastating. Commentators have compared it to the pleasure of drinking hot sugar cane juice: the mouth burns, but one just can't stop. Things taken to their extreme can sometimes appear to transform into their opposites—dry ice can feel hot to the touch. So, too, the intensity of even spiritual love can *seem* painful. We see evidence of this in the lives and writings of saints across different mystical traditions.

> *The Story of Chaitanya Mahaprabhu*
> Once, when Chaitanya was in the Jagannatha Puri temple, an elderly woman, feeling great separation from the Deity of her Lord, climbed a nearby pillar, placing her foot on Chaitanya's shoulder in the process. Chaitanya's assistant was horrified and tried to get her down, only to be met with Chaitanya's rebuke, for he did not want to disturb the lady's reverie. When the lady came to her senses and realised what she had done, she jumped down and begged forgiveness from Chaitanya, who replied, 'Lord Jagannatha has not bestowed so much eagerness upon me', and then entreated her to bless him with such eagerness. It was after learning from Bhaktivedanta Swami about this same principle of love in separation, the yearning to meet one's Lord, that George Harrison wrote the lyrics to 'My Sweet Lord'.

We have probably all experienced the pain of separation, but then we get to feel the joy of union, just as hunger is a component of the enjoyment of eating. This raises the question: if we currently live our lives in apparent separation from the Ultimate Reality, why do so few of us experience this separation as an impetus toward spiritual love? This is true for the dualistic material realm, but in the spiritual realm, the Self's experience of separation *contains* the experience of union, and vice-versa.

How can there be separation in the spiritual realm, where the Ultimate Reality is said to be revealed? Another crooked turn. Separation contains union because one's consciousness becomes totally absorbed in thought of the beloved, and union contains separation because one's consciousness becomes absorbed in the risk of separation.

Those who prefer a reverential relationship with Krishna do not feel the urgent need to always see him because they can perceive his presence internally. For those who are drawn to more intimate relationships with Krishna, concepts of awe-inspiring potency, such as his omnipresence, take a backseat to love expressed in its more intimate forms. 'Blinded' by their natural love of friendship, guardianship, or amorous love, they do not care to estimate the power of Krishna and instead are always anxious for personal exchanges with him—so much so that even the blink of an eye is too long a separation.

The sage Jaimini says that these topics are beyond the power of words or comprehension of the mind, even for those great sages who directly perceive the Ultimate Reality. We can simply catch glimpses of such ecstatic emotions, most notably through recorded outpourings of those who possess them.

MUTUALLY BINDING

Spiritual love is reciprocated and mutually binding for the lover and the beloved. Each individual feels personal happiness suited exactly to their own loving attitude that fulfils their heart's desires—where desire is not about what one *wants* but about what one *wants* to *give*. Such relationships manifest because where there is real love, behaviour is consistent with one's words and thoughts; there is no duplicity. Such inclusivity amidst such diversity is possible only in the spiritual dimension. We can measure our spiritual development by how close we get to this ideal of inclusivity.

The *Bhagavata* describes Krishna as being bound by the unalloyed love of his devotees. The *Bhagavata* explains that Krishna's most incredible feature is how he becomes subservient to his beloveds. The saint Ramanuja was once asked by a devotee what might happen if, after a lifetime of devotion, the devotee could not remember his Lord at the time of death. Ramanuja meditated upon this and later replied that if, after a lifetime of devotion, he could not remember his Lord at the time of death, his Lord would remember him. For such is the Lord's nature: he is mutually bound to his devotee.

As Kaviraja Goswami reflects, 'Glorious is that devotee who does not give up the shelter of his Lord, and glorious is that Lord who does not abandon his servant.'

CHAPTER 19

The Object of Love

'I am unable to repay my debt for your spotless service, even within the duration of this universe...Therefore, please let your own glorious deeds be your compensation.'
—The Bhagavata

'Religion means to know God and to love him.' This simple yet profound statement by Bhaktivedanta Swami breaks down sectarian boundaries. Having established spiritual love as the goal, the *Bhagavata* asserts that knowing the personhood of Ultimate Reality—the all-attractive nature, form, and activities—in sufficient detail can cause our unalloyed spiritual love to emerge.

Since living beings are categorised as marginal energy, and since Krishna, the personal feature of the Ultimate Reality, is the source of that marginal energy, our relationship with Krishna is most important. The ultimate repositioning of our love involves activating that relationship.

We can love a person; we cannot love an abstract concept. If we limit ourselves to the Ultimate Reality as an ambiguous, impersonal feature, our concept may remain just a concept. For this reason, in the *Bhagavad-gita*, Krishna says, 'Those who fix their minds on my personal form...are considered by me to be most perfect...For those whose minds are attached to the unmanifested, impersonal feature of the Supreme, advancement is very troublesome.'

CHARACTERISTICS OF THE DIVINE

The personality of the Ultimate Reality is described differently around the world, depending on whether the names are 'official' (referring to power, majesty, or role, such as Creator, All Mighty, and Controller) or 'intimate' (referring to aspects of his personality or activities, which in the *Bhagavata* tradition include names such as Krishna, Rama, and Govinda).

According to the sage Parashara, the personhood of Ultimate Reality is defined as possessing six characteristics to an unlimited degree: beauty, wisdom, strength, wealth, renunciation, and fame. The *Bhagavata* also describes other attributes, such as absolute independence, omnibenevolence, omnipotence, and omniscience. And when it comes to Krishna, he is described in even greater detail, his unique characteristics being unlimitedly 'beautiful, playful and delightful'. The saint Vishvanath Chakravarti tells us that the last word of all scripture is *raso vai sah*: Krishna is the infinitely expanding embodiment of divine pleasure and, thus, the reservoir of *all* pleasure.

Perspective and insights into the personality of the Ultimate Reality are some of the most important and unique gifts of the *Bhagavata* tradition. Here, we can only touch upon a fraction of the indications of Krishna's personality with a cursory and wholly unsatisfactory glimpse of what is described in the *Bhagavata*.[48]

---

48) For further descriptions of Krishna's personality, form, and activities, see *Krsna*, by A.C. Bhaktivedanta Swami.

CONTRADICTIONS

Krishna is full of contradictions that can be resolved only with the eyes of love. The *Bhagavata* describes stories of baby Krishna stealing butter from his own home and from his neighbours. Why should he, who possesses everything, want to steal? It describes how Krishna runs in fear of his mother, knowing she will chastise him. Why should he, whom even death fears, fear his mother? How can the master of everything be subservient to his beloveds? How can the supreme autocrat give up his independence? Such questions cannot be answered by ordinary logic; for those who desire a loving relationship, Krishna is dictated to only by love. And whatever he does, he does to foster such loving relationships.

Krishna does not diminish himself by placing love above majesty; rather, these dealings bring joy to the world. For millennia, people have developed their love for him just by hearing about his activities. This might seem to contradict his qualities of supremacy, but through the loving eyes of the devotee, Krishna being controlled by love is simply another of his perfections.

THE POWER OF ATTRACTION

Depending on our aspirations, Krishna facilitates what we desire, treating us how we wish to be treated. For those who desire a reverential relationship with Krishna, he manifests his potency and power to inspire that type of worship. For those who desire a loving relationship imbued with intimacy, Krishna's sweetness is the quintessence of his qualities. His form, words, and activities attract the pleasure-seeking senses of the living being away from all other objects of desire.

How do Krishna's activities have such an effect? Stories from the *Bhagavata*, the *Ramayana*, and the *Mahabharata*, speak of great tragedy and pain. For example, Rama's exile to uphold his father's vow is one of the most tragic scenes found in any literature and is known by practically everyone in India, regardless of religion.[49] As noted by one commentator, even the most hard-hearted of people are softened by hearing of Rama's departure. And even that slight softening of the heart is a form of spiritual awakening, for it elicits emotions directed (even if unknowingly) toward the Ultimate Reality. And just like a small rudder can change the direction of an entire ship, a slight adjustment in our consciousness can change the course of our lives.

LOVE RULES

Many religious scriptures, including the Vedas, include demands for ritual sacrifice. But while there are transactional or ritualistic ways through which we can begin to engage with the Ultimate Reality, Krishna cares little for the formality of offerings. Rather, he is won over by offerings of love, no matter how trivial or materially insignificant. Though the rules of sacrifice and offerings are indeed stated in the various scriptures, Krishna breaks his very own rules for the sake of his loving devotee. Therefore, the *Bhagavata* says loving devotional service, *bhakti*, is the life of all rules, for it informs, underpins, and reconciles all others.

---

49) The *Ramayana* tells of how King Dasaratha was held to an old promise he had made to one of his wives to fulfil any two of her wishes. She called upon him to banish Rama, his eldest son and prince regent, and instead install her son as king. To uphold his father's vow, Rama agreed and left for the forest. Dasaratha died in separation almost immediately thereafter.

A GOD WHO DANCES

Krishna is not the abstract god of philosophers. He is a blissful, not an angry, God. The God described when Nietzsche said, 'I would believe only in a God that knows how to dance.' Where 'dancing' is 'lightness in what is most difficult'—Krishna is beyond all types of 'work' and is depicted and meditated upon as revelling with his beloveds. None of this is to say that other representations or features of the divine are not simultaneously true and manifest, but that this is how Krishna is depicted in the *Bhagavata* as the repository of all pleasure and the all-attractive partner for loving exchanges. As soon as there is a small step toward a reciprocal exchange by the living being's free will, the Ultimate Reality draws the Self closer by attraction. At this point, Krishna's qualities take prominence—his responsiveness to the mood of his beloved, his concern for his beloved, and his desire to serve them and submit to their control.

SEEING THE BEST IN US

Krishna's nature is to seek and accept our love, meaning he sees the best part of us and essentially ignores the rest. What we *do* is, therefore, a secondary consideration—if what we do is sincerely out of love for Krishna, we can assume he wants it. As he says in the *Bhagavad-gita*, 'If one offers me with love and devotion a leaf, a flower, fruit or water, I will accept it.' So, it is not a guessing game as to what he wants; the emphasis is on our motive. He wants our love, and the rest is detail.

A famous episode in the *Mahabharata* tells us how Krishna refuses a dinner invitation at the palace of the conspiring Kuru prince and instead accepts the invitation of more humble hosts. Vidura and his wife Sulabha are so overwhelmed with love that while peeling bananas to offer Krishna, they throw away the fruit and offer the skin, which Krishna duly accepts. He sees beyond their faults to extract the essence of their attempt and he does the same with all of us.

In exchanges of love, we seek the other's pleasure, so as we progress in our spiritual love, we may ponder what choice or activity would most please Krishna. When this question is inspired by love, it increases that love. But when our motivation behind an act of service is selfish, Krishna accepts the act and ignores the tainted motive and, in doing so, still sees the best of us.

The intense desire to see Krishna impels Krishna to reveal himself. The *Bhagavata* describes how the child prince Dhruva practised intense and austere meditation—not out of love but to acquire extraordinary material opulence. However, because Dhruva was sincere and not duplicitous, Krishna accepted his acts of austerity and meditation. Gradually, as his consciousness awakened and he experienced spiritual reality, Dhruva's desires evolved from the material to the spiritual. In the end, he received both. Such is the perfect nature of Krishna's reciprocation: despite his transcendental position, out of love and compassion, he continues to accept offerings comprising material elements and born of mixed motives. Accordingly, any activity or gesture, no matter how seemingly small, never goes in vain.

The highest levels of unalloyed spiritual love, free from material demands, are characterised by mutual dependence between the lover and beloved. In the words of the *Bhagavata*, 'The supreme *dharma* for all humanity is that by which one can attain love of the transcendence.' The root meaning of the word *dharma* is 'that which sustains one's existence', and that is the type of love toward which the *Bhagavata* urges us.

THE SERVANT LEADER

In some religions, the followers seek to become subservient to God. A common vision of God is that of one who commands his followers. This perspective is not denied in the *Bhagavata*, though there is also more to it than that. Krishna is more eager to fulfil the desires of his devotees than to receive their service. He is the prototypical servant leader, another display of his supreme personality. Bhaktivedanta Swami compares this to when a Supreme Court judge goes home and allows their child to ride on their back. None of this diminishes the stature of the judge; rather, it exposes the judge's innermost desires and intimate personality. In any loving, reciprocal relationship, the lover and beloved are both eager to engage in the service of the other. Thus, both Krishna and the devotee are simultaneously victorious and conquered.

Krishna only seems to personally involve himself in matters of love. As the young boy Prahlada from the *Bhagavata* says, 'Whatever an unalloyed devotee wants, Krishna doubtlessly grants because he has no duty other than to fulfil the desire of his devotee.' But if unalloyed love is selfless, what possible desires could such a devotee harbour? These desires centre on the devotee's aspirations for ever-increasing reciprocations of loving service. And if his devotee desires anything, Krishna fulfils it beyond any expectation—he is not satisfied just fulfilling their desires; he wants to give them far more. Ultimately, conquered by their love, he gives his very self.

SUPPORTING YOU ALONG THE WAY

Even if a spiritual seeker is not yet on the transcendental plane and still harbours some material desires, they can rest assured that even a faint contact with Krishna has invited him into their lives. They can continue their efforts to gradually distance themselves from selfish motives, knowing that Krishna will take care of them more than they are able to do themselves. He may act in unexpected ways, but the result will be the gradual exhaustion of material desires and the proportionate escalation of spiritual love. The *Bhagavata* says that Krishna maintains his devotees just as fishes, tortoise, and birds respectively nourish their offspring by watching them, meditating upon them, and keeping them physically close.

Even offensive people are not cast away, for as one such offender said, 'If a person falls forcefully to the ground, the earth again supports him. In the same way, the distress of one who commits offences is destroyed simply by remembering you.' Recognising this, Brahma prayed, 'Does a mother take offence when the embryo within the womb kicks? Is there anything real or unreal outside of the Lord's abdomen?' The *Bhagavata* assures us that as soon as we remember Krishna, our success is guaranteed; even if our motive is impure, Krishna will reciprocate by helping us adjust it.

HIDE AND SEEK

Absorbed in matters of love, Krishna only indirectly engages with his external energy, such as during the process of creation. In those rare times, his activities are outwardly manifest; at other times, the laws of material nature carry on, like a potter's wheel keeps spinning after being set in motion. Krishna himself remains hidden from view. However, as the all-pervading feature of the Ultimate Reality, and as transcendental knowledge, he is always accessible, always waiting to draw us into his embrace.

The invisibility of the Ultimate Reality confounds those who insist that mundane thought and effort should suffice for us to force his audience. However, although the Ultimate Reality partially manifests for the physicalist and the impersonalist, a personal relationship and audience with Krishna can be forged only with love.

> On the verge of death, Gajendra, who did not have a clear idea to whom he was praying, called out in desperation:
>
>> 'I offer my obeisances unto the Supreme Person. Because of him, this material body acts due to the presence of spirit, and he is, therefore, the root cause of everyone...and has entered the heart of every living being. Let me meditate upon him...He is both the supreme cause and the supreme result, the observer and the witness, in all circumstances... An artist onstage is not understood by his audience; similarly, the activities and features of the supreme artist cannot be understood... He is the witness in everyone's heart, who enlightens the individual soul and who cannot be reached by exercises of the mind, words, or consciousness...The material world is just like a shadow resembling you. Indeed, one accepts

this material world as real because it gives a
glimpse of your existence...You appear as the
reservoir of all pleasure and the protector of
the surrendered souls. You possess unlimited
energy, but you are unapproachable by those
who are unable to control their senses.'

Although this prayer lacks a clear definition of whom Gajendra was appealing to, it was heartfelt and thus sufficient to draw Krishna swiftly to the rescue.[50]

Uddhava's prayers to Krishna provide further hope:[51]

'Who could reject the dear most object...
could be so ungrateful, knowing the benefits
you bestow? Who would reject you and accept
something for the sake of material enjoyment,
which simply leads to forgetfulness of you?
For this, transcendental poets have difficulty
expressing their gratitude to you! You have
proven your friendship to the living beings
in two ways: you accompany the Self as the
Superconsciousness in the heart—a place
that is closer to the Self than its own breath.

---

50) Adapted from *Srimad Bhagavatam* Canto 8, Chapter 3.
51) Adapted from the rendition in *Saranagati*, volume 92, and *Srimad Bhagavatam* Canto 11, Chapter 29.

> You are always present and accessible, and if someone turns to you, you reciprocate to facilitate their spiritual progress. And secondly, you come as the spiritual guide. Krishna, you have not forgotten me, even though I wanted to forget you. You came with me, although I wanted to leave you. You are present in the heart as the most reliable friend.'

The *Bhagavad-gita* proclaims that we can be peaceful if we acknowledge Krishna as our friend, benefactor, and well-wisher. When we realise that we cannot enjoy anything separate from or in the absence of Krishna, that it is Krishna who is the ultimate proprietor—the owner and controller of all, endowing us with free will as well as direction—and that Krishna is the eternal friend and only real benefactor of all living beings, we feel relief. This knowledge calms our incessant desires for self-gratification, claims of proprietorship, and ego-driven illusions of benefiting others. We no longer feel the urge to force our agenda or to strive in ways that, in the long run, are not good for ourselves or others. We can be peaceful knowing that there is strength beyond our limited capacity and recourse beyond our *karma* and destiny. We can choose to turn to this friend and benefactor only in hours of need—as we would a transactional supplier—or we can choose to build a relationship.

THE QUESTION OF SUFFERING

Why would Krishna, an unconditionally loving personality, create a place of suffering such as the material world? We have discussed Krishna's accompaniment of every living being as a patient presence within the heart, awaiting our reciprocation. We have learned about his unconditional love, that there is nothing we can do that will make Krishna love us more, nor anything we can do that can make him love us less. We have heard of Krishna's energy pervading the material cosmos as further evidence of his accessibility. The issue of suffering is one of the most significant and persistent objections to believing in an all-powerful and benevolent God. Let's look at the issue of suffering and its relationship with free will.

As Bhaktivedanta Swami said, the whole world is full of Krishna's singing, but some people want to dance independently, and some want to dance with him. The choice is ours. If we want to 'dance independently', Krishna allows us to do so. But in doing so, we must take full responsibility for our actions, which also means living through all the reactions that follow over multiple lifetimes. There is no independence without responsibility. Krishna gives us the choice. We have noted that Krishna remains aloof to the workings of the material world and intervenes in our lives only when invited. This means that the suffering we observe in the world is not the desire of a sadistic or impotent God.

But why does Krishna not intervene earlier, as soon as we first call out to him? Because our desire to call out to him needs to be deeper than our desire to avoid him. The cultivation and deepening of this desire is the journey of spiritual life.

Also, snapshots in time can be misleading. A simple rope can cause fear for someone who mistakes it for a snake; so too can death for one who thinks it is the ultimate end. The *Bhagavata* provides numerous examples of how Krishna's non-appearance and even his seemingly contrary acts always produce optimal outcomes. At the beginning of the spiritual journey, capable of seeing only proximate causes and effects, we can't tell what is in our best long-term interest. This changes with our movement from Ignorance and Passion to Goodness and with our own developing spiritual insight.

Krishna's aim is, without revoking our free will or providing false options, to convince us to return to his embrace. He appeals to us individually, and what is optimal for one person may not be for another. For some spiritual seekers, he might allow the gradual depletion of material wealth because this will further encourage them on their spiritual path. For others, it might be the opposite. In either case, it boils down to what the individual really wants at their most fundamental level: do they want the material world, in which case the material laws of nature take over, or do they want Krishna, in which case he intervenes. If we choose the latter, obstacles become a 'stairway' on which we can progress to our constitutional position in the spiritual realm.

But if a spiritual seeker faces obstacles, say poverty, how do we know if it is the material laws of nature playing out, or if it is Krishna's intervention? The *Bhagavata* tells us that we can know by the effect it has on the individual. Krishna's interventions don't leave any subtle residue of desire or seed for future *karmic* reactions. We know that *karma* moves from subtle desires to physical acts, the acts reinforcing the desires and sowing seeds of new desires. Even when we overindulge in something and become fed up with it, this can only be a temporary reprieve. With Krishna's interventions, neither providing something nor taking it away causes further entanglement in the *karmic* web. The fingerprint of Krishna's interventions is the recipient's joy, either because the recipient directly relishes them or indirectly because the recipient understands them as Krishna's participation in their lives.

Another common name for Krishna is Hari, meaning 'to take away' or 'to steal'. The devoted believe that Hari takes away their distress and misery. The more cautious or non-devoted believe he takes away material enjoyment. But Krishna declares that his real interest is in stealing away our minds and hearts, according to the individual's readiness. Until we are ready, he desires us to continue our spiritual search and keep advancing until we reach our desired destination.

Back to the young ladies of Krishna's village. They are an example of the most exalted lovers of divinity. Once, these most intimate of Krishna's associates, who held deep, amorous love for him, challenged him as to why he did not more quickly or sufficiently reciprocate their love. A beautiful poetic debate ensued until Krishna finally admitted that he does not immediately reciprocate because he wants to intensify the spiritual aspirant's loving devotion. Thus, Krishna claims that his neglect is not neglect but the true reciprocation of our deepest and purest desire.

However, the *gopis* protested: this might make sense for those who were not yet completely absorbed in Krishna, but they were. They could not think of anything else, even if they wanted to! What of them? Krishna concluded by acknowledging that he had indeed not fully reciprocated their love. But this was not because he was ungrateful or unwilling but because he felt unable to do so. He was unable to repay the debt of their matchless loving service, marked by their complete and exclusive dependence on him.

Krishna can never repay his debt to those who love him unconditionally. He renders small favours as tokens of his affection, but ultimately, all he can do is remain their helpless, insolvent debtor. Their love forces him to break the vow he made in the

Bhagavad-gita: 'As all surrender unto me, I reward them accordingly.' Their own glorious love must be their compensation.

The *gopis*' example is the epitome of selfless love for all others to follow. Understanding Krishna's soft and innermost heart, which caused their love to shine forth for the benefit of all living beings, they revelled in bliss—as is always the eventual result of Krishna's interventions.

CHAPTER 20
Living Yoga

'One who earnestly waits for your mercy, all the while patiently tolerating the reactions of his past misdeeds and offering you respect with his heart, words and body, is surely eligible for liberation, for it has become his rightful claim.'
—The Bhagavata

We learned about the general types of yoga and the yoga ladder in Chapter 11. The original goal of yoga was spiritual, though many people have used it for material ends. Yoga helps to tame the restless mind and nurture attachment to transcendence. In Chapter 18, we learned more about the top of the yoga ladder, *bhakti*, or *bhakti-yoga*, as the process of loving service. In this chapter, we will explore some of the practicalities of *bhakti-yoga* and *ashtanga-yoga*.

Spiritual love, inherent in every living being, is not something to be gained from outside; rather, it is revealed from within. The most essential principle for its revelation is our sincere and intense desire for it. Yoga is there to help us clear the path for spiritual love to shine forth. As we have seen in previous chapters, yoga gradually transforms what the mind considers pleasurable, and by changing our tastes and preferences, it brings the mind and senses under control.

Krishna calls *bhakti-yoga* 'the most secret of all secrets' and 'the king of knowledge' because a) it yields direct perception of the Self and all three aspects of the Ultimate Reality, b) failed attempts never destroy it, and c) it is easily and joyfully performed. All Vedic texts, including the *Bhagavata* and the *Bhagavad-gita*, agree that the path of loving devotion is the easiest and most effective of yoga systems. In the *Bhagavad-gita*, Krishna, after all his explanations of the different yoga systems, provides concluding advice:

> 'Hear still further the greatest secret of all, my supreme message: you are so much loved by me! Therefore, I shall speak for your well-being. Be mindful of me with love offered to me…Truly you shall come to me—I promise you this, for you are dearly loved by me. Completely relinquishing all forms of *dharma*, come to me as your only shelter. I shall grant you freedom from all misfortune—do not despair!'

Bhakti-yoga, or offerings of love, is the fast-track yoga system. It creates a positive feedback loop: the mind's engagement with transcendence helps it to withdraw from materialistic consciousness, which in turn prompts further engagement with transcendence. Meditation, an action of the mind, is not the ultimate goal, nor is the mind's withdrawal or nullification. Rather, it is positive engagement of the spiritualised mind—loving service—that expresses the Self's inherent nature and innermost desires. When we force the mind, that is *nirbija-yoga*, lifeless yoga; when the spiritualised mind is naturally and unrestrictedly absorbed in transcendence, that is *sabija-yoga*, living yoga.

WATERING THE SEED

The mind is like a restless child—we can try instructing or forcing it to 'stop' and 'behave' or provide it with something that captures and redirects its attention. The practices of *bhakti-yoga* are the waters that nourish the dormant seed of love within our hearts so that, with careful attention, they sprout and flourish.

Chaitanya highlighted five *bhakti-yoga* practices that you can bring to your daily life:

- **Connect:** so susceptible are we to peer and social pressure, that whom we connect with, and how, is critical to our spiritual journey. The *Bhagavata* advises us to surround ourselves with spiritually insightful people—people of good character who are non-judgmental and are genuinely interested in our well-being.

- **Chant:** the fundamental and subtle nature of sound makes it an excellent medium for bridging the material and the spiritual. For this purpose, sacred sound plays a profound role in many spiritual paths. Every day, we experience how sensory input can be transformative, causing psychological and physiological changes. This is also true at a spiritual level; the *Brahma-sutra* states that we are liberated by spiritual sound.[52] Different sounds evoke different moods, and spiritual sounds, such as mantras, can evoke spiritual awareness. The *Bhagavata* emphasises the repetition of such powerful sounds—particularly the names of the divine, with a focus on the name Krishna.

---

52) Transcendental sound is unlimited, deep, full of intricacies and subtlety, and difficult to comprehend. It is said to manifest on four different levels: within the life air, mind, intelligence, and senses, three of which are internal and so are not perceivable by the sensory ear.

- **Study:** hearing and reading sacred texts provides a philosophical grounding for faith and a window into spiritual reality, descriptions of which, especially the transcendental nature and loving exchanges of Krishna, prompt a shift in what the mind considers desirable and undesirable. These descriptions become the bow that propels the arrow-like Self toward the target of loving service and constitute a most effective process for elevating the mind. As we learned in Chapter 3, sacred texts such as the *Bhagavata* can reveal transcendence, but the fullness of this reality becomes perceivable when we develop the 'ears to hear and the eyes to see'.

- **Sacred Places:** like sacred sounds, sacred places profoundly affect our consciousness. While we may not all be able to reside in a place of pilgrimage, we can meditate on the presence of the Ultimate Reality everywhere and so make our homes, places of work, and even our bodies sacred places.

- **Sacred Images:** images are a powerful means to draw and hold our attention. Different traditions use objects such as icons, relics, paintings, and deities to create a focus of worship and reverence. Expressing gratitude or reverence to these objects has been a practical way for many people to shift their state of consciousness. The form of such expressions will, of course, vary by tradition and geography; they may include offering articles of worship, prayer, bowing down, and so on.

When we incorporate these practices into our daily lives, even mundane activities can become spiritualised. Something like gardening can become a spiritual meditation: when we see consciousness and the presence of the Ultimate Reality within every being, when we grow flowers for the divine, when we act as custodians of nature, and so forth.

Simple acts can become the essence of religious practice if performed without selfish motivation. Over time, duty is transformed into affection and affection into love. Through these processes, we can make use of the temporary and mundane to achieve the eternal and transcendent.

When we water a tree's roots, all parts of the tree are watered. Likewise, the *bhakti-yogi* achieves success by trying to please their beloved. The *Bhagavata* declares: 'One who accepts this path [of loving service] will never blunder...Even while running with eyes closed, he will never trip or fall.'

'With eyes closed' here means ignorance of the rules and rituals of various scriptures. The path bestows fearlessness because it focuses on the essence. Fear evaporates as we connect ourselves and everything around us to the Ultimate Reality. We are reminded that nothing can ever be separate or independent of that reality. Freed from fear and confident in our spiritual identity, we can more easily relinquish material attachments and engage everything in loving service.

ASHTANGA-YOGA

Ashtanga-yoga is a method for controlling the senses and mind, aiming to divert them away from the mundane to the Self, and then reconnect the Self with the Ultimate Reality. Notably, even the early stages of *ashtanga-yoga* include versions of the abovementioned practices: learning from a spiritual guide, philosophical reflection, mantra recitation, residence at a sacred place, and worship of a sacred image. Only when a yogi is on the platform of full absorption (*dhyana*) may the cessation of external activity be potentially beneficial.

There are eight (*asht-*) stages (*anga*) of *ashtanga-yoga*. The first four are prescriptions (*yama*), proscriptions (*niyama*), controlling posture (*asana*), and controlling breath (*pranayama*). The first two stages are a commitment to an ethical life. Somewhat conveniently ignoring these two preliminary but essential first steps, the third and fourth stages (postures and breathwork) are what has become popularised around the world as yoga. Once posture and breath are under control and no longer distract us, the following four stages gradually become possible—withdrawal of the mind from sense objects (*pratyahara*), preliminary meditation (*dhyana*), advanced meditation (*dharana*), and full realisation of the object of meditation (*samadhi*).

In this eighth and final stage of yoga, *samadhi*, one realises the form of the Ultimate Reality within the heart. This establishes a direct connection (and even communication) between the Self and the Superconsciousness. In *samadhi*, the yogi is so focused on the object of meditation that they have no awareness of themselves or even that they are meditating. The *prana* (life air) becomes fixed in one of the six *chakras*, which leads to concentration of the mind on the Ultimate Reality.

The yoga master Patanjali confirms in his *Yoga-sutra* that the target of all yoga is connection with the Superconsciousness that resides in our hearts. From that point of connection, the yogi chooses whether or not to progress to engagement in loving service.

During yoga, we get gradual relief from the disturbances of material desire, but that is not sufficient to satisfy the Self. The Self needs not only relief from pain but also the *positive* engagement of its inherently blissful and loving nature. So, while yogic trance may stop all material activities and even bring us in contact with

Ultimate Reality at the last stage of *samadhi*, *bhakti-yoga* both stops material activities and engages the Self in spiritual activities. That is why it is the fast-track yoga system. When something material is repurposed for transcendence, it becomes spiritualised—this is why *bhakti-yoga* subsumes and is the culmination of *ashtanga-yoga* and all other yoga paths. As we learned when discussing the yoga ladder, the end goal of all yoga is *bhakti*. We can achieve it either directly or as the final goal of *ashtanga*.

We know from the yoga ladder that the aim of some yogis is the impersonal aspect of Ultimate Reality, some the imminent Superconsciousness, and some the transcendent person. The impersonal is generally approached through *jnana-yoga*, the imminent through *ashtanga-yoga*, and the personal through *bhakti-yoga*. And just as *bhakti-yoga* subsumes the other yoga systems, its destination, the personal aspect of the Ultimate Reality, subsumes both the impersonal aspect[53] and the imminent aspect.[54]

Krishna summarises the yoga process to Uddhava: one gradually controls the life air using *pranayama* and raises it to the lotus chakra of the heart. *Pranayama* is the fourth stage of *ashtanga-yoga*, and it involves deep inhalations and exhalations with long holding periods. One can exhale, hold, inhale or do it in the opposite direction. The yogi then places the form of his object of meditation on that heart lotus and meditates upon each limb, beginning with the feet and culminating with the face. When the mind is elevated, with half-closed eyes, the yogi should concentrate on the tip of the nose and see Superconsciousness, the form

---

53) *Bhagavad-gita* 14.27: 'And I am the basis of the impersonal *Brahman*, which is the constitutional position of ultimate happiness, and which is immortal, imperishable and eternal.'
54) *Bhagavad-gita* 10.42: 'With a single fragment of myself I pervade and support this entire universe.'

of divinity within. One should continue this meditation until the mind becomes fixed.

It is typically easier for the yogi to concentrate on the sound, activities, and form of divinity. Chanting mantras consisting of names of the divine, hearing and reading scriptural stories, and worshipping a deity form of the divine are all potent and integral parts of yoga. When one has achieved the stage of unwavering meditation, one can then withdraw the consciousness, after which the yogi can give up the practice of meditation, having advanced beyond meditation to engage in a loving relationship. Superconsciousness is no longer merely the object of meditation; it and the yogi are now in unity, like the sun and its rays.

OBSTACLES ON THE PATH

Sometimes, the weeds of subtle material desires are almost indistinguishable from the seedlings of love. If we indulge our base desires or neglect our spiritual practice, we water the weeds, and they can grow stronger and outgrow our fledgling spiritual love. We must cultivate and protect the seeds we want to nurture.

The sage Haridasa Thakura said that at dawn, before the sun is fully visible, darkness is dissipated, and the fear of thieves vanishes. Likewise, even in the early stages of *bhakti*, our *karmic* reactions begin to dissipate, and fear flees. And when the sun finally rises, everything becomes visible, and we go about our work: we perceive the Ultimate Reality and engage in loving service. Just as a fan keeps spinning for a while after being turned off and gradually comes to a stop, our material desires persist even after *bhakti-yoga* disconnects the *karmic* 'current'. However, with time, these desires eventually diminish and cease. We need to have patience till the sunrise.

PROGRESS CHECKS

As we take up the practice of yoga, it's important to have ways to verify our progress. How do we know it's really working? This will help us reflect not only on how we are doing so far but also on what we need to do next. There are three broad markers by which we can test our spiritual progress:

1) Our motives, sensual preferences, and standard of happiness cause us to:
- Be motivated by Goodness.
- Experience peace, increasing happiness and fulfilment.
- Restrain the senses and refrain from habits that harm others or oneself.
- Be free from self-destructive feelings such as insecurity and self-pity.
- Be conscious of our impact on others and the environment.
- Feel happiness in the happiness of others and pain in others' pain.

2) Our experience of the Ultimate Reality causes us to:
- Perceive the Ultimate Reality within and around us.
- Avoid hypocrisy, as perception of the Ultimate Reality removes the separation between our internal and external experiences.
- Experience increasing levels of positive emotions, such as humility and forgiveness.

- Be inspired to act with spiritual intent.
- Connect with other living beings and the natural world.

3) Our engagement in loving service causes us to:
- Deepen our desire to serve.
- Want to connect with and impact the hearts of others and be able to do so.
- Have clarity and focus on the essential and eternal.
- Prioritise dedicated loving service over serving oneself.
- Have sustained, focused meditation.

CHAPTER 21
Putting It All Together

'Acts of sacrifice, charity and austerity are never to be given up; they should always be performed. Indeed, sacrifice, charity and austerity purify even the great souls.'
—Bhagavad-gita

The rules and regulations of scripture are subordinate to two basic principles: to always remember Krishna and never forget him. This formula reveals a profound truth of universal spirituality: it all depends on the state of our consciousness. Regardless of any shortcomings in ritual or process, everything becomes faultless if conducted in good consciousness, with sincere spiritual intent. All the other rules of scripture are created to support these two basic principles.

Bhaktivedanta Swami explained attachment to material things as material consciousness and attachment to spiritual things as spiritual consciousness. In other words, consciousness is the platform of attachment. If we are conscious, we will be attached to *something*. We cannot just stop our basic functions of thinking, feeling, willing, or even doing, but we can gradually redirect our purpose. By working for a higher purpose, we begin to see how we can engage everything—our thoughts, words, and deeds—in the service of the Ultimate Reality.

Scriptural rules often encourage our hard work and effort, urging us out of the stagnation of Ignorance. After all, fulfilling any of our desires requires us to make sacrifices, big or small.

At the dawn of creation, the first word Brahma heard was *tapa*, meaning 'austerity'. This not only directed him to perform asceticism to facilitate the process of secondary creation but also indicated the need for all living beings to work hard for any material or spiritual gain. Commitment to hard work is required as we strive for spiritual realisation if it is to be steady and long-lasting. Brought face to face with the temporal nature of the world at a funeral, for instance, we may resolve to be less materialistic, only to return to our habitual behaviour the next day. To maintain spiritual realisation requires hard work. Like for any meaningful goal, we must be willing to perform some austerity and make some sacrifices. Thankfully, the science of habit change shows that even modest steps in this direction can build confidence and establish a positive feedback loop, overall leading to significant outcomes.

MAKE AN EFFORT

We often learn new things by conscious effort and eventually develop effortless ability—a bit like learning to ride a bike. Many religions require you to follow a set of rules and rituals, but hopefully, this leads to increasing levels of joy and spontaneity with heartfelt expression. Alongside the hard work required, the *Bhagavata* acknowledges the importance of nurturing such heartfulness through expressions like singing and dancing. Such means of spirituality keep us inspired and joyful. Most importantly, they offer us a taste of our goal; the spiritual world is a place of bliss.

UNIVERSAL PRINCIPLES OF RELIGION

Spiritual traditions sometimes mistakenly think that an effective way to become more universal is by watering down their message. But this is just a race to the bottom—by removing their distinctiveness, they may be stripped of their essence. As we learned in Chapter 1, in genuinely spiritual traditions, the deeper you go, the closer you move to a truly universal essence. A tradition's message should broaden, not narrow, as you move closer to its core truths. As Bhaktivedanta Swami wrote, 'The principles of religion are not the dogmas or regulative principles of a certain faith. Such regulative principles may be different in terms of the time and place concerned. One has to see whether the aims of religion have been achieved. Sticking to the dogmas and formulas without attaining the essence is no good. A secular state may be impartial to any particular type of faith, but the state cannot be indifferent to the principles of religion as above-mentioned.' He was referring to truthfulness, self-discipline, compassion, and clarity. Who could argue with that?

Truthfulness involves being honest with others and, even more crucially, with oneself. Self-discipline is the ability to create a gap between stimulus and response. Compassion includes recognising that the needs of others are more important than one's own and acting with this understanding. Clarity—cleanliness, purity—is being guilt-free and clear-eyed, acting and thinking with spiritual awareness.

The *Bhagavata* concludes that the most beneficial and sensible practice is whatever will strengthen one's spiritual love. For many religious people, *impiety* is anything that contradicts their religious scripture. The *Bhagavata* defines impiety from a broader perspective: anything that obstructs our loving service.

GRADUAL PROGRESS

Most people, however, are not interested in giving up all their material desires in pursuit of a spiritual goal, and so for them gradual elevation is prescribed, beginning with basic social norms and the universal virtues of truthfulness, self-discipline, compassion, and clarity. In this context, people can pursue their material goals—primarily economic development and sensual pleasure—alongside their spiritual pursuit.

We have already discussed stepping stones and the yoga ladder, and we now turn to a common everyday challenge related to this principle: since we spend so much of our time at work, how can we make our career or vocation an integral part of our spiritual journey? How do we connect work life to spiritual life?

> ### King Nimi and Chamasa
> King Nimi asked sage Chamasa how those who are unable to quench their material desires and are not inclined toward spiritual life can still benefit spiritually. The sage explained that the answer lies in a societal framework that allows for individualisation and moderated sensual gratification, with the ultimate purpose of gradual material detachment and spiritual attainment. By such regulated enjoyment and

> by acting piously, one can neutralise the cycle of *karma*. As Krishna told Arjuna, one can attain perfection through performing their own work.
>
> Chamasa cautioned, however, that if the purpose is not kept clear, people may exploit such allowances and become absorbed in the material aspects of religiosity. They may forget their essence and even consider themselves superior to others, having developed a false sense of security due to their so-called piety. Chamasa says that they are 'killers of their soul' because they prematurely give up the process, thinking themselves already cured.

To avoid becoming 'killers of the soul', as Chamasa puts it, we must maintain a clear spiritual purpose and deter base hedonism by dedicating all our work to a greater purpose. The *Bhagavata* explains that we are meant to be the assisting hands and senses of divinity working in the world.

ONE SIZE DOES NOT FIT ALL

With the *gunas* as its foundation, the *Bhagavata's* social framework enables individuals to use their unique strengths, likes, dislikes, and motives to support their material and spiritual development. Krishna presents a cooperative social structure in which each part supports the other, like the different parts of our body—an ideal balance of individualism and collectivism.

We all come to this world with a past and a destiny, but also with unlimited potential. Traditionally, it was the teacher's duty to observe each child's psychology and educate them accordingly. The role of education was to encourage each child's strengths and natural instincts so that they could succeed in all areas of their life—academic, physical, emotional, and spiritual—while nurturing truthfulness, self-discipline, compassion, and clarity, benefitting both the individual and society.

Among its many meanings, and in a social context, the Sanskrit word *dharma* indicates the contribution a person can make to society. For a child, it may include being a good student. The *dharma* of parents includes raising healthy children. A teacher's *dharma* is to educate; a police officer's is to protect others. As we saw above, it is the universal *dharma* of all people to strive for truthfulness, self-discipline, compassion, and clarity.

Each stage of life and work brings new obligations and a shift of *dharma*, and inevitably, our diverse *dharmas* come into conflict. Some *dharmas* take priority some of the time, but not always. A key deciding factor for which duty takes precedence is motive. For example, one who strives always to be truthful might, for instance, be doing the wrong thing if they knew that the truth would help a murderer find their victim.

> Striving to fulfil our *dharma* requires that we contemplate our various responsibilities. In the mode of Ignorance, this calculation is made indifferently; in Passion, begrudgingly; in Goodness, with dutiful effectiveness. But recall that because the most essential *dharma* of the Self is love, it is to this end that all other *dharmas*, if in conflict, must yield.

THE FRAMEWORK

The *Bhagavata* outlines four broad stages of life, each with its own purpose and underlying *dharma* and each with scope for differentiation based on an individual's personality, aspirations, and circumstances:

- **Student life:** meant for study, developing self-discipline, and cultivating one's higher purpose in life. Learning is a lifelong project, but this first stage focuses specifically on education and preparation, including academic and vocational training.

- **Married life:** meant for enjoying the world ethically, providing charity and shelter to all living beings, and applying what we learn in student life. This stage is about engagement with and contribution to society.

- **Retired life:** meant for deepening spiritual practice and contributing to society without selfish or material motives. This stage is about reflection on our life experiences and reaching for deeper spiritual realisation.

- **Renounced life:** meant for increased austerity and teaching other members of society. This stage is about being dedicated to helping others on their spiritual journeys.

By systematically progressing through these stages, we progress toward our spiritual goal without having to give up the world.

YOUR PERFECT JOB

The Bible's Golden Rule is to treat others as you wish to be treated. The Vedic Platinum Rule (as Milton Bennett called it) is to treat others as they wish to be treated. Both have utility, and the difference is worth noting. The implications are that equality in the West often means the same thing for everyone because I assume you must want what I want. Whereas in the East, equality often means the capacity to accommodate individual desires because you may want something different to what I want. The Vedic tradition adopted differentiation, or individualisation, as intrinsic to all social needs. This included health (Ayurveda treatments depend on your specific physiological makeup) and education (Vedic schools had checkpoints where the provision for skills, experience and knowledge were recalibrated according to a child's preferences and emerging strengths).

The *Bhagavata* outlines four archetypal occupational categories to appeal to different personality types and motivations, with the premise that everyone can be a contributing member of society:

Role	Social Contribution	Motivated By	Leadership Style
Employee	Aesthetics/Functionality	Service	Informal/Servant leader
Entrepreneur	Wealth creation	Money	Plutocratic leader
Executive	Protection/Justice	Power	Warrior leader
Educator	Knowledge/Ideas	Influence	Thought leader

We may or may not see a clear fit at first, but the framework can help guide us toward an occupation that best aligns with our motivations and aspirations. The above is a simplified version of a framework that identifies the roles and responsibilities of each stage of life and category of occupation. Leadership is included in the table above as an indication of the broader framework and because it cuts across all categories—from how one leads a family to how one leads a nation. For all categories, the most fundamental principle of leadership is to be honest—first and foremost with oneself, then with others. This includes leading by example and a lack of hypocrisy. Second, the proof of good leadership can be found in the lives of those who follow that leader. For example, citizens of knowledge, good character, and spiritual insight are, for instance, signs of good national leadership. And third, it is a leader's duty to widen their scope of concern beyond themselves and their family. The wider the scope of concern, the greater the capacity for leadership. Society today would benefit from applying such a lens to our selection of leaders and our methods of holding them accountable.

This framework depends upon us choosing work according to our nature. Krishna advised Arjuna about the dangers of repressing our nature because of perceived imperfections: 'Duties prescribed according to one's nature are never affected by negative *karmic* reactions. Every endeavour is covered by some fault, just as fire is covered by smoke', and, therefore, 'It is better to do one's own duty imperfectly than another's perfectly.'

Even though sometimes the duties that arise from such work may be troublesome, we should not abandon them for what seems to be an easy way out but does not match our nature. If we do, we repress our nature and will eventually be pulled back towards it. Imperfect but authentic execution of one's own duty is better than perfectly but artificially imitating another's duty: we should not pretend to be something we are not. We all have an important and unique role to play. And by the honest dedication of our work, we safely rise up the yoga ladder and develop our connection with Ultimate Reality.

A CORRUPTION

Tragically, this spiritually motivated societal framework became corrupted over time and led to centuries of discrimination and abuse. Rather than a dynamic social structure that catered to individual needs, preferences, and psychophysical make-up, it became obsessed with birthright.

Approximately 500 years ago, Sanatana Goswami wrote that there was no rule against women or members of any social strata receiving *diksha*, the Vedic ceremony that ordains one as a *brahmana*, someone most interested in understanding the Ultimate Reality. This was in line with the teachings of Chaitanya but opposed the prevalent caste system, which was based on birthright. Sanatana Goswami's view was also in line with Krishna's statements in the *Bhagavad-gita* that one's proclivities define one's occupation—i.e. that we should find work we enjoy and for which we have a natural propensity, without deference to birth.

Discernment is a sign of intelligence, but discrimination based on prejudice is a sign of ignorance. Prejudicial attitudes are an extension of our false ego, the thinking that whatever I am—whatever nationality, race, or religion—must be the best, if for no other reason than because it is what I am. By this thinking, anyone who does not belong to 'my' category must be inferior.

The *Bhagavata* highlights many examples of saintly personalities with different appearances and backgrounds and those who broke the mould. For example, it points to marriages between members of different social strata and to children who do not follow the positive or negative example of their parents. If we want to be genuinely spiritual, we must insist on moving beyond discrimination, including the discrimination that exists within and between religions.

CHAPTER 22
Help Is at Hand

'Devotees like your good self are verily holy places personified. Because you carry the Lord within your heart, you turn all places into places of pilgrimage.'
—The Bhagavata

In a postmodern culture of individualism, some may feel that taking guidance from others lessens one's worth. Or you may feel that transcendence being guarded by gatekeepers diminishes the universality of spiritual life. This is understandable, given how religious authorities in more than one tradition have subjugated and exploited others. But let's not throw the baby out with the bathwater. The role of the spiritual teacher can be compared with good spectacles: they are meant to help us see better, bring things into focus, and not get in the way. Likewise, a spiritual teacher must not get in the way of someone's connection with the Ultimate Reality but rather enhance it.

We each have our own limited perspectives, unconscious biases, and habits of body and mind. Changing any of which is a mammoth task, even with sustained effort. Relying on our endeavours limits us to our minds and all the clutter contained therein, and when we're stuck, it's hard to get unstuck without help. That's why building connections with spiritual guides is so important, no matter how experienced we might be. Someone further along the path may be able to encourage us and help us see the bigger picture, point out upcoming hazards, or simply provide a helping hand. This kind of positive connection is one of the most potent means for spiritual attainment; for those aspiring for loving exchanges in the spiritual realm, it is an essential aspect of the ultimate goal itself.

The *Bhagavata* compares the effect of such a connection to how a crystal reflects the qualities of a nearby object. Positive or negative, we reflect the qualities of the people we associate with. Those with deep spiritual insight, within whom spiritual love has awakened, can help us achieve the same. And such goodwill, particularly when it comes from those who are most interested in our real welfare, can have a positive effect on our lives.

A spiritual teacher helps transform their students' theoretical knowledge into realised knowledge. As stated in the *Bhagavad-gita*, 'The self-realised souls can impart knowledge unto you because they have seen the truth.' One no longer 'falls into illusion'. The *Bhagavata* explains that the depth of our spiritual relationships determines the degree to which that knowledge manifests in our hearts. A unit of energy can be considered 'equal' to the totality of energy if it can channel our access to that totality. Similarly, those who live in a deep connection with the Ultimate Reality can channel it for us.

Once, upon meeting a group of great sages, Krishna offered his respects, saying, 'Mere bodies of water are not the real sacred places of pilgrimage, nor are demigod images of earth and stone the true worshippable deities. These purify one only after a long time, but saintly sages purify one immediately upon being seen.'

Through these words and his own example, Krishna instructed the world on the importance of positive association.

HOW TO FIND THE RIGHT GUIDE

We all need guides on our spiritual journey. And as we have seen in previous chapters, leadership by example is crucial. Socrates said, 'Let him that would move the world first move himself.' To test someone's qualification as a guide, we can apply some of our tests for spiritual progress:

- Are they honest? Do they walk their talk?
- Is their life devoted to loving service?
- Does the person display control over their senses?
- Are they materialistic or desirous of personal adulation, or are they content in spiritual life?
- Are their students of good character and encouraged to be independently thoughtful?
- Do they try to minimise harm to all life forms?
- Do they focus on the spiritual essence?

We may not be able to answer all these questions conclusively, but if we are true to ourselves, we can probe our intuitive responses. The *Bhagavata* gives us the responsibility to test any prospective spiritual teacher (while giving teachers the responsibility to test each prospective student). Faith, after all, is 'where we place our heart', not something to be given or taken lightly.

INDICATIONS OF A GENUINE TEACHER

So important is the principle of finding a genuine teacher that the following text appears twice in the *Bhagavata* (one of only two verses that do): 'The value of a moment's association with a devotee of the Lord cannot be compared even with the value of attaining the heavenly planets or liberation from matter, and what to speak of worldly benedictions in the form of material prosperity.'

The *Bhagavata* provides several helpful characteristics of a genuine spiritual teacher:

- **Humility:** *humus* refers to the essential, nutrient-rich earth that feeds life. It is from humility that the *Bhagavata* says that virtue sprouts; if we are not humble before something greater, we tend to become captured by something lower. It has nothing to do with low self-esteem: 'Humility is not thinking less of yourself but thinking of yourself less.'[55] In the material realm, we try to prove ourselves better than others; in the spiritual realm, everyone competes to prove the greatness of others. The humility of spiritually realised persons softens our hearts and thus encourages us on our spiritual journey.

- **Fidelity:** genuine spiritual teachers don't feel the need to upend all that has gone before them and create a new ideology of their own. When introducing his new approach to spiritual practice, Buddha referred to the ancient principles of *ahimsa*, *dharma*, *karma*, and *samsara*. There may be the need to adapt tradition to time, place, and circumstance, but this should be

---

55) *The Purpose Driven Life* by Rick Warren.

done while also honouring the good that has preceded us. This, of course, requires humility.

- **Selflessness:** an unswerving commitment to the benefit of others is another hallmark of a genuine spiritual teacher. The *Bhagavata* insists that working for the benefit of others 'with our life, wealth, intelligence, and words is the duty of every human being.' For the spiritually advanced, this often means making personal sacrifices so that others may suffer less.

- **Magnanimity:** a genuine spiritual teacher must also be magnanimous, serving generously and without distinction. The *Bhagavata* compares Narada, its archetype spiritual teacher, to the sun, which rotates throughout the universe for the benefit of all, without discrimination. Magnanimous persons consider even their most offensive opponents to be fitting recipients of their compassion, prayers, and best wishes.

- **Facilitation:** driven by compassion, spiritual teachers facilitate their students' spiritual journeys and engage them in loving service. Because they experience and live their lives in harmony with spiritual reality, when we follow in their footsteps, we can catch a semblance of what they experience, and in their company, we may experience moments of spiritual emotions such as fearlessness and deep compassion.

ONE BUT MANY

Spiritual teachers come in all shapes and sizes. As we saw from the mendicant Dattatreya, there is no limit to the number or source of teachers from whom we can take inspiration. The spiritually advanced are all too rare, but the *Bhagavata* says that though such great souls may be distanced by geography and time, varied in means, and diverse across traditions, they are one in purpose. They are also one in purpose with *Bhagavata* itself—the reason why advanced transcendentalists are sometimes called '*Bhagavata*'. Bhaktivedanta Swami referred to Joan of Arc as 'Joan of Arc of *Srimad Bhagavatam*.' *Bhagavata* is derived from the word *bhagav*, which relates to *Bhagavan*, 'the absolute possessor of all opulence', so anything in relationship with *Bhagavan* is *Bhagavata*. And so, if Joan of Arc had an awakened relationship with God, she is also *Bhagavata*.

Our parents are our first teachers, and the *Bhagavata* shows how peers can also be powerful sources of spiritual guidance. Both are enabled with intimate knowledge of us, will have learned from their own similar challenges, and have a license to be honest.

Not all our guides and teachers will be at the same point in their spiritual journey. Some, even those trying their best on the spiritual path, slip up along the way; the *Bhagavata* says that even the self-realised may be temporarily afflicted by illusion. They may not yet have a profound realisation of the Ultimate Reality to impart to us nor a well-developed philosophical understanding to answer all our questions. But their sincerity of purpose and their concern for us help make up for any lack and allow them to act as our effective well-wishers. In the synergistic dynamic of a sincere spiritual exchange and dialogue, the *Bhagavata* tells us that the realisation that arises can surpass both speaker and listener; the sum is greater than the parts.

THE ULTIMATE TEACHER

Of course, in addition to our external guides, there is our internal one: the Superconsciousness that resides within each of us and awaits our sincere attention. If we are sincere, it is only a matter of time before we reach our destination. With this sincerity of purpose, we will be drawn to those who are meant to guide us, and increasingly, as we mature in our spiritual practice, we will be able to depend on internal confirmation.

Concluding Words

Krishna summarises his teachings to Arjuna in the *Bhagavad-gita* with four seed verses: 'I am the source of all spiritual and material worlds. Everything emanates from me. The wise who perfectly know this engage in my devotional service and worship me with all their hearts. The thoughts of my pure devotees dwell in me; their lives are fully devoted to my service, and they derive great satisfaction and bliss from always enlightening one another and conversing about me. To those who are constantly devoted to serving me with love, I give the understanding by which they can come to me. To show them special mercy, I, dwelling in their hearts, destroy with the shining lamp of knowledge the darkness born of ignorance.'

The *Bhagavata* presents a bold vision of universal spirituality, inspiring spiritual seekers to press forward and deepen their awareness of their essential spiritual identity. This is the most exciting and transformative journey upon which one can embark. Help is at hand, though; we need only take the first step. As Rumi said, 'As you start to walk on the way, the way appears.'

The choice is always ours. As Krishna says in closing to Arjuna, 'Have you heard this with single-minded attention?...Having fully grasped this, with nothing overlooked, then act as you so choose.'

May you, dear reader, find an abundance of loving reciprocation as you walk your path.

SELECTED BIBLIOGRAPHY

Bhaktivedanta Swami, A.C. *Bhagavad-gita As It Is*. Los Angeles: Bhaktivedanta Book Trust, 1989.

Bhaktivedanta Swami, A.C. *Srimad Bhagavatam*. Los Angeles: Bhaktivedanta Book Trust, 1989.

Schweig, Graham. *Bhagavad Gita: the beloved Lord's secret love song*. New York: Harper Collins, 2010.

Dalela, Ashish. *Material and Spiritual Natures: A Scientific Commentary On Sankhya Sutras*. Shabda Press, 2021.

ACKNOWLEDGEMENTS

Editing: Professor Carl Herzig, Becky Alexander, Nilamani Gor
Proofreading: Emily Wells, Nilamani Gor, Kirti Butkovic
Illustrations: Ekadashi Ryan
Design and layout: Jhanvi Rajani, Matthew Whitlock, Ravi Talsania
Advice during the process: Jay Shetty, Professor Graham Schweig
Feedback on an early draft: Jan Hilary, Dr James Biddulph, S.B. Keshava Swami, Pradip Gajjar, Sonal Gor, Sunita Halai, Isha Kusumgar
Support with planning: Raaj Raniga, Sahil Agarwal, Meera Agarwal
Filming: Rajesh Hirani (Filmwork Studios)
Sponsorship: Dharma Endowment Fund
Encouragement to publish: Sacinandana Swami, Radhanath Swami, Sivarama Swami, Visakha Devi

And to the staff and students at Avanti Schools Trust, who allowed me to test much of the content of this book with them, as well as everyone at The Vedanta retreat centre and OMNOM who gave me access to their venues and audiences to do the same.

ABOUT THE AUTHOR

Nitesh has been interested in mystic India since childhood. During his teens he searched for answers within different traditions. In 1993, while at medical school, he became deeply moved by spiritual activism when he founded a youth group that fronted the campaign to save arguably the most significant Hindu temple outside of India from being closed by the British government, culminating in protests that drew tens of thousands outside the Houses of Parliament. He spent all his time at the temple organising the campaign, while also learning about philosophy and meditation. The campaign was eventually won, but the time away from his studies meant he failed medical school as a result! But it was well worth it. He returned to university, graduated, and then worked in start-ups before going on to complete an MBA from London Business School.

Fatherhood prompted him to begin thinking about education, and he was left feeling disappointed with the lack of a holistic approach in the education system. He decided it was time to establish a different type of school—one based on spiritual principles and character formation while also delivering educational excellence. In 2005, his proposal won government funding to establish the first school in what would become the Avanti Schools Trust. While he worked to establish the school in his spare time, he built a career in management consultancy and held Managing Director level roles in investment banking and industry, including co-founding the Dow Jones Dharma Index. All the while, he continued deepening his spiritual understanding and practice.

During this time, he also explored how his career might relate to his spiritual practice, and this led him to write his first book,

The Dharma of Capitalism, which explores how we can apply spiritual principles in the corporate world.

In 2012, Avanti opened its fourth school, and Nitesh became its CEO. He has since led Avanti to become a leading government-funded academy trust with both faith and community schools. Avanti has been noteworthy in its holistic approach to education and in developing unique curricula for personal development, yoga, meditation, philosophy, religion, and ethics. In 2018, Nitesh was awarded an OBE for his services to education.

Nitesh's guiding principles for Avanti schools have been used to establish several other ground-breaking charitable start-up projects that are aligned with well-being, education, and social enterprise.

You can connect with Nitesh by visiting: www.niteshgor.com

OTHER BOOKS BY THE AUTHOR

The Dharma of Capitalism
Published in USA by Winans Kuenstler Publishing (2011), UK and international by Kogan Page (2012)

At a time when the business world is still adjusting to the impact of the financial crisis, leaders and decision-makers at all levels need to rethink their attitudes and strategies. Looking for new ways to conduct business, a number of global companies have already started changing their business models. The objective is not only to become more sustainable and responsible but more profitable in the long term. In *The Dharma of Capitalism*, Nitesh Gor explains why doing the right thing is more than a noble idea or a compliance issue and why it can be both practical and profitable. Filled with practical advice and real-life examples, *The Dharma of Capitalism* is a thought-provoking, process-based toolkit that will help you evaluate every aspect of your business and achieve profit with purpose rather than profit for profit's sake.

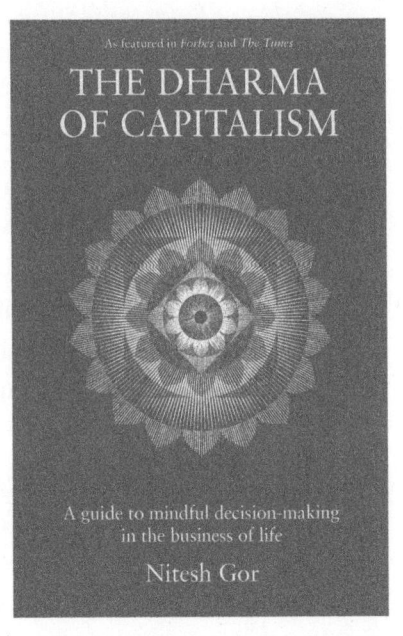